Animal Economics

Directly and Indirectly Accounting for Animal Welfare

NICOLAS TREICH

Toulouse School of Economics and INRAE

CAMBRIDGE
UNIVERSITY PRESS

CAMBRIDGE
UNIVERSITY PRESS

Shaftesbury Road, Cambridge CB2 8EA, United Kingdom

One Liberty Plaza, 20th Floor, New York, NY 10006, USA

477 Williamstown Road, Port Melbourne, VIC 3207, Australia

314–321, 3rd Floor, Plot 3, Splendor Forum, Jasola District Centre, New Delhi – 110025, India

103 Penang Road, #05–06/07, Visioncrest Commercial, Singapore 238467

Cambridge University Press is part of Cambridge University Press & Assessment, a department of the University of Cambridge.

We share the University's mission to contribute to society through the pursuit of education, learning and research at the highest international levels of excellence.

www.cambridge.org
Information on this title: www.cambridge.org/9781009699303

DOI: 10.1017/9781009699334

When citing this work, please include a reference to the DOI 10.1017/9781009699334

First published 2026

A catalogue record for this publication is available from the British Library

A Cataloging-in-Publication data record for this book is available from the Library of Congress

ISBN 978-1-009-69934-1 Hardback
ISBN 978-1-009-69930-3 Paperback

Animal Economics

Why does animal welfare matter? For some, it is because people care about animals; for others, it is because animals themselves are morally relevant. Given the importance of welfare in economics research and the debates around climate change and biodiversity loss, more economists are becoming interested in the economics of animal welfare. *Animal Economics* provides a general introduction to this new field. It explores the complexity of the behavioral attitude of humans toward animals using behavioral economics and explains how existing economic theory can be applied to understand animal welfare as an externality. Combining theory and empirical research to address key issues in animal welfare, including ethical perspectives, public opinion, market demand, and policy design, this book builds on economics principles to explore how to implement optimal policies that reflect human proanimal concerns and the moral status of animals.

NICOLAS TREICH is a research associate at the Toulouse School of Economics and National Research Institute for Agriculture, Food and the Environment in Toulouse, France. A pioneer in the emerging field of animal economics, he has authored over a dozen publications in leading economics journals and has delivered numerous keynote lectures on the economics of animal welfare.

Contents

Figures

Tables

Preface

My interest in animal welfare started around 2015, and looking back, I remember being struck by two things.

First, I was struck by the scarcity of attention given in economics to animals. Economics is all about humans. This anthropocentrism seems deeply ingrained in economic thinking. It is never challenged, even within fields like environmental or agricultural economics where animals are often involved in the analysis. Animals are absent from economic inquiry, or at best relegated to the status of mere "objects" viewed solely as food, resources, biodiversity, or amenities.

The second striking revelation was more personal. It is about the recognition of my own ignorance and biases. Despite considering myself someone who genuinely cares about animals, I had been largely unaware of the immense scale of animal suffering in this world. At the time, I consumed animal products without perceiving significant ethical concerns. However, my newfound interest in animals led me to investigate farm animal welfare. Through this investigation, I was confronted with the harsh reality that most farm animals endure. It became evident to me that I had been consistently underestimating the extent of the problem.

These observations probably served as a catalyst for my work on animal welfare. I believe that animal welfare is one of the most pressing issues that the world faces today. The implication is clear: If economists are interested in welfare in this world, at least some of them should work on animal welfare. So, why not me?

Over the course of almost a decade, I have immersed myself almost full-time in this subject, studying and producing several research papers on animal welfare in economics. Now I feel ready to consolidate my findings and insights, presenting them in the form of an introductory book on animal welfare economics. Notably, this work has been greatly shaped by my collaboration with Romain Espinosa, whose insights have been invaluable in this novel scientific adventure. This book draws heavily on our common work as well as on his own work. Thank you, Romain.

Economics research on animals is still in its early stages of development, and current understanding may be subject to change as new research and discoveries emerge. It is entirely possible (and in fact desirable) that this book becomes outdated relatively quickly. Due to the dynamic nature of the subject matter and the ever-evolving nature of scientific understanding, I consider that this book can only serve as an introduction and exploration to the topic at this point of time. I thus encourage readers to stay curious and open-minded, continuously seeking up-to-date information from reputable sources as the field makes progress.

This book is also closely tied to the course on animal welfare economics that I have been teaching at the Toulouse School of Economics since 2019. The course is offered at the master's level and caters to students specializing in environmental economics and ecology. Consequently, this book serves as a valuable resource to accompany and support the content covered in the course. I would like to express my gratitude to my students for their unwavering interest and the multitude of pertinent questions they have posed throughout the years.

For this class, I have made lecture slides that largely align with the chapters of this book. These slides will be available on my webpage and may serve as resources for those seeking additional support or supplementary material while exploring this new field of animal welfare economics. Slides can be beneficial for individuals interested in acquiring an overview of the subject or even for those looking to conduct a concise course centered around this topic. I encourage anyone to use these slides as needed. I believe that this book, together with the set of slides, could work well to provide a fifteen-hour course included in a broader course in environmental, ecological and/or agricultural economics, or in a course about topics in behavioral economics, public economics, or social choice.

Acknowledgments

Writing a book requires a lot of time and support in various forms. It requires, in particular, a favorable research environment. I first want to thank my institutions, the Toulouse School of Economics and the French National research institute on Agriculture, Food and Environment, as well as the Institute for Advanced Studies in Toulouse and the FDIR chair, which have provided the working environment, intellectual atmosphere, administrative support, and flexibility that have allowed me to investigate this novel area of research. I would like to acknowledge research funding from the French ANR under ANR-24-CE26-2813-02 (SentientBCA). In particular, I would like to express my gratitude to my colleagues Christian Gollier and Jean Tirole for their leadership at the Toulouse School of Economics for more than two decades. Their work has been a constant source of inspiration, both in their roles as prominent researchers, institution builders, and as persons.

Second, I want to thank a few people who have directly contributed to this book. In particular, I want to thank Elisabeth Klages and Nicolas Loiseau for excellent research assistance. Elisabeth read the entire book and provided feedback on both the substance and on the quality of the writing (note also that some sentences were written with the help of ChatGPT to correct grammatical errors as English is not my first language). Elisabeth also made the calculations underlying Figure 1.1 (see Chapters 1 and 10) and checked the accuracy of the citations to published studies, which eventually remains my sole responsibility. Nicolas reproduced most figures featured in this book, converting colored figures from different sources to grayscale format and ensuring a consistent style throughout.

Further, I want to thank those who have commented on parts of an early version of the book: three anonymous reviewers, Olivier

Armantier, Drew Burd, Richard Damania, Emilie Dardenne, Jojo Lee, Marcus Mergenthaler, Rafael Schütz, Monica Saavoss, and Romy Sutra, as well as the indexer Ruth Martin. Special thanks to Nicolas Delon and Luis Mota Freitas, who read almost the whole book and provided very useful comments throughout. Finally, I also want to thank conference and seminar participants, as well as various journal editors and anonymous referees, who have provided feedback on my research papers on animal welfare over the past decade. While this feedback was sometimes critical, it was usually thoughtful, stimulating, and friendly.

Moreover, many colleagues and friends through formal or informal discussions have helped me sharpen my ideas on the topic. I cannot cite everyone, of course, and will certainly forget many people. Let me nevertheless mention several persons who have been instrumental in this intellectual, as well as personal, journey. This includes Matt Adler, Yassin Alaya, Olivier Armantier, Laurent Bègue-Shankland, Lewis Bollard, Sylvie Borau, Heather Browning, Tom Bry-Chevalier, Mark Budolfson, Florence Burgat, Alexis Carlier, Roland Cash, Sylvain Chabé-Ferret, Pascale Champalaune, Laetitia Charalambides, Frédéric Cherbonnier, Emilie Dardenne, Francesca De Petrillo, Marion Desquilbet, Maya Eden, Romain Espinosa, Bob Fischer, Marc Fleurbaey, Jérôme Foncel, Christian Gollier, Philip Good, Brigitte Gothière, Jim Hammitt, Nina Hestermann, Moshe Hoffman, George Homs, Elise Huchard, Olof Johansson-Stenman, Lisa Kramer, Jochen Krattenmacher, Kevin Kuruc, Yves Le Yaouanq, Carole Mare, Lydia Mechtenberg, Anouch Missirian, Pierre Mormède, Céline Nauges, Howard Nye, Sébastien Pouget, David Reinstein, François Salanié, Cécile Sarabian, Paul Seabright, Arthur Silve, Jean Tirole, Karine Van der Straeten, and Erez Yoeli. I would also like to thank my wife Céline and my daughter Inès. As always, I bear all responsibility for any errors or misinterpretations contained in the book.

PART I Preliminaries

The book has three parts, the preliminary part as well as Parts II and III. This preliminary part consists of two chapters, both significantly longer than the others. They offer foundational knowledge about the book's subject matter and animals in general. Readers eager to dive directly into the core content may choose to skip them for quicker access to the main contributions. First, I explain the motivation for this book and preview some key ideas (Chapter 1). I also attempt in this preliminary part to put the book into perspective, in particular with respect to the economics literature and policymaking issues. This first chapter may be viewed as an introduction to the book in general, although it does not provide a summary of the book per se. The main objective of Chapter 1 is rather to identify the contribution and the originality of this book with respect to economics research in general so that readers can get a sense of what they can, or cannot, find in this book.

Then, I focus on animals (Chapter 2). Some readers may not know much about animals. I discuss their number, their category, their importance for the economy as well as their moral and legal status. This chapter aims to provide readers, especially readers who are economists, with preliminary knowledge about the subject of animals in general. The information presented is necessarily very selective and directed. There is a vast body of literature in life sciences, philosophy and law related to animals and their welfare. Obviously, I cannot cover a lot in such a relatively short chapter. Instead, my aim is to present some key ideas and references, acknowledging that this exploration is only a starting point for interested readers. The topics are also selected in terms of their potential to be translated into economics concepts. Indeed, some of the knowledge presented in this preliminary part will be useful later in the book when I come back on some issues but approach them through an economic lens.

1 Introduction

1.1 WHY THIS BOOK?

Nonhuman animals, hereafter "animals," are omnipresent in human life. They provide us with food and clothing, they are used in research, and they offer entertainment and companionship. And of course they are everywhere in the world.

This book proposes an economic analysis of animals and their welfare. But let me ask first: Is animal welfare a pertinent subject for an economist? A basic answer is to recognize that the suffering experienced by animals is often predominantly influenced by economic factors. Animal agriculture provides a good illustration. Over the past century, we have witnessed a marked intensification of industrial animal agriculture. The cause of this evolution is clear: efficiency gains. In the present day, on a global scale, over 80 percent of farmed animals find themselves in factory farms. Deprived of basic elements like sunlight, fresh air, free movement, and natural behaviors such as mating, these animals are denied what we consider essential components of a normal life. Throughout their existence, they endure a persistent state of low welfare precisely because humans get an economic benefit from that situation.

But this raises a much more general and much more difficult question: Is animal welfare an important issue? The state of the world is concerning on multiple fronts. Hundreds of millions of people still live in extreme poverty, there are wars in multiple parts of the world, and the looming threats of climate change and biodiversity loss could greatly affect future generations. The answer to this question depends on how to judge what is "important," and in particular whether we should care about animals while there is such a huge amount of human suffering in the world. Reflecting on this judgment is very difficult and even controversial, but this is precisely one major objective of the research program on the economics of animal welfare.

For economists, the key metric for assessing what matters is welfare. As illustrated in Figure 1.1 (black curve), the global welfare of major categories of farmed land animals – chickens, pigs, and cows – exhibits a negative trend. This figure is derived from data provided by the Food and Agriculture Organization of the United Nations and uses a welfare assessment method that will be detailed in Chapter 10. The observed decline in animal welfare parallels the surge of industrial farming over the last sixty years. This trend reflects the changes in the number of animals raised for food. Since the early 1960s, the quantity of animal-based food production, and consequently the number of animals, has increased drastically. For instance, the average annual chicken consumption in the United States has increased from less than 10 pounds to about 70 pounds per person. This trend shows no signs of stopping. This book will extensively discuss not only the "quality" of animal lives but also the "quantity" of animal lives, namely the number of animals that we produce for food.

The black curve on Figure 1.1 also highlights that overall global welfare of farmed animals is negative, based on the specific measure

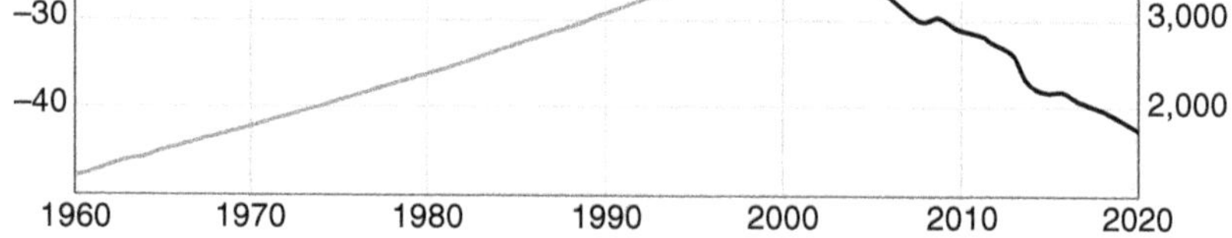

FIGURE 1.1 Global welfare of farmed animals over time (black curve) and Human Development Index (HDI) over time (gray curve).
See Chapter 10 for more information about how this figure has been created.
Source: Food and Agriculture Organization and Human Development Reports of the United Nations, Prados De La Escosura (2015) and Espinosa and Treich (2024)

of welfare adopted in this book (again, more on this later). A negative welfare level essentially means that existence is worse than nonexistence, that life is not worth living. This observation thus strikingly indicates that, all else being equal, it would be better if these animals did not exist at all! This book will extensively discuss the notion of life worth living. This notion turns out to be instrumental in various theory parts. Furthermore, note on Figure 1.1 that total welfare is declining at an increasing rate, suggesting that the problem is rapidly worsening. This trend underscores a sense of urgency and calls for more policy action and more research.

For comparison, I have also included the evolution of the Human Development Index (HDI) over the same period; see the gray curve in Figure 1.1. The HDI is the most well-known index for measuring the overall development and welfare of humans, considering three main dimensions: health, education, and wealth. The figure shows the global HDI, which exhibits a consistently increasing trend. Note that regional HDI (Arab states, East Asia and the Pacific, South Asia, Europe and Central Asia, Latin America and the Caribbean, and Sub-Saharan Africa) also show increasing trends over the period. Hence, despite various catastrophic events in the world and mounting concerns on multiple fronts, human welfare has been steadily improving on average both globally and regionally. This upward trend starkly contrasts with the decreasing and concave pattern observed earlier for animal welfare. The point is that while the overall quality of life tends to improve for humans in the world, it has sharply deteriorated for animals, with human actions contributing to the decline of animal welfare.

This book will present how to model and quantify animal welfare in an economically meaningful manner, and even in a way that allows for a direct comparison with human welfare. It will make progress on the path to answer the question of the direct comparison of welfare of humans and animals, and in particular whether animal welfare concerns are important compared to human welfare. As a preview, our preliminary calculations suggest that the animal welfare costs associated with intensive animal production far exceed its economic benefits for humans, often by several orders of magnitude (Espinosa and Treich 2024). In a nutshell, this research suggests that intensive animal production should essentially be phased out.

This result should not come as a surprise. When we seriously consider the welfare of animals, we confront the reality of billions and billions of animals enduring extremely low levels of well-being. At its essence, economists' calculations thus acknowledge that the consumer surplus derived from meat consumption pales in comparison to the interests of other animals. In other words, the fleeting pleasure of consuming meat is "relatively trivial by comparison with the interests of, say, a pig in being able to move freely, mingle with other animals, and generally avoid the boredom and confinement of factory farm life" (Singer 1980, page 333). To put it bluntly, industrial farming condemns animals to lives of boredom and suffering in exchange for saving a few cents per kilogram of meat, and thus in exchange for a trivial gain in human welfare. This means that the loss to animals seems completely disproportionate compared to the gain to humans. Of course, such a strong claim needs to be carefully explored and assessed, and this determination is precisely one of the objectives of the book. In particular, a key question is whether a compromise can be found between the interests of humans and animals.

Furthermore, note that the impact of humans on animals is not limited to farmed animals. Many human actions and policies, directly or indirectly, affect animals and their welfare. Consider climate policy, for example. Climate change affects animal habitats, migrations, and food availability, as well as potentially increasing disease and parasite transmission. Simply put, climate change profoundly affects nature in general and animals in particular (Parmesan 2006, Ripple et al. 2024). It therefore seems important to consider climate impacts on both humans and animals and then explore optimal climate policy in an integrated nonanthropocentric framework (Budolfson and Spears 2020).

Other domains are also worth investigating. In biomedical research, the use of animals raises ethical questions about their treatment and whether the expected benefits to human health outweigh the costs in terms of animal welfare. Is it acceptable that animals are used in research for some relatively "minor" human health issues, such as alopecia (hair loss) in aging men? Should we stop animal research on a specific disease if it has not proven effective for decades, or if the probability of discovery is *ex ante* very small? These are difficult questions. The tradeoff becomes particularly challenging when considering alternative methods, such as *in vitro* testing or computer simulations, which can reduce or eliminate animal suffering but are not yet fully capable of replicating the complexity of living organisms.

As another example, consider conservation policies that involve culling invasive species to restore native ecosystems. Animal welfare is typically an overlooked aspect of these policies. Killing animals in the name of conservation is morally problematic because the life of any individual animal matters morally. The evaluation of these policies should thus consider the tradeoff between the benefits to biodiversity and the negative impact on the welfare of the affected animals.

Overall, the impact of human activities on animal welfare is immense, yet it remains significantly overlooked. This oversight extends not only to the field of economics but also to many other domains. For instance, it is particularly concerning to see major environmental frameworks, such as the United Nations Sustainable Development Goals and the Earth System Boundaries literature, pay almost no attention to the issue of animal welfare. These initiatives aim to address global sustainability, yet they fail to account for the welfare of billions of sentient beings affected by human actions. That is, they fail from a moral viewpoint.

One major difficulty though is that we currently do not have the tools to quantify our impacts on animal welfare (Budolfson et al. 2023, 2024, Sunstein 2024). This makes it difficult to assess and compare the welfare impacts of policies on animals and humans on a common scale, and thus to make informed and transparent tradeoffs. This perhaps also contributes to the source of the problem. When something is not counted, it eventually does not count. There is thus a need for the development of novel methods to integrate animal welfare into decision analyses. This integration would enable policymakers and various stakeholders to make more informed and ethical decisions that consider the welfare of both humans and animals.

More fundamentally, there is also a need to explore how existing economic theory can address the conceptual issues raised by accounting for animal welfare. Whether animal welfare is considered an externality, a public good, a merit good, or another economic concept, I will show how to apply or adapt standard economics principles to better understand animal welfare issues and, in particular, to design optimal policies. There is no need to start from scratch. It is essential to understand how existing tools, particularly those already employed in public economics and environmental economics, can be harnessed to advance our understanding of animal welfare. This theoretical aspect is likely the main contribution of this book to economics. It includes developing a simple model of animal consumption – what I call the "canonical model" – which is adapted several times to fit different economic concepts.

Another crucial aspect for economic research concerns the lack of understanding of how humans exactly care about animals. Opinion polls and survey studies often suggest that citizens care a lot about animals in general. However, the situation is complex. According to Faunalytics, only about one-quarter of United States donors donate to animal causes (https://faunalytics.org/giving-to-animals-new-data-who-how/). Moreover, donations to animal-related organizations are mainly directed toward companion animal shelters and protection, with much less attention given to noncompanion animals. Research by Animal Charity Evaluators indicates that farmed animals receive less than 1 percent of total donations to animal charities, despite representing more than 99 percent of domesticated animals globally (https://animalcharityevaluators.org/donation-advice/why-farmed-animals/). Why do people seem to care about some animals and not others?

Even for a specific category of animals such as farmed animals, people's behavior is not easy to decipher. Consider, for instance, the opinion survey based on more than 20,000 participants in the European Union: A large majority of Europeans (91 percent) agree that it is important to protect the welfare of farmed animals (Eurobarometer 2023) (see Figure 1.2). However, market data often provide a very different picture. Typically, the demand for animal-friendly products in food markets is very limited. Overall, the "gap" between public opinion and market demand when it comes to animal welfare is a complex issue that likely involves a variety of psychological, social, political, and economic factors. Further research, in particular research in behavioral economics, is needed to better understand these factors and develop strategies to bridge this gap and improve animal welfare.

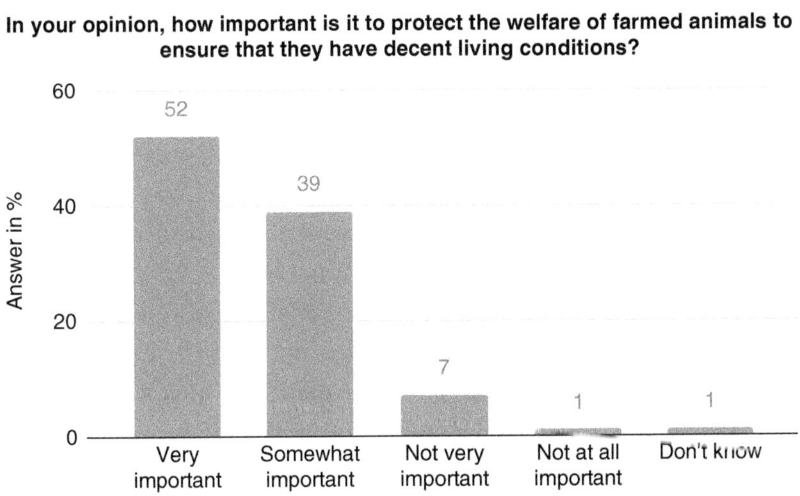

FIGURE 1.2 European citizens' agreement about the importance of protecting farmed animals.
Source: Eurobarometer (2023)

Presently, the economic literature on animal welfare is scarce, and essentially limited to studies on the willingness to pay (WTP) for animal welfare and on the production cost to improve animal welfare (Bennett 1997, Lagerkvist and Hess 2010, Norwood and Lusk 2011, Bennett et al. 2012, Grethe 2017). This literature is published in field journals in agricultural or environmental economics. In the "top- 30" journals in economics, only three papers contain "animal welfare" or "animal well-being" in the title or abstract (i.e., Blackorby and Donaldson 1992, Fleurbaey and van der Linden 2021, Mechtenberg et al. 2024), and not a single paper contains basic keywords such as "vegetarian," "vegan," "sentience," "anthropocentrism," or "speciesism" (based on a search at https://econ-paper-search.streamlit.app/ in December 2024). Other fields, such as animal ethics and animal rights law, are already well developed in philosophy and law, respectively. A similar trend should follow at some point in economics. The inclusion in 2023 of new entries K38 (Animal Rights Law) or Q18 (Animal Welfare Policy) in the *Journal of Economic Literature* classification is an indication that the economics profession is becoming increasingly interested in this area.

The existing literature on animal welfare, predominantly found in philosophy, law, and animal sciences, has undoubtedly generated a vast repository of valuable knowledge. However, it often lacks in terms of economic arguments, despite economics being at the very core of the problem, as argued earlier. This point was eloquently made sixty years ago by Ruth Harrison, a pioneer and visionary of the farm animal movement, in her seminal book *Animal Machines* (Harrison 1964, cited in Bollard 2023): "if one person is unkind to an animal it is considered to be cruelty, but where a lot of people are unkind to animals, especially in the name of commerce, the cruelty is condoned and, once large sums of money are at stake, will be defended to the last by otherwise intelligent people."

The centrality of economic aspects to the problem of animal welfare can be disheartening for the admirable animal advocacy community, which is often guided by moral arguments rather than economic logic. As some have argued, the actions of this community may have had only a modest and diffuse impact compared to the powerful influence of long-term economic and demographic trends (Weisskircher 2024). These trends include the rise of industrial farming, driven by the demand for affordable meat and animal products, the globalization of food markets, and the economic incentives that prioritize efficiency and profit over animal welfare. Despite the passionate efforts and moral convictions of animal advocates, their influence is frequently overshadowed by these larger economic forces, which shape industry practices and consumer behavior on a global scale. Consequently, achieving significant improvements in animal welfare requires addressing these underlying economic drivers and integrating animal welfare considerations into a broader economic framework.

In their influential book *Zoopolis*, Donaldson and Kymlicka (2011) argue that traditional animal advocacy has been largely ineffective. They propose a new societal organization based on a redefined relationship with animals, including granting citizenship status to domesticated animals, sovereignty to wild animals, and denizenship to liminal animals (i.e., animals that live in and around human settlements). However, their visionary framework may sound quite unrealistic within the current societal structure. One critical oversight in their work is the economic feasibility of their model. Transitioning to a system where animals are granted various forms of citizenship and legal rights would require substantial financial resources, infrastructural changes, and ongoing maintenance.

The bottom line is this: Incorporating economic analyses and tools could make moral or political proposals more practical and actionable, ensuring that the changes envisioned are not only ethically sound but also economically viable. This approach is exemplified by the success of cage-free campaigns, which target producers instead of politicians, leveraging market forces to drive change. Overall, I contend that more research in economics is needed to better understand our attitude toward animals and our impacts on their welfare. There is currently a lack of cohesive integration between the literature in social, political, and human sciences and the literature in life sciences on animal welfare. It thus seems useful to establish a comprehensive and unified framework that encompasses the concepts developed in philosophy and other sciences in the humanities with the insights derived from animal welfare and cognitive sciences. Economics can play a pivotal role in achieving this synthesis.

Here is an illustration of this claim. In the canonical model of this book, I propose a simple normative model that encompasses parameters addressing the degree of antispeciesism (as discussed in the philosophy literature, see Chapter 2), another parameter that evaluates the relative weight of a species based on specific cognitive capacities (as explored in animal cognition, cognitive ethology, and comparative psychology), and an additional parameter that measures levels of animal welfare (as studied in the animal welfare sciences literature). This model can be calibrated and ultimately yields a monetary value for animal welfare that can be compared to other monetized costs or benefits for humans. As a result, various decisions or policies that affect animal welfare can then be quantitatively evaluated in a benefit-cost analysis. Moreover, the assumptions can be varied, and uncertainty may be introduced, to check the robustness of the evaluation.

The primary purpose of this book is thus to introduce economic concepts pertinent to the study of animal welfare, with the aim of accelerating the production of theoretical and empirical methods that incorporate animal welfare into economic analyses. I hope that this book will facilitate the creation and development of a novel field within economics, while fostering a more ethical approach to policymaking that considers the welfare of both humans and animals. This book aims to inspire economists, especially young scholars, by encouraging them to think about the role of animals in the economy and, for some, to pursue research on animals and their welfare. By doing so, it may contribute to nurturing a new generation of experts capable of addressing the intricate challenges arising from animal welfare in our present and future world.

Finally, I believe that the book also holds broader relevance for social and behavioral scientists as well as scholars in fields such as environmental, biological, or animal sciences who wish to gain insights into some economic aspects of the subject. This interdisciplinary approach not only enriches our understanding of animal welfare issues but also fosters collaboration among experts from various fields, ultimately advancing the objective of creating more effective and economically sound policies. In sum, it seeks to promote the use of economic methods in policy analysis, to identify gaps in current analyses and to encourage interdisciplinary collaboration to advance this objective.

1.2 ANTHROPOCENTRISM IN ECONOMICS

Economists study humans' actions, humans' beliefs, humans' exchanges, humans' strategic interactions, and so on. Buchanan (1964), for instance, defined economics as the study of exchange activities among human societies. Other well-known definitions, as listed in Table 1.1, are also explicitly human centered. But

Table 1.1 *Definitions of economics by famous economists*

Economist(s)	Definition of economics
Alfred Marshall (1890, Book I, Chapter 1, §1)	"Economics is a study of mankind in the ordinary business of life."
Lionel Robbins (1932, page 15)	"Economics is the science which studies human behavior as a relationship between ends and scarce means which have alternative uses."
Paul A. Samuelson and William D. Nordhaus (1998, page 4)	"Economics is the study of how societies use scarce resources to produce valuable commodities and distribute them among different people."

the key point is that economics is also centered on the welfare of humans. The complete citation from Marshall (1890, Book I, Chapter 1, §1), which serves as the opening sentence of his classic work, highlights this focus on welfare: "Political Economy or economics is a study of mankind in the ordinary business of life; it examines that part of individual and social action which is most closely connected with the attainment, and with the use of the material requisites of wellbeing." To give another example, Angus Deaton, the 2015 Nobel laureate in economics, wrote in an op-ed that the proper basis of the economics discipline is "the study of human welfare" (Deaton 2022).

Hence, what matters in economics is a better understanding of human societies, and what matters normatively is human welfare. In short, economics is the study of humans, "for" humans. Economic studies consider humans as the sole wellspring of welfare, a phenomenon often referred to as anthropocentrism. Indeed, anthropocentrism means that humans alone possess moral value. Economists typically consider that humans, all humans, and only humans have moral value.

The assumption of anthropocentrism is almost universal in economics. One might think this assumption can be justified since economics primarily deals with issues unrelated to animals, allowing their welfare to be safely ignored in economic analyses. On the surface, this seems reasonable. What is the problem after all if research in finance or industrial organization, say, ignores animal welfare? Note however that many industries rely directly on animals (e.g., industries in food, clothing, and health), warranting some caution. Moreover, considering all the indirect impacts of human actions, as through the use of natural resources such as land, the impacts on animals seem potentially huge in many cases. Overall, the direct and indirect impacts on animals of human activities may be substantial. Actually, a recurrent theme in this book is that animals are often invisible (or rendered invisible), and the consequences of human actions on them are not even considered.

Perhaps more problematic is the fact that anthropocentrism is also the rule in other fields in economics such as environmental economics or agricultural economics, where animals are explicitly considered part of the research subject. For example, in economic studies of biodiversity, animals are usually viewed as protected species. However, in these studies the welfare of individuals in these species does not usually matter. At best, animal welfare only matters as a byproduct of biodiversity preservation. Similarly, farmed animals are simply inputs that contribute to agricultural production. In these fields, animals are perceived as mere "objects": They are viewed as food, resources, or commodities. They are not acknowledged as individuals or sentient beings. In other words, the capacity of animals to experience pain or pleasure is simply ignored. Animal welfare is largely disregarded in environmental and agricultural economics.

In essence, the widely prevalent welfarist approach in economics, frequently advanced as a substantial normative asset of the discipline and the cornerstone of significant economic domains such as growth, optimal taxation, and climate or agricultural policy, harbors a critical flaw: It exclusively considers human welfare. Some readers may perceive this section as overly critical, assertive, or even unfair toward the discipline of economics. I understand that. However, I see this flaw as a major normative limitation within the discipline of economics. I believe it is important to emphasize this limitation forcefully because it has been the norm in the discipline.

I believe that a change is needed. It is not just a theoretical or conceptual problem. As the book will argue in some empirical parts (see, for instance, the computation of so-called animal welfare levies in Chapters 7 and 10), the policies that usual anthropocentric economic analysis recommends are often very far from maximizing total welfare precisely because they adopt this restricted view of welfare. Sometimes, a change in the policy modestly affecting the welfare of humans would drastically improve the welfare of animals. It is important to identify those policy changes that can really make a difference.

Animal welfare, in its own right, has thus not received proper attention in economics (Johansson-Stenman 2018). At best, economists focus on how improving animal welfare can enhance consumer surplus, thus assigning instrumental value to animal welfare. The intrinsic value of animals has been overlooked in environmental valuation, which primarily relies on humans' WTP and is thus rooted in anthropocentrism. It is important to note here that human preferences for animals may poorly align with the actual welfare of animals (Budolfson et al. 2024, Espinosa 2024), undermining the effectiveness of an instrumental approach in improving animal welfare. Even attempts in environmental valuation to go beyond altruistic preferences, such as discussions on existence value, still remain entrenched in anthropocentrism by relying on human preferences regarding the existence of animals or other species.

The spectrum of normative considerations about which species hold intrinsic value essentially hinges on where we place the moral dividing line. But where should that line be drawn? Within an anthropocentric framework, this line is typically placed between humans on one side and everything else – animals, plants, and inanimate objects – on the other. For sure, humans are not always treated equally under certain systems, but they are generally accorded at least some moral value. However, the common division between humans and all the rest appears rather arbitrary when we consider that animals, like humans, possess a brain and nervous system, and often can experience positive and negative welfare. Biologically, animals are much closer to humans than they are to plants, let alone inanimate objects.

In this book, I extend moral consideration to animals, but not to plants. I will justify this choice. Animals, including humans, have complex organ systems such as nervous, circulatory, respiratory, and digestive systems. These systems perform similar functions across various animal species. In contrast, plants have fundamentally different structures and systems, such as xylem and phloem for nutrient and water transport, and lack complex organs like brains or hearts. Cellular complexity is also very different between animals and plants. Plants undergo different biological processes such as photosynthesis, different modes of reproduction (like flowering and seed production), and growth patterns (like phototropism and gravitropism). Plants and animals have evolved separately for at least 600 million years. The bottom line is that, given the relative biological continuities between humans and animals, it appears difficult to justify a moral discontinuity that assigns moral value solely to humans and puts all other animals and plants in the same category located outside the moral community.

The anthropocentric position adopted in economics can be viewed as a corner moral case. There is little doubt that this position is morally dubious. For instance, Fleurbaey and Leppanen (2021, page 258) forcefully argue that "anthropocentrism in normative concepts is suspect, unfounded, ominously similar to the old religious and racist doctrines that gave the White Christian Man the right to own the Earth, and apparently too weak as a normative compass to fight pervasive destruction in the age of mass extinction." Some critics would characterize the anthropocentric position as "speciesist" (Singer 1975), which refers to the unjustified and biased treatment of beings based on their species membership (or more precisely to "anthropocentric speciesism"; see Horta 2010).

Now, this raises another question: Why have economists consistently ignored animal welfare? This is a difficult question, and I am not aware of any research on this. I conjecture that the main explanation is a simple one: Like most people, economists are "speciesist." By this, I mean our instinctive moral intuitions that consistently prioritize our own species. As advanced by Jaquet (2021), the notion that only humans hold moral importance may be primarily influenced by "tribalism," namely our inclination to prioritize ingroup members over outgroup members. In essence, I am saying that economists may naturally lean toward human-centric perspectives simply because economists are humans.

But there is an additional problem. Economists are not only anthropocentric, but they also seldom acknowledge the existence of this anthropocentric approach as an important hypothesis, let alone engage in discussions justifying it as a reasonable standpoint. It seems that economists are not even aware of this bias. As an example, consider the working paper of my esteemed colleague at Toulouse School of Economics Jean Tirole titled "Assumptions in economics" (Tirole 2019). In this paper, anthropocentrism is not even mentioned among the assumptions. Jean Tirole, the 2014 Nobel laureate in economics, is one of the most prominent and respected economists worldwide. He has produced various seminal papers in many fields of economics and has contributed several major textbooks. His capacity to contemplate crucial aspects of our discipline is beyond dispute. Nonetheless, I regard this omission as rather ordinary, as it merely mirrors the prevailing conventional mindset within the field of economics. It exemplifies the deeply ingrained nature of the speciesist bias, highlighting how it tends to persist in the background, largely unchallenged and not even mentioned in our discipline. When a problem is not acknowledged, it is difficult to go forward and to change the status quo.

This omission is particularly disturbing in the works in economics that attempt to reflect on equity issues. Let me take a couple of examples to illustrate. In the domain of welfare economics, a pivotal concept is the "veil of ignorance" proposed by John Rawls and John Harsanyi. This concept is built upon a thought experiment wherein individuals tasked with making political decisions must imagine themselves devoid of knowledge about their own identity. This exercise is designed to help them transcend their self-serving biases and, in turn, foster moral impartiality. Within this framework, various examples are provided in the economics literature, where people are asked to envision themselves without knowledge of their gender, ethnic background, economic status, class, abilities, or talents. They are sometimes encouraged to consider extreme scenarios where they could be slaves, physically handicapped, mentally challenged, and more. Yet, strikingly, I have never seen any example prompted to consider themselves as animals. Thus, while this thought experiment induced by the veil of ignorance effectively surmounts numerous mental barriers, it notably falls short when it comes to overcoming species-based biases. The veil of ignorance concept, as it is usually presented in economics, thus exhibits anthropocentric speciesism. In animal ethics, Rowlands (1997) notably advocates for the moral consideration of animals within a contractarian framework by utilizing the concept of the veil of ignorance.

A related concept is that of Adam Smith's "impartial spectator." The impartial spectator represents an imagined observer or judge who is able to view situations from a neutral and unbiased perspective. Bowles and Halliday (2022, page 255) refer to the concept repeatedly in their excellent textbook to introduce the social welfare function used in economic models. They give the example of fishermen imposing externalities on each other, and emphasize that the solution is given by the impartial spectator wishing "to determine fishing time and distribute fish so as to maximize a social welfare function." The point here is the same as earlier. The impartial spectator is not really impartial but rather speciesist, only considering the welfare of fishermen and ignoring that of fish. Interestingly, Bowles and Halliday mention animals in several places in the book, emphasizing for instance that "our physical capacities are hardly remarkable compared to other animals" (page 19). The authors even correct Adam Smith who suggested that only humans can exchange goods, emphasizing that "species of fish exchange services in what are termed 'biological markets'" (page 344). Still, the normative approach in their book inevitably remains anthropocentric.

As a final example, consider Tony Atkinson (2015)'s classic book "Inequality." This book, cited thousands of times on GoogleScholar, and authored by a scholar who has significantly shaped the field of economic analysis of inequality for the past half century, is undoubtedly a reference on the topic. As usual however, the book is all about inequality among humans. Well, when introducing the topic of income distribution, the author writes (page 37): "Barbara Wootton, an English economist and social campaigner, wrote that one of the incidents that led her to write The Social Foundations of Wage Policy was the discovery that the elephant giving rides at Whipsnade Zoo earned the same amount as she did as a senior university teacher." Although Atkinson recognizes that he has wondered about the relevance of the comparison, I find it interesting that he nevertheless introduces the topic using this anecdote. This is interesting because inequality is obviously not solely confined to income matters here; it also revolves around the treatment of a sentient being as a slave (and who does not actually "earn" the money). This highlights the often unnoticed or seemingly inconsequential treatment of animals in our world, a phenomenon that may elude even those with high expertise in matters of fairness and ethics.

In my paper with Alexis Carlier (Carlier and Treich 2020, page 2), we start with the following classical storyline of the invasion of Earth by a superior species.

> Imagine that a super-intelligent species invades Earth. The superior intelligence of these aliens allows them to take over political power. Current living humans cannot make sense of their technology, knowledge, art or culture, nor can they comprehend their moral rules and legal obligations. Alien society is wealthy, egalitarian, and to a large extent much better than existing human societies. Some aliens are economists who study how to allocate resources and design incentives. In particular, welfare economists have designed and applied sophisticated fairness concepts, but these concepts only concern aliens, not humans. Alien environmental economists study how to preserve the environment and humans and (nonhuman) animals from extinction, and their studies thus contribute to maintaining biodiversity on Earth. Aliens only police their society. If animals commit violence towards humans in the natural environment, aliens do not interfere. Aliens like to eat humans but they care about human welfare to some extent. For instance, while most

humans raised for food live inside big production factories, some are free-range, which is better for their welfare but increases the price of human meat.

The point with our story is simple. It is to propose a reversal of perspective. This is a standard technique used in science fiction books or movies (e.g., *The Planet of the Apes*). Our objective is to stimulate a reflection on our anthropocentric speciesism, and in particular about the induced research bias in economics. On rare occasions however, there is an attempt to justify the anthropocentric approach. Most often, human exceptionalism is the only justification. However, as I will argue more in detail later on, this justification is problematic. Even if we were to acknowledge our exceptional status, as I have already said, there exist biological continuities between humans and animals that do not warrant a "moral discontinuity," conferring exclusive moral value solely upon humans. Humans may count more than other animals, even much more; but they cannot count infinitely more.

Consider for instance the recent Review by Partha Dasgupta on the economics of biodiversity (Dasgupta 2021). Interestingly, the Review specifically defends its anthropocentric take. However, as I argue elsewhere (Treich 2022), the defense is problematic. For instance, the Review says (page 49):

> ...there are nevertheless good reasons for concentrating on what one may call the instrumental value of biodiversity. One reason is that there are innumerable systems of thought that go beyond an anthropocentric perspective. Many people argue that life itself has intrinsic value, never mind that only a few among the 8 to 20 million species (of eukaryotes) on Earth are known to feel, never mind to have self-awareness. There are also many systems of belief – alas, all too readily overridden by cosmopolitan society – in which objects that to the cosmopolitan are inanimate, are sacred. They may house life, but they are not life; nevertheless, they are sacred. Uluru in Australia is a famous example. It is

> sacred to the Pitjantjatjara, the Aboriginal people of the area surrounding it. And there is the river Ganges, sacred to Hindus (Box 2.8). But the narratives underlying their sacredness differ.

I find several issues with this defense. First, it is acknowledged that there are "innumerable systems of thought" or "many systems of belief," implying the existence of a multitude of worldviews. I concur with that. However, this does not inherently justify dismissing all alternative perspectives and exclusively favoring the anthropocentric view. Why not also consider certain nonanthropocentric viewpoints that may hold particular relevance? Second, the argument that only a few species "are known to feel" or "have self-awareness" is turned on its head here. These "few" species include at least mammals, birds, and fish (more on this later). This concerns a large range of species and, in turn, billions and billions of animals. Third, as I have argued before, putting animals, plants, and inanimate objects (such as the stone of Uluru or the river of the Ganges) in the same category is problematic. Only animals have, like us, a brain and a nervous system. Finally, this emphasis on what is "sacred" or "sacredness" as a possible alternative to anthropocentrism is in fact symptomatic of an anthropocentric view of the world (since people decide what is sacred); this actually illustrates the underlying resistance to depart from this view. Again, this emphasizes that even our leading scholars in (environmental) economics struggle to think outside of anthropocentrism.

There might of course exist many other factors that explain anthropocentrism in economics and beyond. So far, I have discussed the speciesist bias. Another important factor is politics for instance. The influence of political forces driven by human concerns skews our research agenda and research outcomes, perpetuating a human-centered approach. I have heard so many times that animals cannot be a research priority given all the problems humans face in the world. Essentially, it is all about pushing back that research agenda to a time that will never come. This political influence seems likely in the domains of agricultural and resource economics where limited funds have been allocated historically to the study of the welfare of farmed animals per se compared to other aspects such as animal productivity, animal health, or even the perception of animal welfare by consumers and farmers. As a researcher working for the French National Research Institute on Agriculture, Food and Environment, I know quite well from my personal experience that the research in this area is not fully independent from agricultural politics.

As another factor explaining anthropocentrism, there is the difficulty of the research effort. I quite like the following post by Dani Rodrik in September 2023: "the Economics profession underinvests in imperfectly identified analyses of big/important/relevant questions relative to well-identified but comparatively uninteresting questions." Indeed, my impression is that the economics profession tends to allocate few resources toward exploring "imperfectly identified" analyses. I believe that complexity aversion may play a significant role here. It is very complex to study the well-being of other species, and to integrate this well-being into economic analyses. There is in particular a persistent belief that animal mental states are inscrutable, akin to a black box impervious to scientific inquiry, or inconsequential in explaining behavior. The research topic is not even well defined. It is not clear a priori how the problem of animal welfare can be approached from an economic perspective, and what it can give in terms of interesting economic insights.

1.3 DIRECT VERSUS INDIRECT APPROACH

Let me go back to the initial question about the importance of the topic of animal welfare. There are essentially two reasons why animal welfare matters: for the people who care about animals, and for the animals themselves. It turns out that these two reasons are conceptually very different, and necessitate different approaches. Moreover, there is a pedagogical advantage in studying them separately, as it helps to avoid conflating different aspects of the issue.

Since this distinction drives the whole organization of the book and the methods used, it is important to explain it in detail.

Part II focuses on the direct approach, meaning that this is the "for the animals themselves" part, while Part III focuses on the indirect approach, meaning that this is the "for the people who care about animals" part. These parts are largely independent and can be read separately or even in reverse order. Actually, since Part III uses a more conventional anthropocentric perspective, it might be considered a more accessible starting point for some readers, in particular economists. I chose to start with the nonanthropocentric part since this follows a long philosophical tradition. Also, this perspective represents a significant methodological advancement in economics, and is one of the key novelties of this book, perhaps deserving primacy.

Conceptually, this distinction between the direct and indirect approaches is related to debates on future generations, particularly within the climate discounting literature (Gollier 2012, Millner and Heal 2023). The direct, or social discounting approach, argues that we should discount the future based on the normative belief that the welfare of future generations should be directly weighed. This approach was famously propounded by Ramsey (1928). It assumes that future generations have an intrinsic moral worth. In contrast, the indirect approach suggests that the welfare of future generations is considered only insofar as it affects the welfare of current generations, typically through parental altruism. Hence, this provides two conceptually different reasons for accounting for future generations, one based on general normative principles, the other on humans' preferences. This is akin to the direct and indirect approach adopted here. As an example of well-known investigation, Farhi and Werning (2007) contrast and explore both approaches in their study of intergenerational insurance and savings problems.

The distinction between the direct and indirect approaches is not entirely new in policy evaluation works. For instance, Sunstein (2024) argues that regulators should account for the value of animals, and interestingly, he draws a parallel between the challenges of valuing animals and those of valuing children. Specifically, he highlights that while one could use the parents' WTP for their child as an indirect valuation tool, it may also be important to consider the child's own welfare. We thus retrieve here the direct and indirect approaches. Sunstein further notes an additional complication: children, like animals, do not possess financial resources, which makes it difficult to apply the direct approach using traditional WTP methods.

Part II proceeds as follows. First, I explain why I favor sentientism as an alternative to anthropocentrism. Perhaps, the reader has already encountered the terms "sentientism," "sentience," or "sentient." In short, sentientism is the moral consideration of all (and only) sentient species, namely those species who can "feel." I then discuss the attempts for estimating welfare for sentient species, followed by the fundamental difficulty of comparing these utilities across different species. Undoubtedly, this is a very challenging objective. I then study how to aggregate these scores through a multispecies social welfare function. Finally, I will be in a position to present some theoretical and empirical nonanthropocentric economic approaches, and discuss issues regarding the ethics of animal populations. It is worth noting here that my normative assumptions can also be approached in a more descriptive manner. Indeed, the formal model includes the anthropocentric approach as a special case, allowing me to systematically compare both anthropocentric and nonanthropocentric outcomes.

To repeat, the key point is that the direct approach acknowledges the intrinsic value of animal welfare. This aligns with the philosophical tradition. This approach entails the direct inclusion of animals in the social welfare function. Under this approach, animals are regarded as individuals, and they have an intrinsic value. The impact of human actions on animals can then be perceived as an "externality," where an externality refers to a cost or benefit imposed on a third party who did not consent to it. Implicitly, economists view externalities as effects on individuals who are worthy of moral consideration. Hence, if animals are worthy of moral consideration, actions impacting their welfare can be seen as externalities in the same way.

However, this direct nonanthropocentric approach presents several conceptual challenges, with a major issue being the assessment of welfare. The conventional approach, based on humans' WTP, is inherently anthropocentric; it assumes that human choices can be used to estimate preferences, making it unsuitable for assessing the intrinsic value of animals. Moreover, using animals' WTP presents significant complexity: Animals do not have income, and using other goods like food or energy as metrics introduces additional challenges since animals do not engage in market transactions of these goods. Thus, the standard economic methods for welfare assessment must be adapted. At its core, the direct approach grapples with the complex issue of interspecies comparison. While comparing human welfare among humans is already very difficult, attempting to compare the welfare of humans and animals or even among different animal species presents immense challenges.

Besides, if one views impacts on animals as externalities, and if policies affect their number, we run into population ethics issues. When actions or policies affect the number of morally relevant individuals, it is not even clear what efficiency means. How can we normatively compare the welfare of 100 individuals with a good quality of life to that of 50 individuals with a better quality of life? In economics, we usually avoid such comparisons as we typically compare situations with the same population size and even the same individuals. In the analysis of the canonical model and subsequent chapters, I will explore how to adapt and reinterpret conventional models of externalities, as well as policy interventions such as Pigouvian taxation, when the externalities involve animals, and thus when the policy issue raises a population ethics problem.

At this juncture, it is important to emphasize that the book aligns with the utilitarian tradition, grounding itself in a consequentialist and welfarist perspective. In short, I assume that only the impacts on the well-being of the individuals involved hold significance.

This reflects the normative view that nothing can be good for society unless the members of the moral community (being humans or animals) are themselves benefitting from it. These impacts are then typically aggregated through a sum of utilities of these individuals. I will often coin this consequentialist/welfarist/utilitarian approach the "utilitarian approach." Utilitarianism has been a cornerstone of ethical discourse for over two centuries, originating from Bentham's seminal works. While many contemporary moral philosophers may diverge from utilitarianism, utilitarianism continues to wield a leading influence beyond philosophy, notably in fields such as welfare economics and legal scholarship (Adler 2019). Interestingly, early utilitarians also made central contributions in animal ethics, as we will see. See Sebo (2022) for a concise discussion and comparison of consequentialist and non-consequentialist approaches in animal ethics and Varner (2012) for an ethics that combines the two.

Let me stress now an important problem with the direct approach. I would call this problem the "fundamental political objection." This objection can be presented as follows. Given that humans hold the predominant political power on Earth, it becomes unclear how animals can have practical significance based on this nonanthropocentric approach. The point is that, in terms of immediate policy or political implications, the direct approach seems to lack substantial traction. This is exemplified in our legal system where animals have traditionally been characterized as "things," and thus are subject to the legal regime of goods, not that of "persons." The legal approach remains inevitably anthropocentric, favoring the interests of humans and where animals only have an instrumental value.

To illustrate the political objection, consider the following argument by the famous legal scholar and judge Richard Posner (2004) (cited in Stawasz 2024):

> [T]o the extent that courts are outside the normal political processes, [an animal-rights] approach is deeply undemocratic. There are more animals in the United States than people; if the

> animals are given capacious rights by judges who do not conceive themselves to be representatives of the people – indeed, who use a methodology that owes nothing to popular opinion or democratic preference – the de facto weight of the animal population in the society's political choices will approach or even exceed that of the human population. Judges will become the virtual representatives of the animals, casting in effect millions of votes to override the democratic choices of the human population.

In a nutshell, Posner contends that it is "undemocratic" to grant rights to animals. Of course, one may argue that this rests on a specieist definition of a democracy. But, in any case, this fundamental political objection may be viewed as a serious drawback of the direct approach. One may wonder: What is the point then of discussing an approach that can hardly be implemented for political reasons? This is a very difficult question to answer. Perhaps, one may think that the direct approach serves as a thought experiment that describes what we could or even should do morally. This thought experiment might be viewed as interesting in itself. It may also spark stimulating conceptual considerations. Moreover, one cannot completely exclude that these considerations might perhaps gradually permeate society and potentially have some impacts. After all, the moral beliefs of people may matter in our society. Note that this also offers connections to other political debates surrounding issues such as the interests of future generations or the historical debates on slavery.

This being said, the political objection provides a justification for developing an alternative approach, that is, the indirect approach. This alternative approach assumes that animals do not have intrinsic value but they matter insofar as they matter for humans. Under this approach, animals are indirectly incorporated into the social welfare function through human preferences, such as altruistic preferences toward animals. While the anthropocentric approach is problematic from a moral perspective, it corresponds to the existing economic approach to animal welfare. It is of course much more realistic politically, and it can hardly be deemed as undemocratic. Although this indirect approach is more conventional than the direct approach, it is also full of challenges and thus very stimulating, as we will see.

The existing literature in economics using this indirect approach is mostly based on studies about the WTP for animal welfare. These studies reveal that many people are willing to pay a significant amount for animal welfare, and that their income, age, and access to information are important factors that explain the level of WTP. However, there is still much to learn about how humans exactly care about animals. WTP studies are useful, but only offer a partial and limited view about humans' proanimal concerns, as they focus on specific decision-making contexts, and focus on pricing. It is thus essential to conduct more research to understand how proanimal concerns manifest in people and society. Moreover, as the indirect approach is rooted in the notion that humans care about animals, the underlying theme is fundamentally behavioral. A purely "homo economicus" approach, which assumes purely self-interested decision-making, would be inadequate in this context. It simply fails to account for the interests of animals in human decisions.

This indirect approach is primarily motivated by a puzzle related to the apparent "gap" between public opinion and market demand when it comes to animal welfare. While opinion polls and surveys often indicate that citizens care about animals, market data suggest that concerns for animal welfare are very limited globally. As a case in point, the expansion of intensive farming units in modern animal agriculture indicates that consumers seem to care little about animals. In a 2008 referendum, about two-thirds of Californians voted in favor of banning battery cages, despite the limited demand for cage-free eggs in the state, which held only about 10 percent of the market share at that time (Norwood and Lusk 2011). To paraphrase Norwood and Lusk, this "California egg paradox" raises the question of why people do not seem to shop like they vote. They call it the vote–buy gap. Further research is thus needed to better understand the psychological, social, political, and in particular the economic factors that contribute to the gap between public opinion and market demand for animal welfare, and to develop strategies to bridge this gap and improve animal welfare.

To conclude this section, I would like to briefly address a potential objection to the differentiation between the direct and indirect approaches. This objection posits that attributing an intrinsic value to animal welfare is essentially another manifestation of human preference, albeit of a different nature. In a broader sense, this objection questions the feasibility of a nonanthropocentric evaluation, given that it is conducted by humans, and in turn questions the separability of the direct and indirect approaches. Some may argue for instance that, since moral reasoning is a distinctive capability of humans, there would be no moral suffering if there were no humans.

I disagree with this objection, although I admit that this is a tricky issue. My view is the following. The direct nonanthropocentric approach builds on a normative foundation that defines what should be the social objective. This normative foundation depends on general normative principles, but does not depend a priori on human preferences toward animals. It is, however, important to acknowledge that only humans (philosophers, social choice experts, mathematicians, etc.) reflect on those normative principles and ultimately conduct this evaluation. Therefore, it is possible, and even unavoidable I would say, that some degree of "human bias" is present in the process. But, again, this is not really about human preferences toward animals, and this does not equate to an inherently anthropocentric bias. While humans do the evaluation, its purpose is not (at least in principle) to do it for human benefit. In sum, the evaluation is inevitably made by humans, but not "for" humans. It thus remains nonanthropocentric according to the very definition of the term.

1.4 PUTTING THE BOOK INTO PERSPECTIVE

Existing discussions on animal welfare often highlight moral, cultural, or ideological perspectives. However, economics, which plays a vital role in shaping human behavior and societal structures, is often neglected in these discussions. Occasionally, when economics is considered in some discussions, it is done so as a sweeping critique of capitalism and of the market economy. Yet such critiques are often broad and quite imprecise, and thus not very constructive. What, specifically, is the problem with capitalism in relation to animal welfare? Are there viable alternative systems, and how would they function in practice? Is there evidence that nonmarket economies have treated animals better?

Let me be clear from the outset: This book is not intended as a direct critique of the capitalist system. There are several reasons for this. First, the relationship between capitalism and animal welfare is a fascinating but highly complex topic, perhaps too ambitious to tackle comprehensively within the scope of a book this size. For insightful perspectives on this issue, see McMullen (2016) and Nibert (2017). Second, a central message of this book is that the root problem is not really capitalism itself, but speciesism. Capitalism, if one views it as a system based on private ownership and individual freedom, would take on a very different form in a non-speciesist society. In such a society, animals would be recognized as individuals, and thus neither be treated as property nor deprived of their freedom. As a result, most issues explored in this book would simply not exist even in such a capitalist system.

The book's primary focus is on examining the potential problems and solutions to issues regarding animal welfare that can arise within the current dominant economic system, namely a market economy. In line with conventional economic analysis, the approach here largely centers on identifying and addressing "market failures," with a particular emphasis on externalities and public good problems affecting animals. Additionally, the book concludes with discussions on broader topics, such as the morality of markets and political aspects, offering further insights directly tied to the issue of the impact of the economic and political system on animal welfare in general.

More precisely, the canonical model presented in this book pictures a market economy with human consumers and producers of animal products. In this model, animals are third parties affected by market transactions. In other words, humans generate externalities on animals. A precursor to this model is that of Blackorby and Donaldson (1992). In that outstanding paper, a social planner chooses the optimal level of meat consumption given that both humans and animals' welfare matter, and this level is compared to the equilibrium outcome. Following conventional economic thinking in the management of externalities, I show that it is possible to introduce a levy on animal products so that humans internalize the externalities of their actions on animals (Espinosa and Treich 2024). This is the standard Pigouvian correction to externalities. Hence, the approach illustrates how to adjust the functioning of the existing economic system to better take into account animals.

Although conventional, this approach requires dealing with specific difficulties related to the fact that the affected parties are animals. One key difficulty (already mentioned earlier) is the following: Altering the price of animal products directly impacts the number of animals consumed and produced, consequently influencing the overall animal population. This poses a well known ethical dilemma because one must compare different population sizes, and in particular one must compare life to nonexistence. The concept of "life worth living" becomes central in this context, and a dedicated chapter on population ethics explores various normative approaches to address this complex issue. Different approaches are presented to tackle this challenge and determine how to evaluate and compare animal populations of different sizes.

Another specific difficulty, also mentioned earlier, concerns the calculation of the externality on animals. This calculation is needed to calibrate the appropriate levy to apply to meat consumption to account for the externalities of meat consumption on animals. How to translate animal welfare into the unit of the tax, namely monetary units? Practically, the evaluation of the externality requires the assessment of animal well-being. This assessment cannot in principle resort to the observation of market prices, as they are controlled by humans. Nor can it resort to humans' WTP approach as I have already stated. Therefore, the difficulty of measuring animal well-being and comparing it to human well-being must be confronted.

I present in this book a step-by-step method to assess animal welfare (Budolfson and Spears 2020, Espinosa 2024, Espinosa and Treich 2024). This can be viewed as an introduction to the topic, since the development of methods to assess animal welfare constitutes a research program on its own, and we are just at the beginning of this program. The proposed approach's advantage is its breakdown of this very complex problem into several simpler components. One component involves calculating an "animal welfare score," which can be understood as a utility level at a specific point in time and aggregated to represent lifetime utility. Another component focuses on comparing this utility level across different species, referred to as "utility potential." Additionally, a philosophical foundation is provided to represent and aggregate the individual welfare of different species within the social objective, or social welfare function. Furthermore, and perhaps most importantly, the book can then formulate specific policy-making insights using a social objective that captures the quantified interests of both humans and animals in society.

A central theme explored in this book revolves around the distinction between quantity and quality. By "quantity," I refer to the quantity of animal lives, that is the number of animals (and possibly the duration of their lives). By "quality," I refer to the quality of animal lives, namely their level of welfare. Various human actions such as food choices, animal testing, or biodiversity preservation can impact either the quantity or the quality of animal lives, and most often both. The book extensively explains why unregulated markets often fail to achieve socially optimal outcomes in terms of both quantity and quality, making regulation essential. It turns out that it is fruitful to separate quantity and quality here, as routinely done in other domains in economics but rarely explicitly done in the works on animal welfare in other disciplines.

It is interesting to examine the literature on animal welfare in food and agriculture sciences versus that in environmental sciences with the quantity/quality distinction in mind. Indeed, the food and agricultural literature on animal welfare is predominantly preoccupied with issues regarding the quality of animal lives, namely the welfare of farmed animals in a specific husbandry system. In contrast, environmental sciences are primarily focused on quantity concerns, such as the preservation of some wild animal populations rather than their welfare levels.

Currently, animal welfare regulations in most countries primarily rely on legislative tools such as norms and guidelines. In the food industry or in medical research, existing regulations focus on the quality aspect alone and are designed to establish a practical and economically manageable minimum level of animal welfare. The research presented in this book is able to compute precisely the tradeoff between the economic cost for humans and the benefit for animals of a regulation improving quality. However, one important message of the book is that the quantity of animal lives must also be regulated, typically by choosing the number of animals produced that is socially optimal. Hence, the book also emphasizes the significance of incorporating instruments that address quantity, such as meat taxation, as part of a comprehensive animal welfare regulation.

Another central market failure in the context of animal welfare is the public good problem arising from the free-rider issue faced by consumers. Consumers may not properly consider that the impact of their proanimal actions also increases the welfare of other consumers who care about animals too, thus leading to underprovision of animal welfare by the market. While this is a recurring theme in economics, it may not have been adequately addressed in animal welfare regulation. Again, in the realm of food consumption, some commentators emphasize the importance of consumers' freedom of choice, and advocate for increased transparency through information schemes, such as labels indicating animal welfare standards. However, it is essential to recognize that such information initiatives alone cannot effectively resolve the public good problem at hand. A fiscal instrument may seem appropriate in a first approximation to deal with this public good problem, following the long-standing literature on Pigouvian taxation.

The book also moves beyond standard market failures such as externalities and public goods as it also extensively discusses "behavioral failures." In particular, it documents the various misperceptions or even misconceptions of humans regarding animals. For instance, people may underestimate animal suffering in industrial farming conditions, and overconsume meat as a result. I show then that animal welfare may then be viewed as a merit good, and that applying a levy on meat may also properly restore optimality under simple conditions.

I extensively discuss the literature on the psychological conflict that arises in individuals who consume meat while also being aware of the moral concerns related to animal welfare. This conflict is coined the "meat paradox." I present an economic approach to this paradox highlighting the effectiveness of meat taxation as a means to make consumers more realistic about the impact of their consumption on animals, which, in turn, reinforces the usual economic impact of taxation. Additionally, the book explains for instance that the commodification of animals in various industries can lead to an erosion of morality. By examining these diverse behavioral failures or problems, the book aims to provide a comprehensive understanding of the issues involved in animal welfare within the context of a market economy. It also identifies gaps in current studies, and ideas for future research.

The book also discusses the links between proanimal and prosocial aspects. There is indeed a large literature in psychology and economics on prosociality that may be relevant. For instance, recent studies have identified an interesting pattern: "moral universalism." This pattern characterizes the extent to which people account for the interests of strangers relative to those of ingroup members.

Indeed, two clusters typically emerge: Some people support redistribution, health care, environmental protection, affirmative action, and foreign aid, while others support military spending, law enforcement, and border protection (Enke et al. 2023). Younger and poorer people, women and less religious people in almost all countries are more universalist in the sense that they more likely to belong to the former group (Cappelen et al. 2024).

Although it remains an open question whether animals are part of this universalism pattern, it would not be a surprise. Studies in psychology have shown that individuals who tend to devalue other human groups (e.g., racism, sexism, homophobia) also tend to devalue animals (speciesism) (Caviola et al. 2019). Evidence suggests that animals are often viewed as the "outgroup," potentially making them targets of prejudice and discrimination possibly stemming from ancestral tribalistic tendencies. On the other hand, empathy toward humans may extend to animals, suggesting potential parallels between proanimal and prosocial findings. Adding to this complexity is the challenge of gauging the well-being of animals from a human perspective. Assessing human welfare is often feasible, since we can rely on introspection to understand what brings happiness and suffering in others and can directly ask people how they feel. However, the issue becomes considerably more intricate when it comes to animals, particularly those who are distant from us in evolutionary terms. This can typically give rise to two opposite biases: anthropomorphism, attributing human characteristics to animals (akin to projection bias), and conversely anthropodenial, denying such traits to animals.

A word now on the method used in this book. Although most content is nontechnical, several chapters in this book employ mathematical models. In particular, I use a so-called canonical model and adapt it in several chapters to discuss various economic approaches to animal welfare. I acknowledge that this technicality may be perceived as a barrier to some readers. The main justification for using these models is the usual one: rigor and precision. Mathematics indeed permits us to explore rigorously the implications of a set of assumptions. It also permits the precise definition of certain concepts. Consider for instance the concept of antispeciesism. This concept is central in animal ethics and more generally in the literature on animal welfare, but the term is often used colloquially. In this book, I will formally characterize antispeciesism as a moral concept. This allows us to reduce the scope for misunderstanding, and to explore the implications of antispeciesism in a meaningful manner. This also, of course, makes it easier to see the limitation of that characterization, and perhaps make progress toward a better characterization. Additionally, the use of mathematics also permits the generation of quantitative estimates through the calibration or estimation of formal models. For instance, I leverage the theoretical model's outcomes to compute the optimal levy in monetary terms that could be applied to meat consumption.

I want to add, however, that the mathematical language employed in this book is basic and consistent throughout, primarily focused on defining an objective to maximize, identifying optimal solutions, and conducting comparative statics analysis (i.e., exploring how the solutions vary with the model's parameters). The computations are straightforward and usually necessitate only one or two lines of mathematical calculus. I overlook some mathematical difficulties that bring little to the depth of the analysis, such as the analysis of second order conditions or of corner solutions. Thus, the book does not contain many technicalities. Only a basic knowledge of mathematics is necessary, and readers can find the essential mathematical concepts in various basic microeconomics textbooks. Furthermore, I strive to provide intuitive explanations throughout the book, ensuring that the implications of the theory are understandable to a broad audience. In some chapters, I even separate the formal analysis from a qualitative discussion of the important aspects. On the other hand, readers who are mathematically inclined will find backup for the main text in the cited sources.

As a minor remark, I have chosen not to include footnotes in this book. It is a departure from my usual practice, and also from the usual practice of the profession. While footnotes are undoubtedly valuable, they can also be somewhat addictive. Once you start adding footnotes, there is often a temptation to include even more, whether it is for additional explanations, side remarks, or extra references. Personally, I find myself relying on footnotes quite heavily in my research papers. Therefore, the decision to ban footnotes serves as a commitment device to focus on essential content and avoid distractions and endless additions. This decision is costly but, hopefully, it will enhance the flow of the text and optimize readability. Let me also mention that I will frequently use verbatim citations, particularly in the literature survey sections (such as 2.4 and 2.5). Often, there is no need to rephrase something that has already been expressed with perfect clarity. Moreover, this practice allows me to give due credit to the original authors.

As I said earlier, the primary audience for this book is undoubtedly economists, or more broadly people interested in the research in economics. Indeed, one central objective of this book is to develop and accelerate the development of the research in economics on animals and their welfare. However, the content may surprise some of these readers, particularly agricultural economists, as it significantly diverges from the existing discussions on animal welfare in their field. Indeed, the book does not devote a lot of space discussing the production costs associated with animal welfare or consumers' WTP for more animal-friendly products. Although these aspects are undeniably essential, they have already been explored in other works such as in the seminal book by Norwood and Lusk (2011). Moreover, these works largely rely on established and conventional economic approaches. They typically consider animal welfare as an "attribute" of a product and essentially study how this attribute affects demand and cost functions. Hence, I do not add much to this conventional approach in this book.

Instead, my book largely adopts a distinctive focus, perhaps resulting in greater methodological challenges posed by animal welfare to economists, and exemplified by the presentation of the direct and indirect approaches earlier. Let me thus re-emphasize: The direct approach departs from conventional economic thinking as it extends social welfare considerations to encompass animals, recognizing their inherent value and well-being. Additionally, the indirect approach investigates a novel topic in behavioral economics: understanding proanimal concerns and their broader implications, and exploring the complex relationships between human actions and beliefs, markets, institutions and ultimately the welfare of animals. Again, this book only provides an introduction to these challenging topics. However, in doing so, I believe that it ventures a step beyond the approaches usually found in agricultural and environmental economics to animal welfare. Overall, I find this book to be highly complementary to the existing work in agricultural economics such as Norwood and Lusk (2011).

Some economists, especially behavioral economists, may also be familiar with the work of John Kagel and his coauthors from the 1980s, where they conducted lab experiments in economics using animals (Battalio et al. 1981, Kagel 1987, Kagel et al. 1995). While this research could also be labeled "animal economics," its objectives are fundamentally different from the focus of this book and are largely unrelated to its content. Kagel and his colleagues performed numerous experiments in which rats and pigeons make choices that affect how much food and water they receive. In these studies, the "price" typically refers to the effort required, such as the number of times a lever had to be pressed by an animal to obtain a specific quantity of a given commodity. The aim is to explore whether the predictions of economic theory apply to animal behavior. That is, it is about using animal experiments to understand human behavior (Kagel et al. 1995). The underlying assumption is that many aspects of human decision-making have a biological component that might be shared with other animal species. Indeed, Kagel (1987) notes that animals often exhibit choice patterns similar to those observed in humans. However, this research is not concerned with animal welfare per se, which is the primary focus of this book. That is, this book is fundamentally policy oriented, considering animal welfare as part of the policy objective.

As mentioned earlier, the early chapters primarily cover animal welfare literature from philosophical and other perspectives, which may not be of interest to all economists. While these chapters provide background, they fall outside the realm of economics. Therefore, readers mainly focused on economics aspects of animal welfare might prefer to skim these sections and proceed directly to Chapter 7. In that chapter, I introduce an economic model, the so-called canonical model, that serves as a benchmark for the subsequent chapters, focusing on the economic aspects of animal welfare. This model, along with its various adaptations, provides a central theoretical tool for understanding, and perhaps teaching, the economic aspects of animal welfare. It should offer a setting that resonates with economists' expertise and interests. I believe that this model facilitates a structured and rigorous approach to the economics of animal welfare.

To conclude this long introduction, I would like to touch on the delicate topic of activism. Am I an activist? Is this an animal advocacy book? These are questions I ponder. To be honest, I guess I align with the activist spirit in the sense that my research strives for an enhancement of animal welfare in the world. But, is this fundamentally different from a scientist advocating for stricter climate regulations? We all lean on scientific foundations. Certainly, there are moral values in the science I employ. Yet, moral values are also inherent in climate policy science, as evidenced by the well documented debate about climate discounting, for example. One peculiar aspect, however, lies in the potential consequence of my advocacy. The optimal policies proposed in this book may frequently favor a "transfer" of welfare from humans to animals. I acknowledge that this outcome poses a challenge in a society that predominantly centers around humans, and it may encounter strong resistance due to the prevalent speciesist bias discussed earlier. We go back here to the fundamental political objection, also mentioned earlier. But is this a problem?

One of my closest friends and colleagues once suggested that I collaborate with someone who may not share the same activist stance, someone who is not personally concerned by the issue of animal welfare. While I can see the point, I found this suggestion somewhat strange. I countered by asking whether he would for instance recommend a female colleague, deeply invested in the gender issue, to partner in a scientific project about gender economics with a male researcher unconcerned by gender issues. It turns out that individuals working on matters of justice, be it gender or minority-related issues for instance, are often females or individuals from minority backgrounds. They possess an inherent drive and motivation to address these subjects, and yes, there is a risk that they produce biased research. However, they also possess a unique insight into the issue which may grant them a critical advantage in generating novel ideas. I do not see why the same would not apply for researchers working on animal welfare.

REFERENCES

Adler MD (2019) *Measuring Social Welfare*. Oxford University Press.

Atkinson AB (2015) *Inequality: What Can Be Done?* Harvard University Press.

Battalio RC, Kagel JH, Rachlin H, Green L (1981) Commodity-choice behavior with pigeons as subjects. *Journal of Political Economy*, 89(1), 67–91.

Bennett RM (1997) Farm animal welfare and food policy. *Food Policy*, 22(4), 281–288.

Bennett RM, Kehlbacher A, Balcombe K (2012) A method for the economic valuation of animal welfare benefits using a single welfare score. *Animal Welfare*, 21(S1), 125–130.

Blackorby C, Donaldson D (1992) Pigs and guinea pigs: A note on the ethics of animal exploitation. *Economic Journal*, 102, 1345–1369.

Bollard, L (2023) We love animals: Why do we torture them? https://farmanimalwelfare.substack.com/p/we-love-animals-why-do-we-torture.

Bowles S, Halliday SD (2022) *Microeconomics: Competition, Conflict, and Coordination*. Oxford University Press.

Buchanan JM (1964) What should economists do? *Southern Economic Journal*, 30(3), 213–222.

Budolfson M, Espinosa R, Fischer B, Treich N (2024) Monetizing animal welfare impacts for benefit–cost analysis. *Journal of Benefit-Cost Analysis*, 15, 1–18.

Budolfson M, Fischer B, Scovronick N (2023) Animal welfare: Methods to improve policy and practice. *Science*, 381(6653), 32–34.

Budolfson M, Spears D (2020) Public policy, consequentialism, the environment, and nonhuman animals. In *The Oxford Handbook of Consequentialism*, ed. DW Portmore, 592–615. Oxford University Press.

Cappelen AW, Enke B, Tungodden B (2025) Moral universalism: Global evidence. *American Economic Review*, 115(1), 43–76.

Carlier A, Treich N (2020) Directly valuing animal welfare in (environmental) economics. *International Review of Environmental and Resource Economics*, 14, 113–152.

Caviola L, Everett JA, Faber NS (2019) The moral standing of animals: Towards a psychology of speciesism. *Journal of Personality and Social Psychology*, 116(6), 1011.

Dasgupta P (2021) *The Economics of Biodiversity: The Dasgupta Review*. HM Treasury.

Deaton A (2022) Is economic failure an economics failure? Le Monde. www.lemonde.fr/en/opinion/article/2022/12/30/angus-deaton-is-economic-failure-an-economics-failure_6009720_23.html.

Donaldson S, Kymlicka W (2011) *Zoopolis: A Political Theory of Animal Rights*. Oxford University Press.

Enke B, Rodríguez-Padilla R, Zimmermann F (2023) Moral universalism and the structure of ideology. *The Review of Economic Studies*, 90(4), 1934–1962.

Espinosa R (2024) Animals and social welfare. *Social Choice and Welfare*, 62(3), 465–504.

Espinosa R, Treich N (2024) The animal welfare levy. *Journal of the European Economic Association*, in press.

Eurobarometer (2023) Attitudes of Europeans towards animal welfare. https://europa.eu/eurobarometer/surveys/detail/2996.

Farhi E, Werning I (2007) Inequality and social discounting. *Journal of Political Economy*, 115(3), 365–402.

Fleurbaey M, Leppanen C (2021) Toward a theory of ecosystem well-being. *Journal of Bioeconomics*, 23, 257–295.

Fleurbaey M, Van der Linden M (2021) Fair social ordering, egalitarianism, and animal welfare. *American Economic Journal: Microeconomics*, 13(4), 466–491.

Gollier C (2012). The debate on discounting: Reconciling positivists and ethicists. *Chicago Journal of International Law*, 13(2), Article 13.

Grethe H (2017) The economics of farm animal welfare. *Annual Review of Resource Economics*, 9, 75–94.

Harrison R (1964) *Animal Machines: The New Factory Farming Industry*. CABI.

Horta O (2010) What is speciesism? *Journal of Agricultural and Environmental Ethics*, 23, 243–266.

Jaquet F (2021) Speciesism and tribalism: Embarrassing origins. *Philosophical Studies*, 179, 933–954.

Johansson-Stenman O (2018) Animal welfare and social decisions: Is it time to take Bentham seriously? *Ecological Economics*, 145(C), 90–103.

Kagel JH (1987) Economics according to the rats (and pigeons too): What have we learned and what can we hope to learn. In *Laboratory Experimentation in Economics: Six Points of View*, ed. A Roth, 155–192. Cambridge University Press.

Kagel JH, Battalio RC, Green L (1995) *Economic Choice Theory: An Experimental Analysis of Animal Behavior*. Cambridge University Press.

Lagerkvist CJ, Hess S (2010) A meta-analysis of consumer willingness to pay for farm animal welfare. *European Review of Agricultural Economics*, 38(1), 55–78.

Marshall A (1890) *Principles of Economics: An Introductory Volume*. www.marxists.org/reference/subject/economics/marshall/.

McMullen S (2016) *Animals and the Economy*. Palgrave Macmillan.

Mechtenberg L, Perino G, Treich N, Tyran JR, Wang SW (2024) Self-signaling in voting. *Journal of Public Economics*, 231, 105070.

Millner A, Heal, G (2023) Choosing the future: Markets, ethics, and rapprochement in social discounting. *Journal of Economic Literature*, 61(3), 1037–1087.

Nibert D (ed.) (2017) *Animal Oppression and Capitalism* (2 volumes). Bloomsbury Publishing USA.

Norwood FB, Lusk JL (2011) *Compassion, by the Pound: The Economics of Farm Animal Welfare*. Oxford University Press.

Parmesan C (2006) Ecological and evolutionary responses to recent climate change. *Annual Review of Ecology, Evolution and Systematics*, 37, 637–669.

Posner RA (2004) Animal rights: Legal, philosophical, and pragmatic perspectives. In *Animal Rights: Current Debates and New Directions*, eds. CR Sunstein and MC Nussbaum, 51–57. Oxford University Press.

Prados De La Escosura L (2015) World human development: 1870–2007. *Review of Income and Wealth*, 61(2), 220–247.

Ramsey FP (1928) A mathematical theory of saving. *The Economic Journal*, 38(152), 543–559.

Ripple WJ, Whalen DN, Wolf C (2024) Trophic cascades and climate change. *Food Webs*, e00362.

Robbins L (1932) *An Essay on the Nature and Significance of Economic Science*. New York University Press.

Rowlands M (1997) Contractarianism and animal rights. *Journal of Applied Philosophy*, 14(3), 235–247.

Samuelson PA, Nordhaus WD (1998) *Economics*. The McGraw-Hill Companies, Inc.

Sebo J (2022) *Saving Animals, Saving Ourselves: Why Animals Matter for Pandemics, Climate Change, and Other Catastrophes*. Oxford University Press.

Singer P (1975) *Animal Liberation: A New Ethics of Our Treatment of Animals*. Random House.

Singer P (1980) Utilitarianism and vegetarianism. *Philosophy and Public Affairs*, 9(4), 325–337.

Stawasz A (2024) Animals in cost-benefit analyses. Available at SSRN 3643473.

Sunstein CR (2024) Regulators should value nonhuman animals. *Journal of Benefit-Cost Analysis*, 15(1), 1–13.

Tirole J (2019) Assumptions in economics, mimeo.

Torres B (2007) *Making a Killing: The Political Economy of Animal Rights*. AK Press.

Treich N (2022) The Dasgupta Review and the problem of anthropocentrism. *Environmental and Resource Economics*, 83, 973–997.

Varner GE (2012) *Personhood, Ethics, and Animal Cognition: Situating Animals in Hare's Two Level Utilitarianism*. Oxford University Press.

Weisskircher M (2024) Fifty years after Peter Singer's Animal Liberation: What Has the Animal Rights Movement achieved so Far?. *The Political Quarterly*, 15(2), 333–343.

2 Animals in This World

2.1 COUNTING ANIMALS

In this chapter, I first present some general figures regarding the number of animals that exist in this world, and the number of those who are exploited by humans. As we will see, the numbers involved are truly staggering, almost beyond comprehension. This puts into perspective the significance of Figure 1.1, which underscores the immense animal welfare challenge we face globally. On a more positive note, these numbers also represent substantial opportunities to alleviate animal suffering. This can be accomplished by reducing the quantity of animals used by humans and also by improving their living conditions. The strategies for achieving this goal serve as a central motivation for this book.

Let me start with farmed animals. Each year, over 70 billion farmed terrestrial animals are slaughtered for meat, with chickens comprising by far the largest portion; see Figure 2.1. Note that this is an underestimation since animals used for dairy products and eggs are not accounted for in this figure. Note also that the trend has been highly increasing over the last sixty years. To help comprehend these figures, the website Our World in Data has provided some illustrative "translations" of these statistics. Approximately 900,000 cows are slaughtered daily globally. If each cow were 2 meters long and lined up end to end, the row would span 1,800 kilometers. In the case of chickens, the figures are even more astounding: A staggering 202 million chickens are slaughtered each day. This means for instance that 140,000 chickens are slaughtered every minute.

Estimating the numbers of aquatic animals is difficult and the figures obtained vary a lot from one study to the other. There is a lot of uncertainty, and a scarcity of studies. Fish production is usually quantified in weight rather than number of individual fish, in

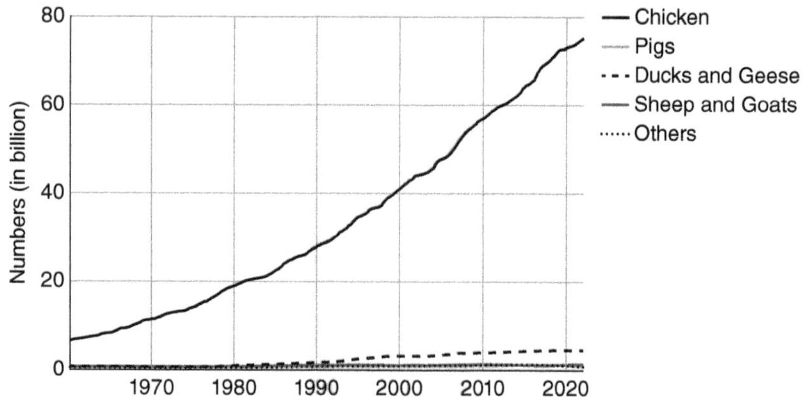

FIGURE 2.1 Yearly number of farmed land animals slaughtered. Source: Food and Agriculture Organization of the United Nations and Our World in Data

contrast to farmed mammals and birds. Using estimates of individual weight at the time of kill, a few recent works attempt to translate these figures into numbers of individual fish.

Franks et al. (2021) estimate for 2018 a population of 250 to 408 billion individual fish from more than 400 species that are farmed in aquaculture. Mood et al. (2023) conduct an analysis of the annual global farmed fish production from 1990 onwards. Figure 2.2 provides estimated ranges for the number of fish, along with the combined figures for birds and mammals slaughtered (as in Figure 2.1). Based on the mid-point estimates for each year, it is found that in 2006, the number of fish surpassed that of birds and mammals, reaching 56 billion. By 2019, this figure had surged to 124 billion, signifying a staggering 1.5-fold increase compared to the numbers of birds and mammals. Mood and Brooke (2024) estimate that about 1,600 billion (or 1.6 trillion) wild fish are caught every year with anchovy accounting for 28 percent of this total. These figures provide lower bounds since they exclude unrecorded captures such as illegal fishing and "ghost fishing" (i.e., any lost or abandoned fishing gear that continues to fish and trap animals).

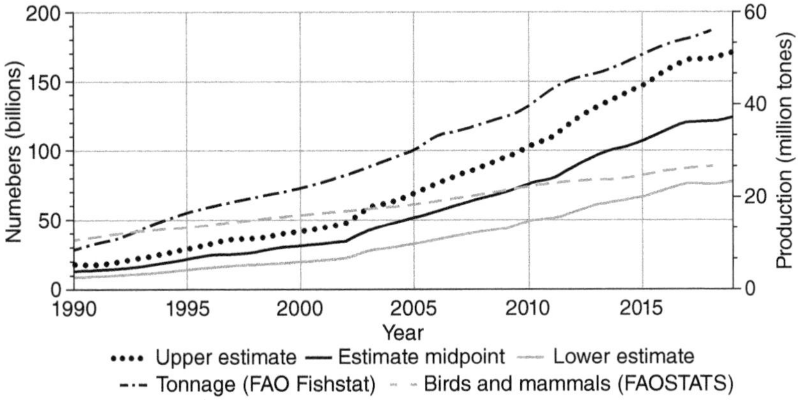

FIGURE 2.2 Farmed fish production in numbers and tonnage.
Source: Mood et al. (2023)

Still, this huge toll regarding farmed land mammals and fish pales in comparison to the annual count of shrimps harvested for human consumption. This number greatly surpasses the combined total of all other vertebrate and invertebrate animals slaughtered worldwide for human consumption. Waldhorn and Autric (2023) estimate that the annual number of shrimp killed for food is in the trillions, with approximately 300 to 620 billion coming from farms and 6.5 to 66 trillion caught in the wild.

The data given in Figure 2.2 represent yearly or daily figures. Another approach is to compute how many farmed animals are raised at any given time. According to Anthis and Reese-Anthis' (2019) estimations, there are approximately 31 billion land animals and a range of 38 to 215 billion farmed fish worldwide at any given moment. Their analysis reveals that fish make up roughly 78 percent of the global farmed animal population, while meat-raised chickens account for 12 percent, and egg-laying chickens constitute 5 percent. In contrast, both cows and pigs each represent a mere 1 percent of this population. Furthermore, there are between 150 and 370 billion shrimps being raised on farms at any given time. Additionally, the Rethink Priorities website estimates between 120 million and 1.2 billion farmed frogs, more than 6 million farmed snakes, and 1.2 million farmed crocodiles alive at any given time.

Let me now turn to wild animals. There are few studies on this topic, so the estimates are very tentative, and much more uncertain than for farmed animals. It appears that biologists have not dedicated extensive efforts to estimating the number of individuals in animal populations. Gaston and Blackburn (1997, pages 615 and 616) write for instance that: "Attempts to assess the magnitude of global biodiversity have focussed on estimating species richness. [...] The total number of individual organisms in the world [...] has been a largely ignored statistic." In this chapter, I will be mostly drawing on the data already presented in Carlier and Treich (2020), as well as on the abundance estimate part in the supplementary material of Bar-On et al. (2018).

Birds – Gaston and Blackburn (1997, page 615) use multiple methods which all give "surprisingly consistent estimates of a global bird population of between 200 billion and 400 billion individuals." Other estimates such as De Juana (1992) find populations of between 100 billion and 400 billion. Updating the methods, Gaston et al. (2003) estimate around 86 billion individual birds. Callaghan et al. (2021), by aggregating species-level estimates for approximately 10,000 bird species, estimate that there are currently around 50 billion individual birds in the world.

Mammals – Matheny and Chan (2005) use wild mammal densities that are 2.25 wild bird densities. Based on population estimates ranging from 200 billion to 400 billion birds, this calculation results in an estimated range of 450 billion to 900 billion wild mammals. Bar-On et al. (2018) estimate much lower figures, with around 80 billion wild mammals, noting that the number of marine mammals is relatively small, estimated to be around 20 million individuals.

Reptiles – Tomasik (2009) uses a handful of published estimates of reptile population to conclude that there are between 100 billion and 10 trillion reptiles.

Amphibians – Tomasik (2009) extrapolates from various estimates of local amphibian population densities to estimate a global amphibian population of 100 billion and 10 trillion.

Fish – Global fish biomass is roughly estimated to range from 1 to 2 billion tonnes (wet mass) according to Wilson et al. (2009). Some argue that early estimation methods, particularly those involving trawling nets, substantially underestimate fish biomass. More recent assessments utilizing acoustic methods suggest that the biomass of mesopelagic fish alone could be as high as 10 billion tonnes (Kaartvedt et al. 2012). Mood and Brooke (2010) find that 77.4 million tonnes of fish corresponds to a range of 0.97 to 2.74 trillion individual fish. Applying these conversion rates to Kaartvedt et al's estimate of 10 billion tonnes gives us a global wild fish population estimate ranging from 125.3 trillion to 354 trillion individual fish. Utilizing an alternate estimation approach to convert biomass into a number of individual fish, Bar-On et al. (2018) proposes an estimate of approximately one quadrillion (i.e., 10^{15}) fish.

Others – Less cognitively complex animals are many orders of magnitude more populous than the previous groups (Williams 1960, Tomasik 2009). Bar-On et al. (2018) estimate that there are about 5×10^{17} pteropods (a subgroup of mollusks), about 10^{18} terrestrial arthropods such as insects and arachnids and about 10^{20} marine arthropods.

To provide yet another picture, let me now present numbers in terms of biomass. In their recent study, Greenspoon et al. (2023) find that roughly 40 percent of the biomass of all wild land mammals is concentrated in just ten species. Among these, large herbivores like the white-tailed deer, wild boar, and African elephant are the primary contributors. Turning to wild marine mammals, baleen whales dominate, accounting for around 60 percent of the total biomass. Figure 2.3 provides a visual representation of the relative number of species, individual counts, and overall biomass within each taxonomic order of wild land mammals. Note that Greenspoon et al. (2023) exclude synanthropic species (mice, rats, pigeons, etc.), that is, species that benefit from and thrive in human environments.

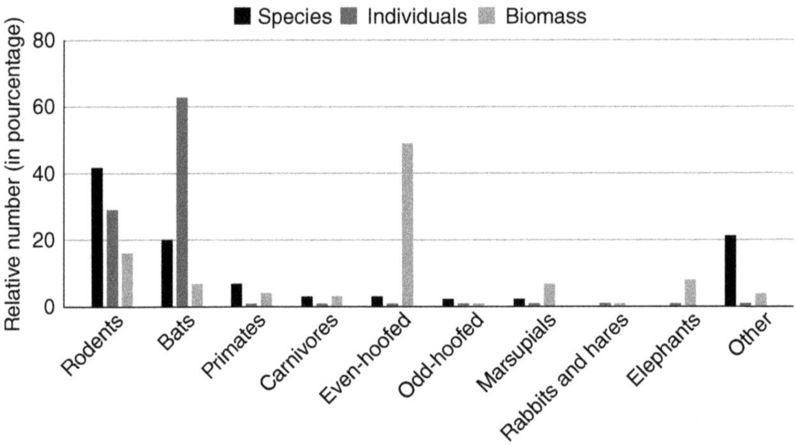

FIGURE 2.3 Relative number of species, number of individuals, and total biomass of each taxonomic order of wild land mammals. Source: Greenspoon et al. (2023)

Perhaps surprisingly, bats make up one-fifth of the species and two-thirds of the individual mammals. However, they contribute less than one-tenth of the total biomass. It is thus important to acknowledge that reasoning in terms of biomass, species diversity, or individual counts leads to vastly different perspectives; see Figure 2.3. Despite wild marine mammals boasting a considerably lower number of species and individuals compared to their land-based counterparts, their collective mass of roughly 40 million metric tons surpasses that of wild land mammals by nearly twofold. For context, common pet species like cats and dogs collectively weigh approximately 20 million metric tons, a figure on par with the combined biomass of all wild terrestrial mammals.

The data presented in this section, while informative, offer a static perspective and do not shed light on the dynamic interplay between evolving animal populations and human–animal interactions. These interactions are myriad and complex, exerting significant influence on both animal populations and their surrounding environments. Figure 2.4 illustrates the concerning downward

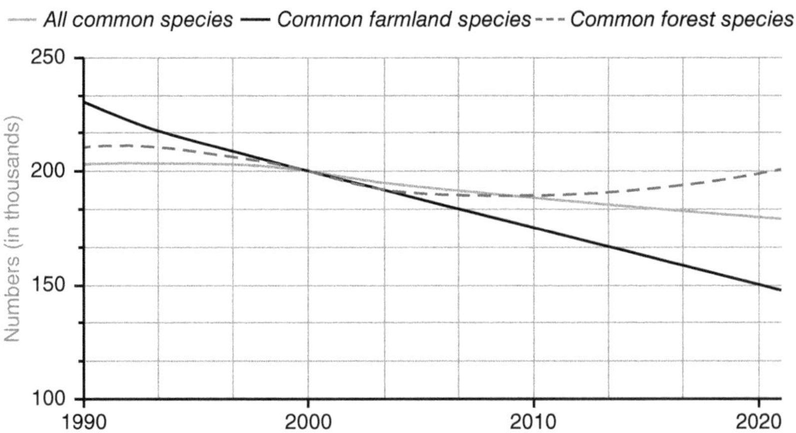

FIGURE 2.4 Evolution of bird population in Europe.
Source: Various NGOs and Our World in Data

trend in bird populations, often serving as a reference for assessing biodiversity decline.

According to the recent global assessment report by the Intergovernmental Science-Policy Platform on Biodiversity and Ecosystem Services (IPBES 2019), the rate of species extinction is currently tens to hundreds of times higher than the average rate observed over the past 10 million years, and this rate is accelerating. Presently, approximately 1 million species face the risk of extinction, with half of them being plants or animals (except insects), and the other half comprising insects. IPBES (2019) identifies five primary direct drivers contributing to biodiversity loss: changes in land and sea use; direct exploitation of organisms; climate change; pollution; and the introduction of alien species.

Undoubtedly, human activities have exerted a profound impact on the ecological balance of our planet, resulting in habitat reduction and the extinction of numerous species. The primary driver behind this is land use, and thus agriculture (and especially animal agriculture) in terms of the economic sector (Wilting et al. 2017). While there is in general no direct conflict between farm and wild mammals, the resources required to raise and feed the growing livestock populations place strong pressure on the natural environment and in turn on wild animals. Therefore, it is central to gauge the extent to which biodiversity has been altered due to changes in resources resulting from human activities. Quantification of shifts in land use patterns has been undertaken, revealing a prevalent trend toward the conversion of natural vegetation into croplands and pasture.

A logical progression in assessing the magnitude of the adverse effects of human activities on biodiversity is to inquire about the extent to which they have diminished the global population figures across major taxa. Notably, croplands and pastures exhibit a significantly simplified ecological structure compared to many of the land-use types they have replaced. Gaston et al. (2003) provide an estimation of the current global breeding-bird population according to land use. As illustrated in Table 2.1, there are substantial disparities between croplands, pastures, and forests. Particularly, tropical forests harbor a remarkably high bird density. Taking these estimates at face value, it can be inferred that about a quarter of the global bird population resides in tropical forests.

Bar-On et al. (2018) present diverse metrics for quantifying human impact on animal populations. Drawing on a multitude of recent local and global studies, they compute the biosphere's biomass

Table 2.1 *Estimates of bird density in different land-use types*

Land use	Bird density (individuals per km^2)
Cropland	300
Pasture	375
Grassland/steppe	450
Boreal forest	575
Temperate mixed forest	800
Warm mixed forest	1,250
Tropical forest	2,500

Source: Gaston et al. (2003)

composition in terms of gigatons of carbon. In terms of biomass, plants dominate both terrestrial and marine life, constituting over 80 percent of all living biomass. In contrast, all animal categories – mammals, fish, insects, worms, birds, and others – account for a mere 0.37 percent of the total biomass. Fish biomass surpasses that of humans by over 100 times, while humans outweigh wild (terrestrial) mammals by nearly 100 times. Notably, the biomass of livestock nearly doubles that of humans. Figure 2.5 underscores the current prevalence of domesticated animal biomass in relation to human and wild animal biomass, emphasizing the extensive indirect impact of human food production on the planet.

Let me now turn to pets. While obtaining exact global figures for pets can be challenging, certain statistics provide a rough estimate of their scale. In the United States alone, there are approximately 300 million pets. The most prevalent among these are fish (105 million), followed by cats (86 million) and dogs (78 million) (Green 2016). Roughly 48 percent of households in the United States have a dog, and 38 percent have a cat. In addition to domesticated

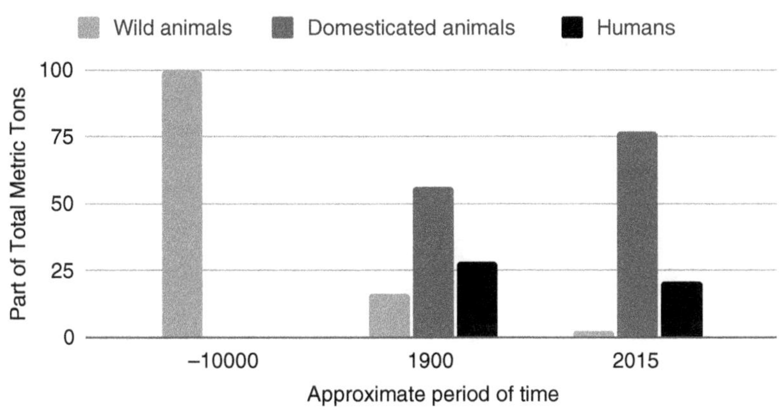

FIGURE 2.5 Estimated biomass of wild animals, domesticated animals, and humans.
Source: Vaclav Smil (2013). Data prepared by Nathan Hagens and Paul Chefurka: www.resilience.org/stories/2018-08-30/the-way-of-exploitation-can-we-do-better/

cats, it is estimated that there may be as many as 70 million feral and free-roaming cats. In the United States shelter system, roughly 7.6 million companion animals enter shelters nationwide each year. Of these, around 3.9 million are dogs and 3.4 million are cats. In the European Union-28 region, as of 2016, 18 percent of households own a dog, while 26 percent own a cat, and approximately 35 percent have some form of pet. If we make a simplistic extrapolation, assuming that the global rate of pet ownership mirrors that of the United States, it would imply a global pet population of 6.8 billion.

Finally, let me consider animals used in scientific research. In 2005, an estimated 115 million vertebrate lab animals were used annually (Taylor et al. 2008). By 2015, this number was extrapolated to approximately 192 million (Taylor and Alvarez 2019). Nonetheless, it is likely that the number of laboratory animals alive at any given time is less than 100 million (Fraser and MacRae 2011). Additionally, a significant number of invertebrates are employed, but specific estimates of their population have not been documented. It is estimated that around 12 million animals are used annually for dissection in US high schools (Green 2016). In total, there were 767,622 animals reported to have been used in US research experiments in 2015, according to the USDA/APHIS. Here is how the figures break down: 172,864 guinea pigs, 138,348 rabbits, 98,420 hamsters, 61,950 nonhuman primates, 74,263 pigs, 61,101 dogs, 19,932 cats, and 140,744 other animals.

2.2 ANIMALS AND THE ECONOMY

Animals have been instrumental in the progress of human civilization. They enable the transportation of both people and heavy goods, as well as the extraction of water and other resources from the ground. Animals provide essential goods like food and leather. They also provide wool for clothing, fat for lighting, and fuel for cooking and heating through manure. Animals such as horses were instrumental in wars. In European civilization, significant strides toward the development of a market economy were first made possible because animals initially alleviated a portion of the population from the constant demands of food production. Popular books such as *Guns, Germs and Steel* by Jared Diamond make it very clear that animals were central in human development, as well as human disease and conflicts. Animals, in many respects, have been our slaves and they have played a key role in the transition from feudalism to capitalism (Murray 2011). In Emile Zola's *Germinal*, the depiction of the harsh conditions endured by both miners and horses vividly portrays the exploitation and suffering inherent in the mining industry, making it a timeless classic.

However, it is also important to notice that reliance on animals has markedly diminished since the onset of the industrial revolution in developed economies. Take, for example, the whale industry. Whale fat once served as a vital source of energy and found extensive industrial applications for humans. As depicted in Figure 2.6, the zenith of whaling in the United States occurred in the mid-nineteenth century. In 1846, the industry employed as many as 735 ships and 70,000 individuals (Coleman 1995). Yet, the discovery, refinement, and widespread availability of abundant petroleum crude

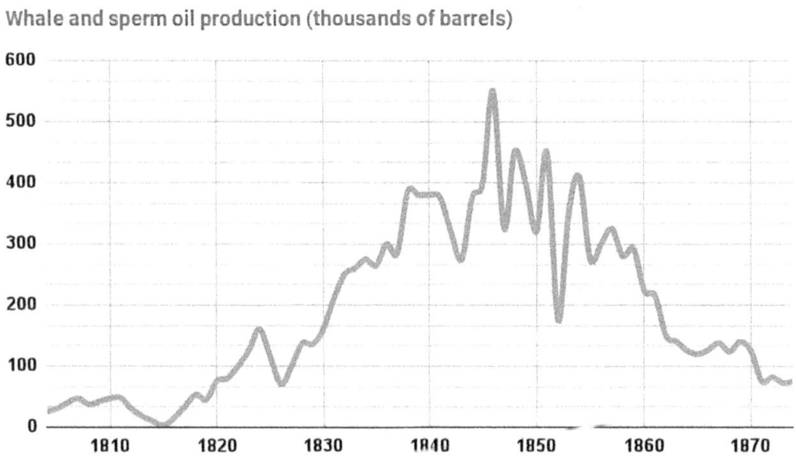

FIGURE 2.6 Evolution of whale oil production in the United States. Source: Coleman (1995) and Our World in Data

oil, which proved more cost-effective than whale oil, dealt a fatal blow to the American whaling sector. By 1890, a mere 200 whaling vessels remained in operation, and less than a century later in 1971, there was no more American commercial whaling.

Numerous other instances follow a similar pattern. Many innovations have gradually led to the displacement of animals from the production process. However, the replacement process was often lengthy and intricate. At times, the development of machines initially coincided with an increased (and not a decreased) use of animals, such as when horse-drawn local transport supplemented the development of trains in France. It is well known that horses were instrumental in the rise of American industrial power in the nineteenth century (Greene 2008). Nevertheless, over an extended period, there has been a significant decline in the use of animals in developed economies. For instance, the mechanization of agriculture and transportation caused the population of horses and mules in the United States to plummet from 21 million in 1910 to a mere 6 million by 1960 (Kilby 2007).

Note the subtlety here in terms of impacts on the number of animals. In some cases, like the advent of petroleum crude oil, more animals, such as whales, may exist since we no longer hunt them. Conversely, in cases like agriculture or transportation, where tractors and cars have taken over, fewer animals exist because we no longer require them, and we thus do not bring them into existence. These considerations will be important later on when we study the social impact of economic activity on the number of animals.

Now, it is crucial to acknowledge that the trends differ significantly for food production, as the global reliance on animals has constantly increased in the last decades. Consider the increasing number of farmed animals already documented earlier; see Figures 2.1 and 2.2. The main causes of this trend seem well known (Parlasca and Qaim 2022). The global human population is expanding, leading to a rise in the consumption of animal products. Furthermore, meat consumption per capita tends to escalate with rising income levels as illustrated in Figures 2.7 and 2.8. Over the last sixty years, there has been a dramatic surge in meat consumption, particularly in countries like China, which has witnessed a boost in affluence due to economic development. Furthermore, the industrialization of agriculture has contributed to a reduction in the cost of animal products. As a nation's wealth grows, so does the level of industrialization in agriculture, leading to more intensive animal production, as exemplified by the trends for chickens and pigs in Figure 2.9.

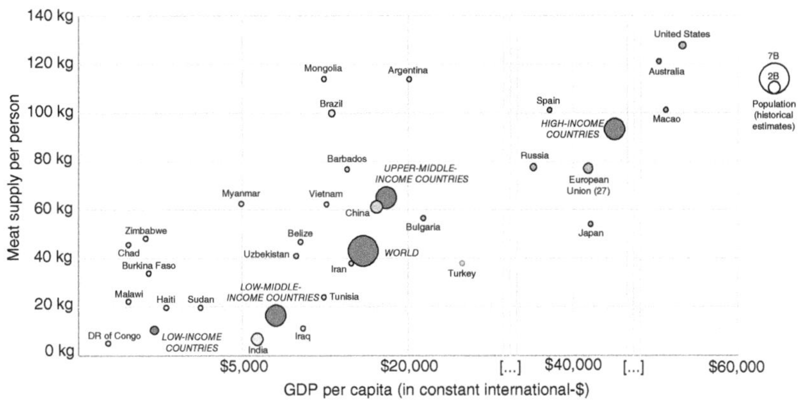

FIGURE 2.7 Meat consumption as a function of GDP per capita. Sources: Food and Agriculture Organization of the United Nations and Our World in Data

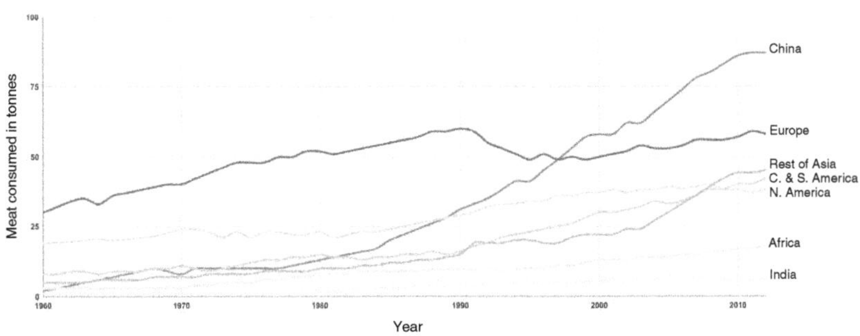

FIGURE 2.8 Total consumption of meat (in million metric tons) in different regions.
Sources: Godfray et al. (2018) and Food and Agriculture Organization of the United Nations

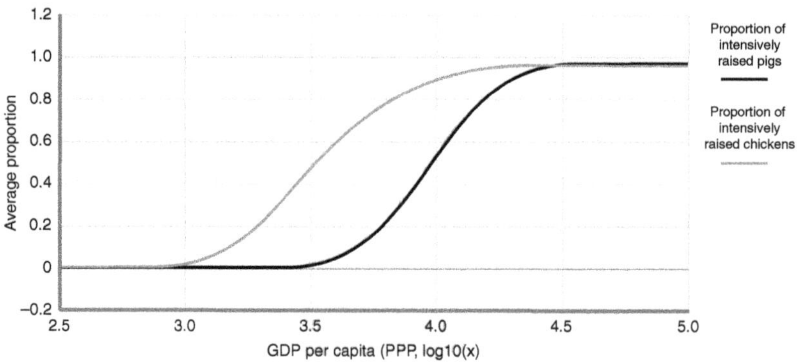

FIGURE 2.9 Proportion of intensively raised chickens and pigs as a function of GDP per capita.
Source: Gilbert et al. (2015)

In light of these trends, it comes as no surprise that the animal farming sector holds a substantial share of our economies. For example, meat production contributes to approximately 6 percent of the United States' GDP, encompassing both direct and indirect revenues. Livestock farming constitutes roughly 40–50 percent of overall agricultural value in North America and Europe. It occupies approximately three-quarters of global agricultural lands in this world, and consumes about one-third of global crop production (Foley et al. 2011). In the European Union, animal farming sustains around 4 million jobs, encompassing both direct and indirect employment opportunities. Overall, the livestock value chains are estimated to employ more than 1.3 billion people worldwide (Salmon et al. 2018).

In low- and middle-income countries, the livestock sector plays a pivotal role as a significant source of income and employment for numerous households (Collishaw et al. 2023). Livestock not only provides essential power in agriculture and transportation but also bestows prestige upon individuals and communities. Additionally, livestock often serves as a means of wealth preservation, functioning as a form of insurance (Herrero et al. 2013). Livestock can also significantly impact social inclusivity and equity. Backyard and small-scale production systems represent vital economic activities for impoverished households with limited financial opportunities (Salmon et al. 2018). Notably, for women in developing countries, ownership of livestock may constitute one of the few productive assets they are allowed to possess (Parlasca and Qaim 2022).

At the same time, it remains uncertain whether this upward trajectory in reliance on animal farming will persist. The relationship between meat consumption and income (see Figure 2.7), exhibits an inverted-U shape, indicating a turning point where meat consumption starts to decrease beyond a certain income threshold (Parlasca and Qaim 2022). Therefore, as nations grow wealthier, we might anticipate further in the future a decline in per capita meat production and consumption rather than a rise.

This shift might be attributed to a combination of health, environmental, and ethical considerations regarding meat consumption, which tend to gain prominence as income levels rise. This inverted-U shape pattern mirrors the well-known Kuznets' curve, originally introduced by Simon Kuznets to depict the relationship between economic development and income inequality. Later, it was adapted in environmental economics to illustrate the connection between economic development and environmental pollution. Global data suggests that the "peak" of meat consumption on the Kuznets' curve typically occurs at per capita incomes of around 36,000 international dollars (Cole and McCoskey 2013). Currently, most of the world population lives in countries well below this peak. Based on common projections using income and demographics, global meat demand should thus continue to rise until 2050, mostly driven by low- and middle-income countries (Parlasca and Qaim 2022).

However, it is not completely clear whether such an increasing trend will continue in developing countries. More and more, it is recognized that the expansion of animal farming is not environmentally sustainable. Policymakers now possess a more advanced understanding of how to influence the consumption and production of animal products. This can be achieved through mechanisms such as integrating agriculture into carbon pricing schemes, implementing subsidies, and more generally enacting regulations. Cultural distinctions also play a significant role and can potentially counteract this trend. For instance, in India, religious and cultural norms have resulted in a distinct development pattern: Over the past half-decade, incomes have surged, and poverty has markedly decreased, yet the level of meat consumption has not seen a significant rise.

Interestingly, Frank (2008) hypothesizes the existence of an "animal welfare Kuznets' curve," with harm to animals initially rising with economic growth, followed by improvement in the treatment of animals after some peak value. However, the author stresses that this hypothesis contradicts a common belief that capitalism is fundamentally associated with animal exploitation. This belief suggests that future economic expansion may lead to an ongoing decline in the level of animal welfare due to increasing industrialization of animal agriculture. As said before, there are strong market-driven incentives to cut costs and thus by implication animal welfare. But, as far as I know, there is no evidence of a systematic link between market economy and animal exploitation. For instance, the Soviet system did not seem to be any better for animals, and Mao's regime seemed especially cruel and efficient at exterminating animals (Frank et al. 2024)

The animal welfare Kuznets' curve appears also consistent with the apparent surge of vegetarianism and veganism in developed economies (The Economist 2020). An early study on vegetarianism per country suggests a U-shape pattern (Leahy et al. 2010), representing a sort of mirror image to the income effects discussed earlier: After a peak income level, more and more households are vegetarians. See Figure 2.10. Also, we have already seen that many innovations have led historically to reducing the reliance on animals. We cannot exclude for instance that novel plant- or cell-based meat may surge in the future, thus further reducing the demand for animal-based food.

I now briefly turn to the role of pets for our economies. More than two-thirds of Americans have at least one pet in their home,

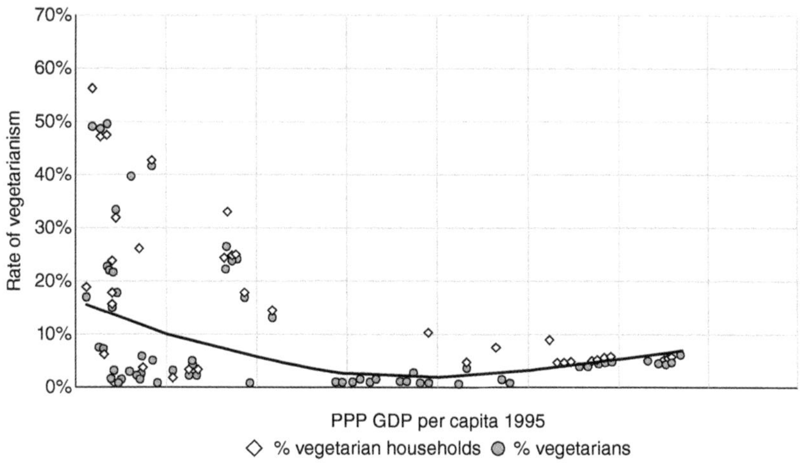

FIGURE 2.10 Rate of vegetarianism and income per capita per country. Source: Leahy et al. (2010)

with dogs, cats, and fish being the most commonly owned pets among American adults. In 2017 households in the United States spent over $69 billion on pets, including over $17 billion on veterinary care (APPA 2018). In terms of ongoing household expenditures, annual averages for dogs in the United States amounts to $1,480 in total which is allocated as follows: $458 for surgical veterinary visits, $242 for routine veterinary visits, $287 for food, $81 for food treats, $228 for kennel boarding, $81 for vitamins, $47 for grooming aids and $56 for toys (Weimer and Vining 2024 using APPA 2021–22 data). Note the importance of health-related expenditures through veterinary visits, representing about half of the dog-related budget.

Given the significance of health expenditures, the pet insurance sector has seen remarkable growth. In 2023, the total premium volume for pet insurance in the United States reached nearly $4 billion, with 5.7 million pets insured representing a 17 percent increase compared to 2022 (NAPHIA 2024). Dogs accounted for the majority of insured pets, representing 80 percent of policies, while cats made up the remaining 20 percent. The average annual premium for accident and illness coverage was $676 for dogs and $383 for cats.

Notably, this represents approximately half the average car insurance premium, underscoring the substantial cost of insuring pets. Note however that the penetration rate of pet insurance still remains low, in the vicinity of 10 percent for dogs and 5 percent for cats. This indicates that while the pet insurance market is growing, a significant majority of pets in the United States remain uninsured. The penetration rate for dog insurance is much higher in other countries like Sweden, approximating 80 percent.

Weimer and Vining (2024) also briefly examine the economics of animal shelters. In the United States, there are approximately 7,000 shelters managed by both municipalities and nonprofit organizations. These shelters are funded through various means, including taxes, donations, and adoption/surrender fees. Overall, Weimer and Vining estimate the total annual shelter costs to be about $2.5 billion. Annually, approximately 3.1 million dogs enter shelters, with about 2 million being adopted and around 390,000 euthanized (interestingly, they note that in the 1970s, over 90 percent of sheltered animals were euthanized). Shelters contribute to about 40 percent of the total supply of dogs in the United States. Unfortunately, for many dogs, shelters represent the end of the line.

Undoubtedly, many people care a lot about their pets and pets thus contribute significantly to the well-being of humans. Numerous survey studies consistently highlight that pet owners often regard their animals as integral members of their family. Endenburg and Bouw (1994) emphasize that the primary motivation for pet ownership is companionship. Research consistently underscores that pets, through their reliance on humans and continuous companionship, can fulfill emotional needs and enhance overall human and pet well-being. Schwarz et al. (2007) study whether pets and children serve as complements or substitutes in a household. They show that the probability of having a dog decreases when there is a child under the age of two, suggesting that dogs and young children are substitutes. However, the probability increases with the presence of an older child, indicating that dogs and older children are complementary. Yet, another form of substitution emerges: The presence of a child over the age of two reduces the amount spent on the dog.

2.3 THE ISSUE OF ANIMAL WELFARE

In this section, I discuss some issues related to the quality of lives of animals, namely their level of welfare. The scope of animal suffering in our world is immense, and I can only offer a brief overview here. For those interested in viewing various images depicting farmed animals and the associated welfare issues, I recommend visiting the website: https://weanimalsmedia.org/ (please be aware that some images may be distressing).

I start with the welfare issues regarding farmed animals, which are fairly well documented. I primarily focus on animals raised in industrial farms under intensive conditions because they represent the vast majority of farmed animals. Animal living conditions in industrial farms were meticulously described in the early seminal Harrison's *Animal Machines* and Singer's *Animal Liberation* books, and have been reiterated over the years. The methods of animal rearing have seen only marginal improvements in the last few decades.

I reside in France and will present some current rearing conditions in my country; but note that they are fairly representative of those found in most other developed countries. See, for example, Norwood and Lusk (2011) for a similar but more detailed description regarding farms in the United States. As mentioned earlier, on a global scale, more than 80 percent of farmed animals are raised in factory farms. In the United States, this proportion is nearly 99 percent, while in France, it hovers around 80 percent.

Chickens – We have seen that the majority of farmed animals are raised in intensive farming, with chickens comprising by far the largest population. This is the case in France, where chickens represent about 75 percent of all farmed animals slaughtered every year, and a large majority of them (about 80 percent) are raised

FIGURE 2.11 Broilers in intensive farming in France.
Source: © INRAE, Nicolas Bertrand

under intensive conditions. Let me describe the living conditions of a "standard broiler" in France. Farmed chickens are hatched in a hatchery and then housed in a large building alongside thousands of other broilers, averaging about twenty per square meter; see Figure 2.11. They do not have access to the outdoors. Over their short lifespan, they undergo rapid growth due to genetic selection, which can lead to significant health issues. The air quality inside these buildings is typically poor, often causing discomfort and various health problems, including skin inflammation. Farmers often resort to debeaking (a partial cut of the chicken's beak) to curb aggressive behaviors arising from the challenging environment. Throughout the rearing period, the litter is usually not changed, resulting in progressive dampness and the accumulation of ammonia from animal excreta. Broilers are sent to the slaughterhouse at around 40–45 days of age. The process of capturing chickens for transportation, regardless of whether it is done mechanically or manually, is a stressful event for the birds. It frequently leads to dislocations and broken bones. At the slaughterhouse, chickens are suspended by their legs before being electrocuted. This suspension stage induces significant distress and suffering, including dislocations of legs or wings, broken bones, and bleeding. Finally, the chickens are stunned by electrocution and then slaughtered. A detailed report on the various and specific farming conditions of chickens in Europe may be found in the European Food and Safety Authority report (EFSA 2023a).

Table 2.2 *Different labeled rearing systems for hens produced in France*

Characteristics	Cage	Barn	Free range	Organic
Egg label (code)	3	2	1	0
Density	750 cm^2 /hen	9 $hens/m^2$	9 $hens/m^2$	6 $hens/m^2$
Outdoor access	No	No	Yes	Yes
Farm size	No limit	No limit	No limit	3,000 hens max

Source: CIWF (2023) – www.ciwf.fr/animaux-delevage/poules-pondeuses/

Hens – The standard farming practices for laying hens vary widely, encompassing methods such as cage farming, barn farming, free-range farming, and organic farming. Table 2.2 provides information about different labeled categories in France and in Europe. Hens are typically kept until they are about 18 months old, at which point their egg production declines, and they are slaughtered. Many die because of salpingitis, an inflammation to the oviduct caused by this constant egg-laying. Since 2012, European regulations have banned conventional cages but still allow so-called enriched cages. These enriched cages provide more space per hen (750 cm^2 compared to 550 cm^2) and include amenities such as perches, artificial nests, dust baths, and scratching areas. In Europe, the respective shares of hens in different systems are as follows (EFSA 2023b): 45 percent in enriched cages, 36 percent in barns, 13 percent free range, and 7 percent organic. See the EFSA report for detailed information about hens' farming conditions in Europe (EFSA 2023b).

Pigs – Over 95 percent of pigs in France are raised in intensive conditions, confined indoors. Within days of birth, the majority of pigs undergo castration, most often without the use of anesthesia. Pigs are typically raised on grating, with approximately one square meter of space per pig. To prevent tail biting among the animals, their tails and teeth are commonly trimmed. They are typically slaughtered at the age of six months. Sows can spend a significant part of their lifetime in a cage; see Figure 2.12. A detailed report

FIGURE 2.12 Feeding of pregnant sows in France.
Source: © INRAE, Alain Beguey

on the various and specific farming conditions of pigs in Europe is described in the EFSA report (EFSA 2022).

Cows – In France, the majority of cows raised for milk or meat have access to the outdoors. While indoors, cows typically have the freedom to move, though on some farms, they may be tethered at the neck to their stalls. Dairy cows are usually inseminated annually from around two years of age and are separated from their calves, typically within one or two days of birth. This separation has been acknowledged to be a source of stress for both the cow and the calf. Over the past decades, the drive for increased milk production has led to intensive lactation, contributing to various health issues such as lameness and mastitis. To mitigate aggressive behaviors on farms, most cows undergo dehorning, a process that entails intense suffering for a brief period. Once their productivity declines, cows are fattened for a short period before being sent to the slaughterhouse at an average age of eight years. Approximately one third of cows are slaughtered without being stunned, often for religious reasons, a process considered very painful. Regarding cows from beef herds, nearly all spend at least six months per year on pasture, a form of farming often regarded as more animal friendly. However, issues related to dehorning, transport, and slaughter are similar for all cows. See this EFSA report about the welfare of cows in Europe (EFSA 2023c).

Veal calves – Cow milk production necessitates the birth of calves. Calves are typically separated from their mothers one or two days after birth. Approximately 40 percent of these calves become dairy cows, while another 40 percent are raised for veal meat and are slaughtered before reaching eight months of age. A few weeks later, veal calves are usually transferred to specialized farms for rearing. The transfer conditions may be particularly difficult. During their first eight weeks, veal calves may be kept in individual pens. After eight weeks, European legislation prohibits the use of individual pens, mandating that veal calves be raised in groups with a minimum of 1.7 square meters per animal. Veal calves are ultimately transported to the slaughterhouse by truck or boat, causing severe animal welfare concerns. See the EFSA report about the welfare of veal calves in Europe (EFSA 2023d).

Following the earlier descriptions, we can confidently conclude that the living conditions for many farmed animals are harsh. The majority of these animals endure high levels of confinement, painful mutilations, and short lives filled with significant pain and suffering. Furthermore, many animals, such as standard chickens, pigs, and veal calves, have very limited positive experiences. They will almost never experience sunshine, grass, fresh air, sex, and many other aspects that are considered part of a normal life for animals. Overall, these animals live in a nearly constant state of low, and often very low, welfare.

Moreover, animal welfare issues can even escalate dramatically during unexpected events. While I may refrain from sharing specific details, the treatment of animals during disease outbreaks can verge on the horrific. For instance, during a swine flu episode in East Asia, reports surfaced of herds of pigs being buried alive. Similarly, in the United States, during supply-chain disruptions, farmers have resorted to prompting heatstroke among their pigs and poultry as a means of depopulation by shutting off ventilation systems in their farms. Again, this is because the agricultural sector proves reluctant to incur additional costs to address animal welfare issues during such events. Legal obligations in these exceptional or urgent circumstances are typically minimal. For example, the American Veterinary Medical Association's depopulation guidelines classify certain heatstroke-based killing methods as "permitted in constrained circumstances" when implementing preferred methods is impractical due to the emergency. Heatstroke-based methods may result in prolonged suffering and often fail to achieve 100 percent mortality (Reyes-Illg et al. 2023).

When confronted with criticisms of poor animal welfare, the farming sector often responds that such claims cannot be accurate, as it is purportedly in the farmers' interest to ensure good welfare for animals. The argument goes that healthy animals are more productive and thus have a greater economic value. However, this response is, at best, incomplete, if not completely false. While there are some natural limits to the ill-treatment of animals in normal circumstances, such as ensuring basic necessities like food and water for survival, investing in comprehensive animal welfare measures comes with a substantial cost. In the pursuit of profit maximization, farmers inevitably face a tradeoff between the benefits and the costs associated with improving animal welfare. The economic logic indeed results in a minimal investment in animal welfare. As we have seen, this economic rationale extends to practices such as confining animals in cages, separating offspring from their mothers, the use of various mutilations, or prematurely terminating animals.

Fish – The treatment of fish in terms of harm may often surpass that of land animals. Wild fish caught in nets can suffer from abrasions, cuts, and bruises as they struggle to escape, while those caught by hooks can endure severe injuries to their mouths and throats. The process of being caught and confined in nets or on lines is highly stressful for fish. Many fish are killed using methods that do not result in immediate death, with most dying from asphyxiation, which can take over an hour. They may be left to suffocate on dry land or on ice, or they may be clubbed or gutted while still conscious. Additionally, many fish are caught as bycatch and then discarded, often suffering injuries during capture that they may not survive even if released.

Regarding farmed fish, the aquaculture industry faces strong animal welfare issues (Saraiva et al. 2019) such as overcrowding, water quality (insufficient oxygenation, high concentration of wastes), diseases and parasites, physical injuries, and nonhumane slaughter methods. Moreover, fish in aquaculture typically lack stimulation and the ability to exhibit natural behaviors, probably leading to boredom and stress. Given the relatively recent emergence of aquaculture, most individual fish in modern aquaculture are not biologically adapted to captive conditions, posing significant welfare risks. For many species, "welfare for most species is likely to be poor across the life cycle: from the high likelihood of malformations and physiological defects at birth to restricted mobility, high aggression, and poor handling throughout development to 'extreme pain and suffering' during slaughter (Saraiva et al. 2019)" (Franks et al. 2021, pages 1 and 2).

The fair-fish database (https://fair-fish-database.net/) consolidates information on around a hundred diverse fish species. Many aquatic species exhibit more intricate social and emotional lives than previously recognized. A comprehensive review by Sneddon et al. (2014) on pain perception indicates that fish and decapods, such as shrimp, display unmistakable signs of the ability to experience pain. Similarly, recent research in various fish species has unveiled sophisticated cognitive abilities, including tool use, individual personalities, and problem-solving skills (Franks et al. 2021).

Insects – A word about insects. The entomology literature has long suggested that insects cannot feel pain. As a result, insects have traditionally been excluded from ethical debates and animal welfare legislation. However, recent research indicates there may be neural as well as cognitive and behavioral evidence for pain in insects (Gibbons et al. 2022). Despite their tiny contribution to global food systems, it is estimated that over 300 billion yellow mealworms (Barrett et al. 2023) and over 370 billion crickets (Rowe et al. 2024) are reared annually in the food and feed industry. Rowe et al. (2024) identify various welfare concerns, such as high stocking densities, which can increase rates of aggression, cannibalism, and behavioral repression among individuals on cricket farms. Animal welfare recommendations for insect farming are lacking, and almost no empirical evidence exists to guide producers in practicing humane slaughter for insects (Barrett et al. 2023, Bry-Chevalier 2024).

Let me now turn to the welfare of pets. The welfare of pets, particularly dogs, involves understanding their physical, emotional, and social needs, but it can be complex due to their dependence on human caregivers and differences in communication. Studies have shown that certain aspects of dog welfare can be compromised even in loving homes. For example, many dogs lack sufficient exercise or mental stimulation, which can lead to boredom or obesity. Additionally, some common practices, like excessive time spent alone, restrictive confinement, or certain types of training, may reduce welfare by creating stress or frustration.

The vast majority of dogs sold over the internet and in pet shops are the products of cruel breeding practices in "puppy mills." These mills, as the name suggests, function as factories that breed dogs at the lowest possible cost. Conditions in these facilities are notoriously inhumane: Dogs are often confined to cramped, unsanitary cages with minimal socialization, veterinary care, or proper nutrition. Cages may even be stacked to maximize space, further limiting each dog's movement. These environments inflict severe physical and psychological trauma, and dogs rescued from such conditions frequently show symptoms of anxiety, fear, and difficulty adapting to normal life. The Humane Society's "Horrible Hundred" report (www.humanesociety.org/horriblehundred) documents widespread neglect and abuse in puppy mills. When a dog's breeding productivity declines, they are often killed or sold for other uses.

Another important domain concerns animal testing. We saw earlier in this chapter the figures in terms of the number of animals used. The level of animal welfare in animal testing can vary significantly depending on factors, such as the specific procedures being conducted, the laboratory practices in place, the country's legislation, and the ethical considerations taken by researchers. But it is a fact that animals used in testing often experience high pain and distress. The conditions in which test animals are kept can be poor, with issues such as inadequate space, lack of environmental enrichment, and isolation.

Numerous countries and institutions have enacted guidelines and regulations to safeguard the ethical and humane treatment of animals involved in research. These directives encompass provisions for appropriate housing, care, and handling of animals, along with requirements to minimize pain and distress during experiments. Animal testing for cosmetics is banned in over 40 countries, yet it remains mandatory for toxicity assessment in the development of new drugs. Although researchers typically must seek approval from ethical review boards before conducting experiments with animals, the actual protection afforded to animals in experiments often falls short. Protection measures are not consistently based on an understanding of animal ethology but rather on the industrial use of animals (McMullen 2016).

Animal testing is a complex and controversial issue. Proponents of animal testing say that it has enabled the development of many life-saving treatments, that there is no alternative method for researching a complete living organism and that there exist strict regulations preventing the mistreatment of animals in laboratories. A poll of thousands of scientists by the Pew Research Center found that 89 percent favored the use of animals in scientific research. The California Biomedical Research Association states that nearly every medical breakthrough in the last 100 years has resulted directly from research using animals. In December 2024, nearly 3,000 researchers published an article in the French newspaper *Le Monde* opposing a proposed amendment that sought to impose a tax on each animal used in research. They argue that animal research remains essential for scientific progress, and that such a tax would penalize French laboratories.

An issue with the argument that animal research is essential is the lack of a counterfactual. We cannot precisely determine what scientific progress would have been achieved with less animal research. Simply pointing out that many discoveries relied on animal research provides no insight into what might have been discovered in a world where such research did not exist. In fact, there is a long history of scientists warning that transitioning away from animal research would lead to catastrophic consequences, including the collapse of medical science (e.g., Visscher 1972). However, these dire predictions have consistently failed to materialize. To explain the resistance of scientists, factors such as self-interest, self-selection, cognitive dissonance, and status quo bias may all play a role.

Opponents of animal testing say that it is cruel and inhumane to experiment on animals and that alternative methods available to researchers such as in vitro testing, computer modeling, and advanced imaging techniques can often replace animal testing. They emphasize that the biological differences between animals and humans can limit the relevance of findings, leading to results that may not accurately predict human responses, potentially wasting time and resources. Another significant issue with animal testing lies in the limited regulatory oversight and lack of transparency surrounding the treatment of animals. Many animal testing facilities operate with restricted public access to information, and there is often minimal accountability for ensuring ethical standards in animal care (https://aldf.org/article/federal-laws-and-agencies-involved-with-animal-testing/).

To conclude, let me briefly discuss wild animal welfare. Wild animals can express natural behavior and have access to reproductive opportunities. However, contrary to romanticized views, the living conditions of wild animals are often harsh. The majority of wild animals belong to r-type species, characterized by prolific reproduction with only a few offspring surviving. Most animals in those species succumb to starvation or become prey, experiencing painful deaths and very short lives. When injured or sick, wild animals do not have access to remedies like antibiotics for infections. Even a small and temporary injury may have dramatic consequences when food is not easily accessible.

Predators also contribute to a cycle of fear and anguish during the prey's demise. Additionally, natural deterrence mechanisms can result in a severe loss of welfare, as discussed in the literature on the "ecology of fear" hypothesis (Ripple and Beschta 2004). However, this hypothesis is still an open research question (Creel et al. 2009). Note also that, in the absence of predators, population numbers may surge to carrying capacity, leading to mass starvation when conditions become less favorable. Hence, the overall welfare impact of predators is not clear. Note also that, unlike the relatively controlled environments of farmed animals, the welfare of wild animals exhibits a high degree of heterogeneity.

In any case, the assessment of wild animal welfare remains a significantly under-researched area. The emotional and psychological needs of wild animals are often overlooked, leading to calls for a more compassionate approach that recognizes their intrinsic value and right to live free from harm (Ramp and Bekoff 2015). The ecological health of wild populations is closely linked to their welfare, as healthy ecosystems support biodiversity and resilience. As awareness grows, there is a pressing need to integrate animal welfare considerations into conservation efforts, advocating for practices that prioritize the well-being of all sentient beings within their natural habitats.

2.4 THE MORAL STATUS OF ANIMALS

While moral discussions on animal welfare may appear recent, the roots of these discussions extend far into history. Religion is a good starting point. In Genesis 1:26 of the Bible, God says: "Let us make man in our image, after our likeness: and let them have dominion over the fish of the sea, and over the fowl of the air, and over the cattle, and over all the earth, and over every creeping thing that creepeth upon the earth." In other words, humans have dominion over animals.

It turns out that all three major abrahamic monotheistic religions (Christianism, Judaism, Islam) emphasize humans' exceptionalism and the human–animal divide. Interestingly, some other religions have a different perspective on the place of animals. Buddhism, for example, revolves around the concept of (non)suffering, with one of its fundamental precepts being the avoidance of harm to living things. Hinduism posits that both humans and animals possess a soul capable of migrating across living beings, challenging the notion of a rigid human–animal divide.

As far as I am aware, the earliest indications of ethical considerations for animals date back to ancient Greek philosophy. See, for example, our discussion in Carlier and Treich (2020). Aristotle, for instance, simply perceived animals as resources: "we may infer that, after the birth of animals, plants exist for their sake, and that the other animals exist for the sake of man ... if nature makes nothing incomplete, and nothing in vain, the inference must be that she has made all animals for the sake of man" (350 BC; cited in Carlier and Treich 2020). Nevertheless, some ancient philosophers already disagreed about whether animals merit moral consideration. For instance, Socrates advances in Plato's *The Republic:* "Would this habit of eating animals not require that we slaughter animals that we knew as individuals, and in whose eyes we could gaze and see ourselves reflected, only a few hours before our meal?" (360 BC; cited in Carlier and Treich 2020). In other well-known texts, Plutarch and Porphyry also questioned the morality of meat-eating habits.

Centuries later, René Descartes in 1649 famously described animals as automata or machines: "it seems reasonable since art copies nature, and men can make various automata which move without thought, that nature should produce its own automata much more splendid than the artificial ones. These natural automata are the animals" (cited in Carlier and Treich 2020) (Note however that Descartes' views are not always consistent and seem much more complex than often presented. See for instance Burgat [2006, in French]). To also illustrate the divergence of perspectives in the Enlightenment age, note that, a century after Descartes, Jean-Jacques Rousseau introduced the concept of "sensibilité" or sentience. He wrote: "It appears, in fact, that if I am bound to do no injury to my fellow-creatures, this is less because they are rational than because they are sentient beings: and this quality, being common both to men and beasts, ought to entitle the latter at least to the privilege of not being wantonly ill-treated by the former" (Rousseau 1754, page 158). Along this line, Voltaire, in 1764, remained unconvinced by Descartes' animal machine hypothesis and wrote a harsh critique.

Immanuel Kant considered animals as things. Animals are not included in his categorical imperative. However, he argued that we have indirect duties to animals (Gruen 2017). According to Kant, the primary reason to avoid cruelty to animals is the potential risk of development of cruel habits that could subsequently be directed towards other people. In the "Lectures on Ethics" he states the following: "If a man shoots his dog because the animal is no longer capable of service, he does not fail in his duty to the dog, for the dog cannot judge, but his act is inhuman and damages in himself that humanity which it is his duty to show towards mankind. If he is not to stifle his human feelings, he must practice kindness towards animals, for he who is cruel to animals becomes hard also in his dealings with men" (Kant 1784 [1997], 212 [Ak 27: 459]).

Early utilitarians, notably Jeremy Bentham and John Stuart Mill, wielded major influence on animal ethics. In 1789, making an analogy to slavery, Bentham contended in his famous line that when determining the intrinsic value of animal interests, the crucial question is not, "Can they reason? Nor, Can they talk? But, Can they suffer?" (chapter xvii, paragraph 6). While Bentham's position regarding animal welfare may be less radical than that commonly attributed to him (Kniess 2019), Bentham saw an intrinsic worth in avoiding animal suffering. This is the key idea. Even contemporary Kantians such as Korsgaard have recognized the moral force of the experience of pain (Gruen 2017): "it is a pain to be in pain. And that is not a trivial fact" (Korsgaard 1996, page 154). The capacity to undergo positive or negative states, such as happiness and suffering, is frequently posited as the primary criterion for moral consideration.

A century later, Henry Sidgwick (1893, page 414) another leading utilitarian, argued that the welfare of sentient beings should matter intrinsically, and thus should enter into the social objective:

> We have next to consider who the "all" are, whose happiness is to be taken into account. Are we to extend our concern to all the beings capable of pleasure and pain whose feelings are affected by our conduct? Or are we to confine our view to human happiness? The former view is the one adopted by Bentham and Mill, and (I believe) by the Utilitarian school generally: and is obviously most in accordance with the universality that is characteristic of their principle. It is the Good Universal, interpreted and defined as 'happiness' or 'pleasure,' at which a Utilitarian considers it his duty to aim: and it seems arbitrary and unreasonable to exclude from the end, as so conceived, any pleasure of any sentient being.

The contemporary literature on animal ethics is huge, and the current section will only mention a few important ideas and authors. The two most widely discussed ethical approaches are the so-called animal welfare and animal rights views (Newman et al. 2017). These views are reflected respectively in the prominent works of the philosophers Peter Singer and Tom Regan.

Peter Singer, renowned for his influential book *Animal Liberation* (1975), contends that, as sentient beings, animals possess interests, such as the interest in avoiding suffering. He asserts that neglecting these interests amounts to arbitrary discrimination, akin to racism. After Richard Ryder first coined the term, Peter Singer popularized the concept of "speciesism" in the following form: "the racist violates the principle of equality by giving greater weight to the interests of members of his own race, when there is a clash between their interests and the interests of those of another race. Similarly the speciesist allows the interests of his own species to override the greater interests of members of other species. The pattern is the same in each case" (page 108).

Shelly Kagan (2016), in a critical response to Singer, defines speciesism as the general view that "the interests of our own species count more than the interests of other species" and proposes a hierarchical view that justifies speciesism and goes on to argue that he is not in fact so much a speciesist as a "personist" (i.e., a perspective that places moral importance primarily on the status of "persons" rather than on membership in a particular species or other characteristics). Kagan (2019) posits different moral statuses for different kinds of beings based on their intrinsic properties. In this framework, moral status is not binary (where beings either have full moral status or none at all) but instead exists on a spectrum or hierarchy. The degree of moral consideration owed to a being corresponds to its place in the hierarchy. Beings with higher cognitive capacities and sentience deserve greater moral consideration and protection compared to those with lower capacities.

A central argument in Singer's writings on the concept of antispeciesism is called the principle of "equal consideration of interests." The essence of the principle of equal consideration of interests is that "we give equal weight in our moral deliberations to the like interests of all those affected by our actions" (Singer 2011, page 21). Singer discusses precisely what this means to have "interests," suggesting that the capacity for suffering and pleasure is a prerequisite. It would be nonsense for instance to say that a stone or a river has interests. Singer (1975) supports the assertion that animals can suffer through an argument by analogy, pointing out that animals share similar nervous systems with humans and exhibit comparable behavior in response to painful stimuli.

Another crucial argument is that of "species overlap," contending that certain humans and animals share comparable sets of morally relevant characteristics, making them similarly morally significant. This is similar to the "argument from marginal cases." In short, if one believes that humans have moral value, but animals do not, then it is likely that there is an inconsistency in the reasoning behind it. For example, one can claim that animals do not have moral value because they do not possess a certain level of intelligence. The logical consequence would be that humans without that level of intelligence also do not have moral value, such as babies or the mentally disabled. Interestingly, Voltaire made a similar argument centuries ago.

Singer is a utilitarian, and more generally he belongs to the consequentialist's school of thought. In traditional ethical theory, a fundamental divide exists between consequentialist and deontological theories. According to consequentialism, what matters is the consequences of our actions. In contrast, deontological theories focus on how actions follow certain principles (e.g., norms and rules) rather than solely the consequences of the actions. For instance, a utilitarian consequentialist might justify animal testing if it leads to significant medical breakthroughs that save or improve human lives. They would argue that the overall benefits to human welfare outweigh the suffering inflicted on animals during the testing process. The focus is on maximizing overall happiness and minimizing suffering across all affected beings. A deontologist would oppose animal testing based on the principle that it is inherently wrong to harm sentient beings. They would argue that animals have rights or intrinsic moral worth that must be respected, and using them as mere means to an end (even for potentially beneficial outcomes) is not morally permissible.

A major proponent of deontological ethics, Immanuel Kant, asserted that moral rules should be guided by the principle that they could be consistently applied as a universal law governing everyone's behavior. However, Kant's ethical approach is typically restricted to humanity. As we have seen earlier, Kant did not ascribe intrinsic value to animals. That is, animals were not part of his categorical imperative. More recently, however, some famous deontologists have shown more sympathy toward animals. Figures like John Rawls and Robert Nozick, for instance, have argued that animals' welfare should be considered, contingent upon not infringing upon human rights.

Tom Regan (1983), perhaps the most well-known deontologist and animal rights philosopher, also adopts an approach that can be characterized as sentientist. He believes that animals are "*subjects-of-a-life,*" who:

> want and prefer things, believe and feel things, recall and expect things. And all these dimensions of our life, including our pleasure and pain, our enjoyment and suffering, our satisfaction

> and frustration, our continued existence or our untimely death—all make a difference to the quality of our life as lived, as experienced, by us as individuals. As the same is true of … animals … they too must be viewed as the experiencing subjects of a life, with inherent value of their own. (Gruen 2017)

As many other philosophers, Regan criticizes speciesism, which he defines as follows: "A speciesist position, at least the paradigm of such a position, would take the form of declaring that no animal is a member of the moral community because no animal belongs to the 'right' species – namely, Homo sapiens" (Regan 1983, page 155). He further contends that certain animals should, in principle, possess the same rights as humans. Advocates of similar perspectives include Francione (2008) and Donaldson and Kymlicka (2011), who posit that animals should not be regarded as mere property.

Regan (1983) asserts that ethical principles should center on the "magnitude of the harm" to affected individuals rather than the aggregated impact, which is the focus of utilitarian theories (Newman et al. 2017). He also puts forward the "worse-off principle," emphasizing the imperative to refrain from causing harm to the most disadvantaged individual. Note that this concept aligns closely with prioritarianism and the well-known Rawlsian principle that we regularly encounter in economics. It is the worse-off principle that prompts Regan to advocate for the complete abolition of slaughter-based agriculture. According to this perspective, even painless death inflicts an incomparably greater harm than the harm humans would endure by abolishing animal agriculture.

Again, diverse schools of thought exist, and space and knowledge limitations prevent an in-depth exploration of extensive ideas within animal ethics. However, a prevailing consensus among philosophers, spanning various traditions such as consequentialism/utilitarianism, deontology, virtue ethics, and phenomenology, for instance, suggests that animal interests hold positive intrinsic value deserving of moral consideration. After centuries of disagreement, it seems that most philosophers eventually agree on this point and, as a result, on the need to make progress in how humans treat them. To underscore this convergence within the philosophy community, and conclude this section, I reproduce in Table 2.3 the Montreal

Table 2.3 *Montreal Declaration on Animal Exploitation*

Montreal Declaration (2023)
We are researchers in the field of moral and political philosophy. Our work is rooted in different philosophical traditions, and we rarely find ourselves in agreement with one another. We do agree, however, on the need for a profound transformation of our relationships with other animals. We condemn the practices that involve treating animals as objects or commodities. Insofar as it involves unnecessary violence and harm, we declare that animal exploitation is unjust and morally indefensible.
In ethology and neurobiology, it is well established that mammals, birds, fish, and many invertebrates are sentient – i.e., capable of feeling pleasure, pain, and emotions. These animals are conscious subjects; they have their own perspective on the world around them. It follows that they have interests: our behaviours affect their well-being and can benefit or harm them. When we injure a dog or a pig, when we keep a chicken or a salmon in captivity, when we kill a calf for his meat or a mink for her skin, we seriously contravene their most fundamental interests.
Yet, all of these harms could be avoided. It is obviously possible to refrain from wearing leather, attending bullfights and rodeos, or showing children captive lions in zoos. Most of us can already do without animal foods and still be healthy, and the future development of a vegan economy will make things even easier. From a political and institutional standpoint, it is possible to stop viewing animals merely as resources at our disposal.
That these individuals do not belong to the species Homo sapiens is morally irrelevant: while it may seem natural to think that animals' interests count less than the comparable interests of humans, this speciesist intuition does not stand up to close scrutiny. Everything else being equal, mere membership of a biological group (be it delineated by species, skin colour, or sex) cannot justify unequal consideration or treatment.

Table 2.3 *(cont.)*

Montreal Declaration (2023)
There are differences between humans and other animals, just as there are differences among individuals within species. Admittedly, some sophisticated cognitive abilities give rise to particular interests, which in turn may justify particular treatments. But a subject's ability to compose symphonies, to make advanced mathematical calculations, or to project oneself into a distant future, however admirable, does not affect the consideration due to his or her interest to feel pleasure and not to suffer. The interests of the more intelligent among us matter no more than the equivalent interests of the less intelligent. To say otherwise would amount to ranking individuals according to faculties that have no moral relevance. Such an ableist attitude would be morally indefensible.
It is therefore difficult to escape this conclusion: because it unnecessarily harms animals, animal exploitation is fundamentally unjust. It is therefore essential to work towards its disappearance, especially by aiming at the closure of slaughterhouses, a ban on fishing, and the development of plant-based food systems. We have no illusion; such a project will not be achieved in the short term. In particular, it requires renouncing entrenched speciesist habits and transforming numerous institutions fundamentally. We believe, however, that the end of animal exploitation is the only shared horizon that is both realistic and just for nonhumans.

Source: https://greea.ca/en/montreal-declaration-on-animal-exploitation/

Declaration, endorsed by over 500 philosophers in 2023. This declaration encapsulates accessible concepts for a wider audience and mirrors a generally compliant position among various philosophers.

2.5 THE LEGAL STATUS OF ANIMALS

Legislation stands as the primary instrument for enhancing animal welfare. The first animal protection laws appeared in the 1800s, and were mostly concerned with public cruelty toward animals as emphasized by the "Act to Prevent the Cruel and Improper

Table 2.4 *Examples of specific legislations in the European Union*

Year	Specific legislation
1957	In the Rome treaty, animals are a commodity, there is nothing about animal welfare
1969	The Council of Europe adopts the Convention on Animals in Transportation
1972	Germany passes its Animal Protection Act
1974	The Council of Europe passes a directive requiring that animals be rendered unconscious before slaughter
2003	The European Union bans the construction of new gestation crates (effective 2013)
2012	The European Union's bans on battery cages go into effect
2015	In French law, animals are defined as sentient beings in the Civil Code (art. 515–14)

Treatment of Cattle" (1822) in the United Kingdom and later the Loi Grammont (1850) in France. Over the years, numerous countries have instituted laws dedicated to safeguarding the well-being of animals and animal populations. For instance, in 1900 there was the Convention for the Preservation of Wild Animals, Birds, and Fish in Africa. See Table 2.4 for some pieces of legislation in the European Union.

In the realm of farmed animals, laws address concerns such as cruelty, neglect, and the establishment of appropriate care standards. These laws often criminalize acts of abuse, neglect, or intentional harm inflicted upon farmed animals. Nevertheless, the enforcement and effectiveness of these laws remain imperfect. Furthermore, in developing countries, animal protection laws are frequently non-existent. Specialized legislation is also in place to protect wildlife, endangered species, and their habitats, encompassing regulations on hunting, poaching, and the trade of wildlife products.

There is significant legislation worldwide regarding invasive species, as they pose one of the major threats to the environment and biodiversity. However, in the legal framework governing invasive species, considerations of animal welfare are, at best, a side remark. Ethical notions are often briefly mentioned in various laws for managing invasive species, but these considerations have rarely led to concrete legal consequences, such as court rulings (Futhazar 2024). Eradicating invasive species is often regarded as the most effective strategy, with little to no consideration given to animal welfare concerns (to the exception of cats in some cases). Hence, the implementation of invasive species regulation remains largely disconnected from animal law, illustrating the strong divide between environmental ethics and animal ethics.

It is important to note that the laws enacted in developed countries are typically riddled with exceptions that significantly narrow their applicability. An illustrative instance is the primary US federal law governing the treatment of animals, the Animal Welfare Act, which expressly excludes "farm animals" from its purview. In the United States, farmed fish lack protection under the Humane Methods of Slaughter Act (HMSA), a situation mirrored in the European Union. Concerning animals used for experimentation, the 2016 Animal Welfare Act provides safeguards but notably excludes birds, rats, and mice, encompassing a staggering 95 percent of animals used in research (McMullen 2016). Protection for animals is sometimes advanced as a general principle such as the 3Rs (Replacement, Reduction, and Refinement) rule in animal experimentation. However, the practical implementation in the legal domain is frequently fraught with ambiguity and yields minimal tangible effects.

Importantly, many OECD countries mention animal sentience in their legislation (such as the 2015 Glavany amendment in France), acknowledging that animals can experience pain and suffering. Likewise, Germany has enshrined the protection of animals as a constitutional objective. The European Union formally recognizes animals as sentient beings whose welfare must be factored in when drafting federal policies (Article 13 of the Lisbon treaty). However,

Sowery (2018, page 31) emphasizes that defining an animal as sentient does not itself create a new legal obligation, and observes "the lack of any discernible impact of the acknowledgement of the 'sentience' of animals in the legislative and policy-making practice of the Union." To paraphrase Sowery, animals have a "curious constitutional status": While they are recognized as sentient, they remain subject to rules that treat them as property.

The systematic classification of animals as property is a major issue. It aligns their legal status with inanimate objects such as cars or furniture. This severely curtails the legal rights and protections extended to animals. Specifically, it implies a prohibition solely on the mistreatment of animals owned by others, while simultaneously permitting the abuse of animals regarded as one's own property. This explains why a key objective among contemporary animal rights advocates is to challenge or even eliminate the notion that animals are considered property. They argue for recognizing animals as beings entitled to rights of self-determination or a certain degree of autonomy. In essence, animals would be acknowledged as "persons" rather than mere property, aligning their status more closely with that of children, a status commensurate with their capacities (Sunstein 2003).

In various sectors like transportation, infrastructure, and environmental management, administrative authorities routinely mandate the production of policy evaluations such as benefit-cost analyses, often providing guidelines for their execution. But, what about the legal obligation to assess policy impacts on animal welfare? Interestingly, article 38 of the European Directive on the protection of animals used for scientific purposes requires "a harm-benefit analysis of the project, to assess whether the harm to the animals in terms of suffering, pain and distress is justified by the expected outcome" (European Union 2010). The European Court of Auditors (2023) recently pressed European policymakers to "consider pricing animal suffering into transport costs and meat prices." However, as we emphasized in the introduction, there is a lack of robust quantitative tools to evaluate policy impacts on animal welfare (Budolfson et al. 2023), and no guidelines to perform this evaluation. As a result, animal welfare is almost always ignored in policy evaluation, resulting in a regulatory blindspot (Stawasz 2024).

Even the "soft law" approach, which encompasses rules, guidelines, or principles that are not legally binding, may encounter resistance when it comes to incorporating animal welfare. For example, animal welfare is notably absent from the United Nations Sustainable Development Goals (SDGs), even though every SDG interacts with animal welfare in various ways (Keeling et al. 2019). In June 2022, over 300 experts signed an open letter recognizing the significant relevance of animal welfare for SDGs. Similarly, animal welfare considerations are usually missing from corporate social responsibility strategies and nonfinancial reporting directives.

A significant legal effort concerns the use of writs of habeas corpus for animals promoted by Steven Wise and the Nonhuman Rights Project (NhRP) in the United States. Traditionally, the writ of habeas corpus has been used to challenge unlawful detention or imprisonment of humans. It was used extensively in the eighteenth and nineteenth centuries to fight human slavery. However, Wise and the NhRP argue that certain animals, such as chimpanzees, elephants, dolphins, and whales possess complex cognitive abilities and self-awareness similar to humans. They in turn argue that imprisoning these animals in inadequate conditions, such as zoos or circuses, constitutes unlawful detention akin to imprisonment. As such, they believe these animals should not be treated merely as property but should be recognized as legal persons with inherent rights. Despite these extensive efforts, it is acknowledged that the litigation efforts associated with the NhRP project have not yet been successful (Wise 2020, Lynch 2023).

So, what is the bottom line? Many laws exist to protect animals in various ways. But, in general, there is a pervasive sense that the legal status of animals is either overlooked or merely serves as an institutionalized mechanism for "animal welfare washing" – a facade that seems to imply legal protection for animals when, in reality, it is lacking. This is especially true regarding farmed animals. The law expert Fabien Marchadier summarizes it well (Marchadier 2023, 67–83):

> The use of reassuring vocabulary, the content of the standards, the delimitation of their field of application, the exemptions which are tolerated organize a system which, far from banning violence against animals, defines the very conditions for its exercise. All these rules are less intended to guarantee a high level of well-being than to establish the amount of suffering inflicted on animals deemed acceptable by producers, breeders and consumers, all showing, to varying degrees and with varying behaviours, a growing concern about the treatment reserved for animals. Together, they form a code of animal exploitation institutionalizing the suffering inflicted on animals.

REFERENCES

Anthis K, Reese-Anthis J (2019) *Global Farmed Factory Farmed Animals Estimates*. Sentience Institute.

APPA (2018) Industry trends and stats. www.americanpetproducts.org/press_industrytrends.asp.

Barrett M, Godfrey RK, Schnell A, Fischer B (2023) Farmed yellow mealworm (Tenebrio molitor; Coleoptera: Tenebrionidae) welfare: Species-specific recommendations for a global industry. *Journal of Insects as Food and Feed*, 1(aop), 1–46.

Bar-On YM, Philips R, Milo R (2018) The biomass distribution on earth. *Proceedings of the National Academy of Sciences*, 115(25), 6506–6511.

Bry-Chevalier T (2024) Comparing the potential of meat alternatives for a more sustainable food system, mimeo.

Budolfson M, Fischer B, Scovronick N (2023) Animal welfare: Methods to improve policy and practice. *Science*, 381(6653), 32–34.

Burgat F (2006) *Liberté et Inquiétude de la Vie Animale*. Éditions Kimé.

Callaghan CT, Nakagawa S, Cornwell WK (2021) Global abundance estimates for 9,700 bird species. *Proceedings of the National Academy of Sciences*, 118(21), e2023170118.

Carlier A, Treich N (2020) Directly valuing animal welfare in (environmental) economics. *International Review of Environmental and Resource Economics*, 14, 113–152.

Cole JR, McCoskey S (2013) Does global meat consumption follow an environmental Kuznets curve? *Sustainability: Science, Practice and Policy*, 9(2), 26–36.

Coleman JL (1995) The American whale oil industry: A look back to the future of the American petroleum industry? *Nonrenewable Resources*, 4, 273–288.

Collishaw A, Janzen S, Mullally C, Camilli H (2023) A review of livestock development interventions' impacts on household welfare in low-and middle-income countries. *Global Food Security*, 38, 100704.

Creel S, Winnie Jr JA, Christianson D (2009) Glucocorticoid stress hormones and the effect of predation risk on elk reproduction. *Proceedings of the National Academy of Sciences*, 106(30), 12388–12393.

De Juana E (1992) Class AVES. In *Handbook of the Birds in the World, ed.* J del Hoyo, A Elliott, J Sargatal. Lynx Edicions.

Donaldson S, Kymlicka W (2011) *Zoopolis: A Political Theory of Animal Rights.* Oxford University Press.

EFSA Panel on Animal Health and Welfare (AHAW), Nielsen SS, Alvarez J et al. (2022) Welfare of pigs on farm. *EFSA Journal*, 20(8), e07421.

EFSA Panel on Animal Health and Welfare (AHAW), Nielsen SS, Alvarez J et al. (2023a) Welfare of broilers on farm. *EFSA Journal*, 21(2), e07788.

EFSA Panel on Animal Health and Animal Welfare (AHAW), Nielsen SS, Alvarez J et al. (2023b) Welfare of laying hens on farm. *EFSA Journal*, 21(2), e07789.

EFSA Panel on Animal Health and Animal Welfare (AHAW), Nielsen SS, Alvarez J et al. (2023c) Welfare of dairy cows. *EFSA Journal*, 21(5), e07993.

EFSA Panel on Animal Health and Animal Welfare (AHAW), Nielsen SS, Alvarez J et al. (2023d) Welfare of calves. *EFSA Journal*, 21(3), e07896.

Endenburg N, Bouw J (1994) Motives for acquiring companion animals. *Journal of Economic Psychology*, 15(1), 191–206.

European Court of Auditors (2023) Review 03/2023: Transport of live animals in the EU: challenges and opportunities | European Court of Auditors. www.eca.europa.eu/Lists/ECADocuments/RV-2023-03/RV-2023-03_EN.pdf.

European Union (2010) Directive 2010/63/EU on the protection of animals used for scientific purposes (article 38). *Official Journal of the European Union*, L276/33. https://eur-lex.europa.eu/LexUriServ/LexUriServ.do?uri=OJ:L:2010:276:0033:0079:En:PDF.

Foley JA, Ramankutty N, Brauman KA et al. (2011) Solutions for a cultivated planet. *Nature*, 478(7369), 337–342.

Francione G (2008) *Animals as Persons: Essays on the Abolition of Animal Exploitation.* Cambridge University Press.

Frank J (2008) Is there an "animal welfare Kuznets curve"? *Ecological Economics*, 66(2–3), 478–491.

Frank EG, Wang S, Wang X, Wang Q, You Y (2024) Campaigning for extinction: Eradication of sparrows and the Great Famine in China, mimeo.

Franks B, Ewell C, Jacquet J (2021) Animal welfare risks of global aquaculture. *Science Advances*, 7, eabg0677.

Fraser D, MacRae A (2011) Four types of activities that affect animals: Implications for animal welfare science and animal ethics philosophy. *Animal Welfare*, 20(4), 581–590.

Futhazar G (2024) The regulation of invasive alien species. In *Oxford Handbook of Global Animal Law*, eds. Anne Peters, Kristen Stilt and Saskia Stucki. Oxford University Press, in press.

Gaston KJ, Blackburn TM (1997) How many birds are there? *Biodiversity & Conservation*, 6(4), 615–625.

Gaston KJ, Blackburn TM, Goldewijk KK (2003) Habitat conversion and global avian biodiversity loss. *Proceedings of the Royal Society of London. Series B: Biological Sciences*, 270(1521), 1293–1300.

Gibbons M, Crump A, Barrett M, Sarlak S, Birch J, Chittka L (2022) Can insects feel pain? A review of the neural and behavioural evidence. *Advances in Insect Physiology*, 63, 155–229.

Gilbert M, Conchedda G, Van Boeckel TP et al. (2015) Income disparities and the global distribution of intensively farmed chicken and pigs. *PLoS ONE*, 10(7), e0133381.

Godfray HCJ, Aveyard P, Garnett T et al. (2018) Meat consumption, health, and the environment. *Science*, 361, eaam5324.

Green C (2016) Animal advocacy by numbers. Faunalytics. https://faunalytics.org/animal-advocacy-by-numbers/.

Greene AN (2008) *Horses at Work: Harnessing Power in Industrial America*. Harvard University Press.

Greenspoon L, Krieger E, Sender R et al. (2023) The global biomass of wild mammals. *Proceedings of the National Academy of Sciences*, 120(10), e2204892120.

Gruen L (2017) The moral status of animals. The Stanford Encyclopaedia of Philosophy. https://plato.stanford.edu/entries/moral-animal/.

Herrero M, Grace D, Njuki J, et al. (2013) The roles of livestock in developing countries. *Animal*, 7(S1), 3–18

IPBES (2019) Summary for policymakers of the global assessment report on biodiversity and ecosystem services of the Intergovernmental Science-Policy Platform on Biodiversity and Ecosystem Services.

Kaartvedt S, Staby A, Aksnes DL (2012) Efficient trawl avoidance by mesopelagic fishes causes large underestimation of their biomass. *Marine Ecology Progress Series*, 456, 1–6.

Kagan S (2016) What's wrong with speciesism? (Society for Applied Philosophy Annual Lecture 2015). *Journal of Applied Philosophy*, 33(1), 1–21.

Kagan S (2019) *How to Count Animals, More or Less*. Oxford University Press.

Kant E (1784) Moral philosophy: Collin's lecture notes. In *Lectures on Ethics*, eds. P Heath and JB Schneewind, 1997. Cambridge Edition of the Works of Immanuel Kant. Cambridge University Press.

Keeling L, Tunón H, Olmos Antillón G et al. (2019) Animal welfare and the United Nations sustainable development goals. *Frontiers in Veterinary Science*, 6, 336.

Kilby ER (2007) The demographics of the US equine population. In *The state of the animals 2007*, eds. DJ Salem, AN Rowan, 175–205. Humane Society Press.

Kniess J (2019) Bentham on animal welfare. *British Journal for the History of Philosophy*, 27(3), 556–572.

Korsgaard CM (1996) *The Sources of Normativity*. Cambridge University Press.

Leahy E, Lyons S, Tol RS (2010) An estimate of the number of vegetarians in the world (No. 340). ESRI working paper. www.econstor.eu/bitstream/10419/50160/1/632222107.pdf.

Lynch MJ (2023) Writs of habeas corpus for nonhuman primates in the United States and the nonhuman rights project: Legal processes and arguments used to secure nonhuman animal rights. *International Journal for Crime, Justice and Social Democracy*, 12(3), 15–26.

Marchadier F (2023) The legal status of animals in European law. In *Animal Suffering: The Ethics and Politics of Animal Lives*, chapter 4, eds. F Burgat and E Dardenne, 67–83. Wiley.

Matheny G, Chan K (2005) Human diets and animal welfare: The illogic of the larder. *Journal of Agricultural and Environmental Ethics*, 18(6), 579–594.

McMullen S (2016) *Animals and the Economy*. Palgrave Macmillan.

Mood A, Brooke P (2012) Estimating the number of farmed fish killed in global aquaculture each year. https://fishcount.org.uk/published/std/fishcountstudy2.pdf.

Mood A, Brooke P (2024) Estimating global numbers of fishes caught from the wild annually from 2000 to 2019. *Animal Welfare*, 33, e6.

Mood A, Lara E, Boyland NK, Brooke P (2023) Estimating global numbers of farmed fishes killed for food annually from 1990 to 2019. *Animal Welfare*, 32, e12, 1–16.

Murray M (2011) The underdog in history: Serfdom, slavery and species in the creation and development of capitalism. In *Theorizing Animals*, eds. N Taylor, T Signal, 85–106. Brill.

NAPHIA (2024) Pet insurance in North America. https://naphia.org/industry-data/.

Newman JA, Varner J, Linquist S (2017) *Defending Biodiversity*. Cambridge University Press.

Norwood FB, Lusk JL (2011) *Compassion, by the Pound: The Economics of Farm Animal Welfare*. Oxford University Press.

Parlasca MC, Qaim M (2022) Meat consumption and sustainability. *Annual Review of Resource Economics*, 14, 17–41.

Ramp D, Bekoff M (2015) Compassion as a practical and evolved ethic for conservation. *BioScience*, 65(3), 323–327.

Regan T (1983) *The Case for Animal Rights*. Routledge.

Reyes-Illg G, Martin JE, Mani I, Reynolds J, Kipperman B (2023) The rise of heatstroke as a method of depopulating pigs and poultry: Implications for the US veterinary profession. *Animals*, 13(1), 140.

Ripple WJ, Beschta RL (2004) Wolves and the ecology of fear: Can predation risk structure ecosystems? *BioScience*, 54(8), 755–766.

Rousseau J-J (1754) Discourse on the Origin of Inequality, Translated by GDH Cole. www.files.ethz.ch/isn/125494/5019_Rousseau_Discourse_on_the_Origin_of_Inequality.pdf.

Rowe E, López KR, Robinson KM, Baudier KM, Barrett M (2024) Farmed cricket (Acheta domesticus, Gryllus assimilis, and Gryllodes sigillatus; Orthoptera) welfare considerations: Recommendations for improving global practice. *Journal of Insects as Food and Feed*, 1(aop), 1–59.

Salmon G, Teufel N, Baltenweck I, van Wijk M, Claessens L, Marshall K (2018) Trade-offs in livestock development at farm level: Different actors with different objectives. *Global Food Security*, 17, 103–112.

Saraiva JL, Arechavala-Lopez P, Castanheira MF, Volstorf J, Studer BH (2019) A global assessment of welfare in farmed fishes: The FishEthoBase. *Fishes*, 4, 30.

Schwarz PM, Troyer JL, Walker JB (2007) Animal house: Economics of pets and the household. *The BE Journal of Economic Analysis & Policy*, 7(1). https://faunalytics.org/wp-content/uploads/2015/05/Citation421.pdf.

Sidgwick H (1893) *The Methods of Ethics*. Hackett Publishing Co.

Singer P (1975) *Animal Liberation: A New Ethics of Our Treatment of Animals*. Random House.

Singer P (2011) *Practical Ethics*. Cambridge University Press.

Smil V (2013) *Harvesting the Biosphere*. MIT Press.

Sneddon LU, Elwood RW, Adamo SA, Leach MC (2014) Defining and assessing animal pain. *Animal Behavior*, 97, 201–212.

Sowery K (2018) Sentient beings and tradable products: The curious constitutional status of animals under Union law. *Common Market Law Review*, 70, 55–56.

Stawasz A (2024) Animals in cost-benefit analyses. Available at SSRN 3643473.

Sunstein CR (2003) The rights of animals. *The University of Chicago Law Review*, 70(1), 387–401.

Taylor K, Alvarez LR (2019) An estimate of the number of animals used for scientific purposes worldwide in 2015. *Alternatives to Laboratory Animals*, 47(5–6), 196–213.

Taylor K, Gordon N, Langley G, Higgins W (2008) *ATLA – Alternatives to Laboratory Animals*, 36(3), 327.

The Economist (2020) Interest in veganism is surging. 29 January 2020. www.economist.com/graphic-detail/2020/01/29/interest-in-veganism-is-surging.

Tomasik B (2009) How many wild animals are there? https://reducing-suffering.org/how-many-wild-animals-are-there/.

Visscher MB (1972) The newer antivivisectionists. *Proceedings of the American Philosophical Society*, 116(2), 157–162.

Waldhorn DL, Autric E (2023) Shrimp: The animals most commonly used and killed for food production. Rethink Priorities. https://rethinkpriorities.org/research-area/shrimp-the-animals-most-commonly-used-and-killed-for-food-production/.

Weimer DL, Vining AR (2024) *Dog Economics: Perspectives on Our Canine Relationships*. Cambridge University Press.

Williams CB (1960) The range and pattern of insect abundance. *The American Naturalist*, 94(875), 137–151.

Wilson R, Millero F, Taylor J, et al. (2009) Contribution of fish to the marine inorganic carbon cycle. *Science*, 323(5912), 359–362.

Wilting HC, Schipper AM, Bakkenes M, Meijer JR, Huijbregts MA (2017) Quantifying biodiversity losses due to human consumption: A global-scale footprint analysis. *Environmental Science & Technology*, 51(6), 3298–3306.

Wise SM (2022) The Nonhuman Rights Project's struggles to gain legal rights for nonhuman animals. In *Animal Ethics and Animal Law*, eds. A & C Linzey, 117–128. Lexington Books.

PART II The Direct Approach

As explained in the preliminary part, the rest of the book is divided in two parts, the direct approach and the indirect approach. The direct approach is about extending social welfare to animals. It is a nonanthropocentric approach that mostly concerns the fields of welfare theory and public economics for the conceptual foundations, as well as animal welfare sciences for various aspects. In this part, I first present the concept of sentientism (Chapter 3), namely the philosophical position that places sentience, that is, the ability to experience feelings such as pleasure and pain, as the foundation for moral consideration. I then discuss in turn different methods for assessing, comparing, and aggregating the welfare of sentient animals (Chapters 4–6).

Once these building blocks are presented, I introduce a simple, canonical model that will serve as a recurring framework throughout the whole book (Chapter 7). This economic model enables the identification of the externality resulting from animal use by humans. It shows that an animal welfare levy, similar to Pigouvian taxation in environmental economics, can restore efficiency. I then extend this canonical model to discuss the optimal individual and social decisions regarding both the quantity and the quality of animal lives (Chapter 8), before turning to the complex topic of (animal) population ethics (Chapter 9). I finally conclude this first part by presenting one method to value animal welfare, and for the sake of an illustration, by performing benefit-cost analyses of a few specific policies affecting the number of animals and their welfare (Chapter 10).

Overall, this part initially sets the basic elements that permit the integration of animal welfare into economic analysis, and explores first theoretically and then empirically the implications of such an integration. The initial sections strongly borrow from other disciplines, while the last sections follow traditional approaches in economics, but with a very novel twist: the integration of animal welfare directly into the social welfare function.

3 Sentientism

3.1 THE MORAL COMMUNITY

The moral community refers to the entities that possess moral status. This is a central issue for the direct approach since it determines which entities should be considered in the social welfare function. There are several possibilities to consider. The first possibility is anthropocentrism, where only humans have moral status. As we have seen in Chapter 1, this anthropocentric approach has been nearly universal in economics, often implicitly assumed without scholars attempting to justify the limitation of their work to human welfare. For instance, many studies in agricultural economics focus on aspects such as husbandry productivity, food security, or the negative externalities of the food system, neglecting to address the intrinsic value of animals.

The most common justification for anthropocentrism is human exceptionalism (Gruen 2017), which argues that humankind possesses distinct capacities compared to other animals that grant moral status. While it is true that humans exhibit unique characteristics within the animal kingdom, the justification of anthropocentrism based on human exceptionalism is fragile in two ways. First, the boundary between humans and other species is much less distinct than assumed in the past. Studies exploring the cognitive, emotional, and social capacities of animals have debunked long-standing assumptions about these capacities once believed to be exclusive to humans, such as the design and use of tools, the prevalence of cultures, the existence of symbolic communication, the capacity for self-awareness, or the ability to impute mental states to others (Webb et al. 2019). Scientific knowledge reveals biological continuities between humans and animals (Sekar and Shiller 2020). Hence, it is not clear why such biological continuities would justify a moral discontinuity where only humans would have moral status.

The second reason, much more powerful in my view, for why anthropocentrism is fragile is the following. Even if we acknowledge that certain capacities are specific to humans, it remains unclear whether these capacities alone justify moral status. Besides, given the diverse conditions of humans, many do not possess usual capacities. For example, most people would still attribute moral status to a human lacking reasoning capacities, such as newborns. This point, akin to the "argument from marginal cases" and already discussed in Chapter 2, is well emphasized in the Montreal Declaration on animal exploitation reproduced in Chapter 2.

The second normative possibility involves granting moral status to all sentient beings, often referred to as the sentientist (or pathocentric) approach. In its narrowest sense, sentience refers to the minimum level of consciousness required to have subjective experiences of the world. There is no universally agreed definition of sentience. Broadly, sentience is the capacity to feel sensations and emotions. It comes from the Latin "sentiens," or feeling. Broom (2014) defines sentience as "having the awareness and cognitive ability necessary to have feelings." Birch (2024) defines sentience as "the capacity to have valenced experiences, such as experiences of pain and pleasure." Sentience is often viewed as the most basic form of cognition, involving a conscious awareness of stimuli without necessarily involving processes of association or interpretation.

Sentience is strongly linked to consciousness or awareness, although it can be viewed as distinct. Self-conscious beings not only experience sensations but are also aware of these experiences. They can reflect on their own thoughts and mental states. Thomas Nagel in his classic paper "What is it like to be a bat?," defines consciousness as the ability to have subjective perceptual experiences, or the ability to have states that it "feels like something" to be in (Nagel 1974). In fact, sentience is often used to mean "phenomenal consciousness," namely the capacity to have any subjective experience at all. But, it can also refer to the narrower concept of "affective consciousness," namely the capacity to experience subjective states with positive or negative valence, such as pain and pleasure.

The distinction between sentience and consciousness is not always clear and consistent throughout the literature. In any case, this distinction will not be central for the rest of the book, and I will generally use the word sentience (unless the cited reference uses a different related term). The crucial aspect is that, from a welfarist perspective usually adopted in economics, sentience is relevant for its implications regarding the ability to have subjective experiences of well-being and to undergo different states of welfare spending on the living conditions. In short, the sentientist approach asserts that moral status should be conferred based on an individual's capacity to experience welfare. Then, the central point is that this capacity is not limited to humans.

In fact, the approach toward sentience adopted in this book is very similar to that adopted by Ng (1995, page 258) in his seminal paper on welfare biology:

> 'Sentients' is usually defined as beings that are capable of subjectively perceiving or feeling by means of the senses. This includes not only beings capable of the feeling of being happy and/or unhappy, but also includes beings just capable of perceiving things without having any affective feeling. In principle, it is possible for some sentients to be capable of perceiving the external world but without feeling happy or unhappy. One could have sensations of perceiving different colours without enjoying or disliking seeing them; one could have the sensation of being touched or even being squeezed without feeling pain or pleasure. Such non-affective sentients really do not have any positive or negative welfare. Their welfare is necessarily zero, just like non-sentients. Hence, for the purpose here, the important dividing line is not between sentients and non-sentients, but between affective sentients and non-affective beings (sentient or non-sentient).

Going back to the different moral possibilities, a third possibility is to grant moral status to all living things, known as the biocentric approach. Proponents of biocentrism argue that moral consideration should be extended not only to sentient animals but also to non-sentient living entities such as plants, fungi, or bacteria. This perspective recognizes the inherent value of all living organisms and emphasizes the interconnectedness and interdependence of ecological systems. Additionally, there is a fourth possibility that advocates for assigning moral value to entire ecosystems, known as the ecocentric view. From this standpoint, moral status should be extended to non-living elements of ecosystems, such as air, rivers, or mountains. This perspective, pioneered by scholars like Leopold (1949) and Callicott (1989), acknowledges the intricate relationships and ecological integrity of natural systems.

3.2 JUSTIFYING SENTIENTISM

In this book, I advocate for the adoption of a sentientist approach for several reasons. First, economics is predominantly a welfarist discipline, meaning that economists are primarily concerned with welfare. Since sentience can generally be understood as the ability to experience welfare (see previous section), embracing a sentientist approach is the most logical and natural extension of usual normative settings in economics.

Second, economists adopting the sentientist approach would align their field with recent strides in philosophy toward antispeciesism. Scholars such as Singer (2011) have contributed to this evolving discourse, emphasizing the importance of considering the interests and welfare of all sentient beings. His primary argument for considering that animals have interests is rooted in their sentience, following Bentham's reasoning: They can suffer and experience pleasure. By embracing a sentientist approach, economists would align themselves with these contemporary developments in philosophy, as illustrated by the Montreal Declaration (2023). From this perspective, sentientism may be viewed as the main alternative to anthropocentrism (Newman et al. 2017).

Furthermore, the adoption of the sentientist approach aligns with the utilitarian framework more seamlessly compared to biocentrism and ecocentrism, which present much larger conceptual gaps and much greater uncertainties. Given current knowledge, it seems elusive to account for the intrinsic values of plants, mushrooms, bacteria and so on, not even mentioning nonliving things such as a river or a mountain. Instead, sentientism recognizes that animals, like humans, have the capacity for subjective experiences and welfare, allowing us to assess and compare different situations based on their impact on well-being.

From an economic standpoint, it would be much more challenging to apply moral valuation to entities that lack the capacity for welfare, as it deviates much further from the foundations of standard economic theory. Therefore, the sentientist approach offers a more practical and compatible extension of economic analysis within the realm of moral consideration. In essence, I assume that welfare requires sentience and that the realm of welfare subjects coincides with the realm of sentient beings. I understand that not every philosopher agrees with this assumption (see for instance Delon [2022] for a different perspective on this issue), but it serves as a practical and valuable premise for the objectives of this book. The feasibility of the approach is important because one key objective is to produce some quantitative nonanthropocentric studies in the not-too-distant future.

Note that even if one argues that biocentrism or ecocentrism are more desirable approaches, the adoption of the sentientist approach can be viewed as an initial and crucial step toward establishing a broader and inclusive normative framework. Recognizing and granting moral consideration to sentient beings who have the capacity for subjective experiences and welfare lays the foundation for extending moral consideration to other living entities or ecosystems. This recognition sets the stage for further exploration and development of ethical frameworks that encompass a wider range of entities and their relationships within the natural world. In this sense, the adoption of the sentientist approach can be seen as a necessary step toward a more comprehensive normative framework.

Obviously, there exist concerns associated with sentientism. This approach aligns with the hedonistic view of welfare and faces various criticisms historically raised against hedonism. Note, however, a subtle distinction between hedonism and sentientism. Some sentientists take sentience as the criterion of moral consideration because they view sentience as necessary for the capacity for welfare, but they do not view welfare as consisting of hedonic experiences. Other sentientists are hedonists, which gives them a more direct route to taking sentience as the relevant criterion. Hedonistic theories of animal welfare interpret welfare as a descriptive concept, where assessing an animal's welfare is solely a matter of accurately representing or describing its mental states (Robbins et al. 2018).

One major criticism to hedonism is reductionism. Critics argue that hedonism reduces life to the pursuit of pleasure and the avoidance of pain, oversimplifying the complexity of experiences and values. A related criticism relates to Nozick's (1974) well known "experience machine," a thought experiment that suggests that people value more than just pleasurable experiences. Nozick proposed a machine that could provide any desired pleasurable experience, yet he argues that many would choose not to plug into it, indicating that we value reality, authenticity, and engagement in actual activities beyond mere pleasure. A further criticism is impoverishment (Haybron 2016): While it is important for our lives to be pleasant, it is also crucial that they are meaningful. That is, it is not only the sum of pleasures that counts.

The key point I wish to emphasize is that these classical criticisms of hedonism, like many others, appear to focus primarily on humans and their welfare. Most objections to hedonism (and, by extension, to hedonic utilitarianism) are human-centered. This makes sense under the widespread anthropocentric approach. However, the use or extension of standard arguments against hedonism often appears unconvincing when applied to animals. For instance, it is not clear how to apply the experience machine to animals. Similarly a "meaningful" life probably makes little sense for many animals, or at least might be something very marginal compared to other needs such as food or reproduction. In sum, I believe that those criticisms against hedonism are largely inappropriate when applied to animals.

Obviously, there may be some disagreement about this defense of hedonism. See, for instance, Purves and Delon (2018) on the question of meaningfulness for some animal lives. Also, there is some evidence that animals may value something other than pain and pleasure, such as in the "contrafreeloading" literature (Inglis et al. 1997). Contrafreeloading is a behavioral phenomenon where an animal chooses to work for food, even when identical food is freely available. Animals, such as rats, pigeons and dogs, often opt to press levers or complete tasks for food rather than simply eating readily accessible food.

Another major criticism to sentientism relates to Nozick's notion of "utility monsters." The utility monster is a hypothetical being used to critique the idea that maximizing overall happiness, welfare, or utility is the best moral approach. In Nozick's hypothetical scenario, the utility monster gains far more happiness from resources than anyone else. The critique is that it would be morally obligatory to allocate most resources to the utility monster, because this would maximize overall utility. As another extreme, sentientism places little importance on species that are barely sentient, which may result in an unjustifiable bias against them.

Personally, I do not find this critique very compelling to disqualify the use of a sentientist approach in general. First, in practice, the concept of a utility monster is highly theoretical and unlikely to occur in reality. Evolutionary forces would unlikely create such monsters, as emotions are "costly" in terms of required resources for an organism (Ng 1995). Second, even if we consider the plausible case of significant heterogeneity variations in utility, which seems very likely when considering the range spectrum of species, I do not see why such heterogeneity should be ignored in general. If an individual suffers much more than another, my intuition suggests that this difference should be accounted for in the social objective. In any case, it is possible to introduce some "weighing factors" to mitigate the risk associated with the presence of utility monsters (and, conversely, of barely sentient individuals) in the moral community. Typically, the sentientist normative objective can incorporate principles of fairness, equality, or diminishing marginal utility, which would mitigate the extreme distribution of resources to the utility monster.

It might also be argued that the focus on sentientism is human-centered. This view is well summarized in Fleurbaey and Leppanen (2021, page 271):

> Human experience revolves around mental states a lot, whereas other species have a different balance between mental and non-mental achievements. Putting exclusive value on the dimension of life that happens to be exacerbated in the human species should perhaps be viewed as biased since it does not have much foundation apart from the (human) intuition that this is a very important aspect of (our human) life.

This sounds like a fair criticism. It may be hard for us to imagine that other species could value other things than those we value. However, at this stage, I view this criticism as a hypothesis and I have not seen any serious evidence supporting it. In any case, this hypothesis certainly warrants caution and modesty, reminding us that only humans can debate these issues, which may create distortions in how we define what is morally sound.

Another argument emphasizes the limitation of an absolute level of happiness as a measure of welfare. This argument has solid evolutionary foundations and is relevant for both humans and many animal species. It is based on the idea of reference points and adaptation (Rayo and Becker 2007). Our brain's hedonic system, shaped by evolution, helps us make decisions that support survival and reproduction. It does this by responding to changes: Positive surprises make us feel good, while negative surprises make us feel bad. Dopamine neurons, which process rewards, work in this way. They do not just react to rewards but also to the difference between what we expect and what we actually get. In a famous experiment, Schultz et al. (1997) find that a monkey's dopamine neurons fire when it receives orange juice. However, when a light signals the juice is coming, the neurons fire at the light instead (the surprise). If the juice does not follow the light, the neurons' activity drop, signaling frustration.

Hence, while our brain encodes the expected value of choices, hedonic feelings essentially reflect prediction errors, that is, positive or negative surprises relative to expectations. A critical consequence of this process is our continuous adaptation to changes in circumstances, a phenomenon known in psychology as the "hedonic treadmill." Unexpected situations bring positive or negative feelings, but we habituate over time. Once new circumstances become the norm, overall satisfaction reverts to a baseline. This suggests that the sum of happiness over time is not really what matters. The key point here is that this process is expected to apply to animals, since they, too, adapt to their environments. The bottom line is that this hedonic adaptation process raises important questions about how we assess animal welfare, particularly in the context of long-term adaptation. There is ongoing research on this issue, in particular in economics.

3.3 WHICH SPECIES ARE SENTIENT?

Once a sentientist approach is adopted, the ensuing question arises: Which species possess sentience? First of all, it is important to note that there is active research on this question too, and that the demarcation between sentient and non-sentient species is not clear-cut. While there are certain species for which sentience is highly probable, there are others where the likelihood of sentience is low, if not nil. For many species, there remains a notable degree of uncertainty regarding their sentience.

Extensive research on neural functioning across various vertebrate species highlights striking similarities in their experiential capacities. For instance, studies have demonstrated that mammals share fundamental emotional systems such as joy, fear, grief, parental nurturance, and playfulness (Sekar and Shiller 2020). These animals possess a nervous system and brain structures that are remarkably similar to those found in humans, and they exhibit comparable responses to various stimuli. Moreover, evidence strongly supports the presence of sentience not only in mammals but also in other species such as birds and cephalopods.

This knowledge was embodied in the famous Cambridge Declaration on Consciousness, which was proclaimed on 7 July 2012 at Cambridge University (Low et al. 2012, page 2):

> The absence of a neocortex does not appear to preclude an organism from experiencing affective states. Convergent evidence indicates that non-human animals have the neuroanatomical, neurochemical, and neurophysiological substrates of conscious states along with the capacity to exhibit intentional behaviors. Consequently, the weight of evidence indicates that humans are not unique in possessing the neurological substrates that generate consciousness. Non-human animals, including all mammals and birds, and many other creatures, including octopuses, also possess these neurological substrates.

This Declaration thus emphasizes a neural and physiological approach to consciousness, suggesting that it requires specialized biological structures, such as those found in the central nervous system of complex organisms. Consequently, organisms with these neurological substrates are considered to be conscious. Emerging scientific evidence has also provided substantial support for the sentience of fish (Brown 2015). In sum, all these species exhibit complex behaviors and display neural and physiological characteristics indicative of conscious experiences. It is extremely likely that they all can feel pain. For instance, this pain appears to lessen or disappear when analgesics are administered, which is a strong indication for pain perception (Bateson 1991, Sneddon 2003).

However, when it comes to other animals, such as insects, earthworms, and certain molluscs, the situation is less conclusive.

Table 3.1 *Likelihood of sentience for some taxonomic classes*

Taxonomic classes	Likelihood of sentience
Mammals	Very likely
Birds	Very likely
Cephalopods	Very likely
Fish	Very likely
Insects	Possible
Plants	Very unlikely

These creatures possess relatively smaller or less centralized nervous systems, making it uncertain whether they possess sentience. Nonetheless, given the scientific uncertainty surrounding their cognitive capacities, an argument can be made for applying the precautionary principle and attributing at least some moral consideration to these species as well (Birch 2017). By erring on the side of caution, we acknowledge the possibility of their sentience and avoid potential harm or disregard of their interests. Note also that categories of animals, such as insects, contain species with very different abilities. Bees' capacities such as communication, navigation, social organization, and even learning and memory (Menzel and Erber 1978), never cease to amaze, for instance. So, the typical taxonomic classes (that I use in Table 3.1) may not be appropriate to provide sufficiently distinctive information about the likelihood of sentience.

The sentientist approach, which grants moral consideration to beings based on their capacity for subjective experiences and welfare, thus broadly encompasses a large portion of animal lives. This approach recognizes that animals, by their very nature, possess the ability to perceive and interact with their environment. In this book, I will most often use the term "animals" instead of "sentient animals." While this may be a linguistic simplification, it is thus not entirely imprecise.

Critically, it is important to recognize that the current understanding of sentience does not extend to include plants. Based on the current state of scientific knowledge, plants are not believed to possess consciousness or the capacity for subjective experiences. In a comprehensive synthesis paper, Taiz et al. (2019) conclude indeed that "the likelihood that plants, with their relative organizational simplicity and lack of neurons and brains, have consciousness to be effectively nil." While plants exhibit complex cellular interactions and signaling mechanisms, they lack the key neurological and cognitive attributes associated with sentience in animals. Therefore, within the framework of the sentientist approach, plants are not part of the moral community. This is why this book talks about animal welfare, and not about plant welfare or ecosystem welfare. In short, "non-sentient animals are not welfare subjects" (Višak 2022), and thus do not have a moral status. As a result, they will not be part of the social welfare function in the economic analysis developed in later chapters.

To conclude this chapter, let me add an important remark about policy implications. This remark is a slight criticism of the focus on the moral community in the philosophical literature, namely of the focus on which species are sentient (see for instance the 2024 New York Declaration on animal consciousness https://sites.google.com/nyu.edu/nydeclaration/declaration). The point is that sentience is often viewed as a binary concept. Either a species is sentient or not. Ethics scholars seldom talk about the "degree of sentience." Fine.

However, for policy issues, what matters is not merely the presence or absence of sentience but whether this makes the difference in terms of global variation of welfare due to policy choices. Therefore, what matters is the number of sentient animals under consideration, especially their capacity to undergo substantial variations in welfare depending on the policy at stake. If a beetle is proved to be sentient but has welfare variations billions of times smaller than that of a pig, should policymakers care about the sentience of this beetle? Worse, the risk is that this focus on who belongs to the moral community distracts policymakers from setting the right priorities, and possibly contributes to maintaining the status quo. When everything matters, nothing matters.

The bottom line is that the key question to me is not so much who belongs to the moral community, but whose welfare is affected and especially by "how much." This point about the "how much" is central in the economic approach of sentientism and will be extensively addressed in the following chapters.

REFERENCES

Bateson P (1991) Assessment of pain in animals. *Animal Behaviour*, 42(5), 827–839.

Bentham J (1780) *An Introduction to the Principles of Morals and Legislation*, eds. JH Burns, HLA Hart, 1970. Athlone Press.

Birch J (2017) Animal sentience and the precautionary principle. *Animal Sentience*, *2*(16), 1.

Birch J (2024) *The Edge of Sentience*. Oxford University Press.

Broom D (2014) *Sentience and Animal Welfare*. CABI Publishing.

Brown C (2015) Fish intelligence, sentience and ethics. *Animal Cognition*, 18, 1–17.

Callicott JB (1989) *In Defense of Land Ethic: Essays in Environmental Philosophy*. State University of New York.

Delon N (2022) Agency and welfare across species, mimeo.

Fleurbaey M, Leppanen C (2021) Toward a theory of ecosystem well-being. *Journal of Bioeconomics*, 23, 257–295.

Gruen L (2017) The Moral Status of Animals. The Stanford Encyclopaedia of Philosophy. https://plato.stanford.edu/entries/moral-animal/.

Haybron DM (2016) Mental state approaches to well-being. In *The Oxford Handbook of Well-Being and Public Policy*, 12, eds. MD Adler and M Fleurbaey, 347–378. Oxford University Press.

Inglis IR, Forkman B, Lazarus J (1997) Free food or earned food? A review and fuzzy model of contrafreeloading. *Animal Behaviour*, 53(6), 1171–1191.

Leopold A (1949) *A Sand County Almanach: And Sketches Here and There*. Oxford University Press.

Low P, Panksepp J, Reiss D, Edelman D, van Swinderen B, Koch C (2012) The Cambridge Declaration on consciousness. Presented at the Francis Crick Memorial Conference, Cambridge, England. https://fcmconference.org/img/CambridgeDeclarationOnConsciousness.pdf.

Menzel R, Erber J (1978) Learning and memory in bees. *Scientific American*, 239(1), 102–111.

Montreal Declaration on Animal Exploitation (2023) https://greea.ca/en/montreal-declaration-on-animal-exploitation/.

Nagel T (1974) What is it like to be a bat? *The Philosophical Review*, 83(4), 435–450.

Newman JA, Varner J, Linquist S (2017) *Defending Biodiversity*. Cambridge University Press.

Ng Y-K (1995) Towards welfare biology: Evolutionary economics of animal consciousness and suffering. *Biology and Philosophy*, 10(3), 255–285.

Nozick R (1974) *Anarchy, State, and Utopia*. Basic Books.

Page L (2024) The aim of maximising happiness is doomed to fail as a public policy. www.optimallyirrational.com/p/the-aim-of-maximising-happiness-is.

Purves D, Delon N (2018) Meaning in the lives of humans and other animals. *Philosophical Studies*, 175, 317–338.

Rayo L, Becker GS (2007) Evolutionary efficiency and happiness. *Journal of Political Economy*, 115(2), 302–337.

Robbins J, Franks B, Von Keyserlingk MA (2018) "More than a feeling": An empirical investigation of hedonistic accounts of animal welfare. *PloS One*, 13(3), e0193864.

Schultz W, Dayan P, Montague PR (1997) A neural substrate of prediction and reward. *Science*, 275(5306), 1593–1599.

Sekar N, Shiller D (2020) Engage with animal welfare in conservation, *Science*, 369, 629–630.

Singer P (2011) *Practical Ethics*. 3rd edition. Cambridge University Press.

Sneddon LU (2003) The evidence for pain in fish: The use of morphine as an analgesic. *Applied Animal Behaviour Science*, 83(2), 153–162.

Taiz L, Alkon D, Draguhn A, et al. (2019) Plants neither possess nor require consciousness. *Trends in Plant Science*, 24(8), 677–687.

Višak T (2022) *Capacity for Welfare across Species*. Oxford University Press.

Webb CE, Woodford P, Huchard E (2019) Animal ethics and behavioral science: An overdue discussion. *BioScience*, 69(10), 778–788.

4 Assessing Animal Welfare

4.1 BACKGROUND ON WELFARE ASSESSMENT

Although no consensus has emerged among animal scientists about the definition and assessment of animal welfare, a wide range of measures have been developed, particularly in the context of farmed animals (Broom 2014). These measures encompass various aspects such as mortality and injury rates, indications of movement difficulties or stereotypies, vocalizations, fear response, group stress, physiological indicators including elevated heart rate, adrenal activity, and reduced immunological response.

As an example, in a well-known study, Mason et al. (2001) provided minks with enriched cages that included a water pool, toys, a tunnel, and other novel objects. They then removed each object, including access to food, one at a time and examined the minks' stress levels by measuring cortisol levels in their urine. The results show that the removal of food and the water pool caused the highest stress levels for the minks, thus providing information about the welfare impact of enrichment. There is a large body of literature focused on assessing pain, as well as emerging research on evaluating play, normal behaviors, and overall happiness in animals. However, a significant challenge lies in consolidating these diverse measures into a comprehensive indicator of welfare.

In economics and social choice, broadly speaking, there are two main families of welfare theories: (i) the experientialist theories where well-being is a matter of experiences, in particular hedonic states and (ii) the preferentialist theories where well-being is a matter of preference satisfaction. Although these theories lead to different measures of well-being, these measures are in general correlated (Clark 2015). There is also the less prominent family of objective goods theories which suggest that certain things are intrinsically valuable, independently of an individual's subjective preferences or choices. See, for example, Adler (2019) for a general introduction as well as Appleby and Sandøe (2002) and Fleurbaey and Leppanen (2021) for pioneering discussions in the context of animal welfare. Empirically, the most standard method in economics to assess welfare is to resort to a preferentialist approach, namely to study individual choices. This so-called revealed preferences approach consists in inferring individual preferences from choice data.

There is a limited but noteworthy body of literature on revealed preferences related to animal choices (Dawkins 2004). For instance, Matthews and Ladewig (1994) examine tradeoffs made by pigs concerning food, interaction with a partner animal, and access to outdoor environments. They measure the amount of effort to obtain each of these commodities, and thus can compute demand curves for each commodity. They find inelastic demand for food, and more elastic demands for the other commodities. There is also the classical work by John Kagel and colleagues mentioned in the introduction where animals participate in economics experiments (Kagel et al. 1995). However, this literature focuses on the choices of animals, not on their welfare. So, how to assess animal welfare?

At this point, it is useful to recall the distinction between "decision utility" and "experienced utility" (Kahneman et al. 1997). Decision utility refers to the value or satisfaction that people expect to derive from a particular choice or action. It corresponds to the anticipated utility that individuals consider when making decisions. Experienced utility refers to the actual utility or satisfaction that individuals derive from an experience after it has occurred. It reflects the real-time emotional or psychological response to an event or outcome. Hence, when talking about animal welfare, I am primarily interested in experienced utility, the genuine impact on the subjective well-being of animals as they experience it. However, traditionally, economics has dismissed the relevance of experienced utility based on two standard arguments: first, subjective hedonic experience is difficult to observe or measure, and second, choices are assumed to provide all necessary information about the utility of outcomes because rational agents are presumed to optimize their hedonic experience when making decisions (Kahneman et al. 1997).

Importantly, research in psychology and behavioral economics in the last decades has made significant progress on how to measure experienced utilities. This research has consistently demonstrated that decision utility and experienced utility are both conceptually and empirically distinct. This implies that decision utility offers only an imperfect measure of experienced utility. This discrepancy arises from a fundamental evolutionary reason: Humans are not inherently designed to make decisions that maximize welfare. This idea is summarized in a very simple way by Kahneman, Wakker and Sarin (1997, page 381): "The effect of natural selection is to increase overall fitness, not necessarily to produce organisms that maximize pleasure and minimize pain over time." Obviously, this idea applies to humans but also to animals.

As is well known in behavioral economics, the revealed preferences approach encounters the common issue of inconsistent choices, which can undermine its reliability as an indicator of welfare. Several studies have demonstrated that animals exhibit similar patterns of consistency and inconsistency in their choices as observed in humans (Ainslie and Herrnstein 1981, Kagel et al. 1995, Schuck-Paim et al. 2004, De Petrillo and Rosati 2023). Moreover, animals are likely to exhibit even greater inconsistencies in their decision-making than humans in various contexts, largely due to their limited cognitive abilities. Specifically, they may possess diminished information processing and learning capacities compared to humans (Cantlon and Piantadosi 2024). However, not everyone may agree with this. For instance, it can be argued that more room for choice and reflection may sometimes make more room for error and inconsistency.

An additional hurdle lies in the valuation of animal welfare in a metric, which is relevant for policy-making. Typically, economists use the money metric, a standard practice in BCA through humans'

WTP. But, how to monetize the welfare impact of animals' decisions? While studies have demonstrated some animals' ability to use tokens (Hackenberg 2009), animals lack a monetary system (De Petrillo et al. 2019). One potential approach to monetize animal welfare from revealed preferences could involve converting food or energy into a monetary equivalent, although this approach remains unexplored as far as I am aware. The best paper I have seen on the potential of this approach is Keeler (2016), who builds on a few revealed preference studies involving salmon. The general problem is that the market prices of food or energy (or any other goods used as a token for animals) are ultimately determined by human choices, making them imperfectly informative about animals' preferences.

Therefore, a gap remains in establishing a common metric to compare the preferences of humans and animals using the revealed preference approach. Fundamentally, the issue is that there is no trade between humans and animals, so that information about trading in the animal world has no economic relevance for the human world. A possible solution might be to simulate a fictitious world where animals would freely participate in market transactions with humans. The simulated prices in this world would then be used to estimate the policy impacts in the real economy. Another solution would be to use the revealed preferences approach to estimate an animal welfare score, representing for instance the fraction of maximal welfare achievement corresponding to current living conditions. These scores could then be compared and translated into a social welfare unit by applying a conversion rate across different animal species (more on this later). Admittedly, these approaches remain very tentative at this stage, and more research is clearly needed in that area.

Fleurbaey and Leppanen (2021) discuss the application of the preferentialist approach to animals. They put forward the equivalence principle (e.g., the equivalent income approach, the standard gamble) as a paramount method in economics to build indices of well-being using individual ordinal preferences. They emphasize the challenge of using the equivalence principle in a multispecies' context. Animals do not have income, and they cannot offer their views about gambles in hypothetical situations. Moreover, different species care about very different functionalities. Humans are good at thinking and dogs at smelling. It is not obvious then how to find a "middle-ground" so that no species appears artificially better off. An application of the approach that takes broad-category functionalities may miss these specialization effects.

In this book, following my work with Matt Adler, Romain Espinosa, and Jim Hammitt, I adopt a different approach, what may be called the social welfare function (SWF) approach. See Chapter 6 and, for instance, Adler (2011, 2019), Adler et al. (2014), Bronsteen et al. (2013), Espinosa and Treich (2024), Fleurbaey and Hammitt (2024), and Dusel and Wieck (2024). The fundamental principle underlying this approach is to assess directly the welfare levels of the individuals (humans and/or animals), quantified through interpersonally comparable measures of well-being. Hence, the idea is to obtain a proxy for the experienced utilities, and compare those utilities through a normative aggregator. It is important to note that the field of economics has a long-standing debate regarding the feasibility of interpersonal comparisons (Adler 2019), and this challenge becomes even more complex when extending comparisons across different species. However, I am optimistic that significant headway can be achieved by merging insights from models in animal sciences and human health, as detailed in the following chapters.

4.2 THE FIVE FREEDOMS FRAMEWORK

Researchers in animal sciences have put forth several frameworks for assessing animal welfare, particularly in the context of farmed animals. The most well-known framework is the Five Freedoms framework, which was initially defined in the Brambell report (Brambell 1965). These freedoms encompass freedom from hunger, fear, disease, discomfort, and the freedom to express natural behaviors (see Table 4.1).

Table 4.1 *The Five Freedoms*

Freedoms	Provisions
1. Freedom from hunger and thirst	By providing ready access to fresh water and a diet to maintain full health and vigour
2. Freedom from discomfort	By providing an appropriate environment including shelter and a comfortable resting area
3. Freedom from pain, injury, and disease	By prevention or rapid diagnosis and treatment
4. Freedom from fear and distress	By ensuring conditions and treatment that avoid mental suffering
5. Freedom to express normal behaviour	By providing sufficient space, proper facilities and company of the animal's own kind

Source: Brambell (1965) and FAWC (2010)

The Five Freedoms paradigm has been instrumental in comprehending, identifying, and mitigating negative welfare states in animals. It can be seen as a tool designed to facilitate assessment of animal welfare in a structured and coherent manner. Going back to the general theories of welfare presented in the previous section, this paradigm may be viewed as sharing aspects of hedonist and objective list theories. It has been used by various institutions and organizations such as the World Organisation for Animal Health (OIE) or the World Association of Zoos and Aquariums (WAZA). The Five Freedoms are also extensively employed for the education of veterinary and animal welfare science students (McCulloch 2013).

Let me provide a few examples illustrating the practical application of the Five Freedoms for some specific animals in various settings. Consider for instance the "freedom from discomfort." In a dairy farm, this may mean that cows are housed in well-ventilated barns with comfortable bedding, such as sand or mattresses, to prevent injury and discomfort. In a zoo, this may mean that enclosures for elephants are designed to be spacious and include features such as mud wallows, bathing pools, and shade structures to ensure comfort. In a laboratory, this may mean that cages for rats and mice are designed to be spacious and include bedding material that allows nesting and burrowing and that environmental controls maintain appropriate temperature and humidity levels. Finally, in a shelter, this may mean that dogs are provided with comfortable living spaces that include a clean, dry sleeping area and protection from extreme weather.

Consider alternatively the "freedom to express normal behavior." In a dairy farm, this may mean that cows have access to pasture or exercise yards where they can graze, socialize, and engage in natural behaviors. In a zoo, this may mean that enclosures are enriched with logs, tires, and other objects that encourage natural behaviors like foraging, playing, and socializing. In the laboratory, this may mean that enrichment items, such as tunnels, wheels, and chew toys, are placed in cages to encourage exploration and play. In a shelter, this may mean that dogs are taken on regular walks, given time to play and socialize, and provided with toys and activities that stimulate their natural instincts.

While the Five Freedoms framework has been widely used and acknowledged both by the production sectors, public agencies and NGOs, some scholars have voiced concerns that they may be too limited in scope as they primarily focus on mitigating negative experiences. Moreover, the freedoms are broad and somewhat vague, which can lead to inconsistent interpretation and implementation. For example, "freedom from discomfort" can be interpreted in many ways, making it challenging to create specific, measurable standards. This vagueness may lead to superficial compliance. Companies often claim they meet the Five Freedoms without substantial changes to their practices.

In response to these concerns, alternative approaches have been proposed to provide a more precise and a more comprehensive evaluation of animal welfare. One notable framework is Five Domains, which goes beyond the Five Freedoms by considering both negative and positive experiences (Mellor et al. 2020, Browning 2022). By incorporating positive aspects of animal well-being, such as opportunities for positive engagement and the ability to experience positive emotions, the Five Domains framework aims to provide a more holistic assessment of animal welfare.

The Five Domains framework focuses on assessing the presence or absence of internal physiological conditions and external environmental factors that contribute to the positive or negative mental experiences, known as affects, crucial for animal welfare. The framework systematically evaluates the internal states and external circumstances of animals across four key domains: "Nutrition," "Environment," "Health," and "Behavior" (Mellor et al. 2020). Subsequently, the various affects generated within these four domains are aggregated into the fifth domain, denoted as "Mental State" (see Table 4.2). In relation to the previous section's discussion, the Five Domains Framework aligns with a hedonic approach. However, Fleurbaey and Leppanen (2021) regard the objective-good concept as the prevailing standard in animal science. This lack of consensus is not unexpected, as frameworks in animal science do not clearly define their underlying welfare concept (Dusel and Wieck 2024).

Moreover, animal welfare frameworks fall short in addressing the tradeoffs that economists typically explore. First, they do not address the relative significance of various welfare impacts on individual animals, even within a single species. As a result, they are not directly useful to make comprehensive assessments regarding the relative merits or drawbacks of different policy options (Budolfson et al. 2023). For instance, how to evaluate the tradeoff between different freedoms or domains, or between the duration and intensity of suffering? Second, these frameworks do not account for comparisons of welfare across different species. Third, these frameworks are not quantitative, and thus cannot be directly used to make comparisons with relevant units (e.g., QALY, money) used in policymaking. How to compare an improvement to the cost in euros of the improvement? How to compare a mild improvement for 1,000 animals to a strong improvement

Table 4.2 *The Five Domains approach*

Physical/functional domains							
Survival-related factors						Situational factors	
1: Nutrition		2: Environment		3: Health		4: Behavior	
Negative	Positive	*Negative*	Positive	*Negative*	Positive	*Negative*	Positive
Restrictedwater/ food, poor food quality	Enough water and food, varied diet	*Unpleasant physical environment*	Pleasant physical environment	*Disease, injury*	Healthy, uninjured	*Behaviour restricted*	Able to express rewarding behavior
Affective experience domains							
5: Mental states							
Negative experiences				Positive experiences			
Thirst, hunger, malnutrition, chilling/overheating, hearing discomfort, breathlessness, pain, debility, nausea, sickness, anger, boredom, loneliness, anxiety, panic, exhaustion				Drinking pleasures, taste pleasures, chewing pleasures, satiety, physical comforts, vigour, reward, goal-directed, calmness, maternally rewarded, playfulness, sexually gratified			

Source: Mellor (2016)

for 100 animals? Hence, if one wants to make these frameworks useful for economic evaluation, additional steps are required. We will see later an example of methods that describes how one can do this.

4.3 LIFE WORTH LIVING

Recognizing the limitations of the Five Freedoms and related approaches, several scholars, as well as the UK Farm Animal Welfare Council for instance, have advocated for a shift toward the concept of "a life worth living," which entails considering the overall quality of life of animals (Mellor 2016). This concept centers around evaluating whether an animal's overall experience of life is positive, neutral, or negative. It is a way to assess welfare beyond mere survival or basic needs, taking into account both the pleasures and pains animals may experience throughout their lives. The idea implies that an animal's welfare should reach a threshold where its existence brings more positive than negative experiences.

Webster (2016) acknowledges the significance of this concept, particularly in situations where veterinarians must engage with pet owners facing the difficult decision of euthanasia. He also raises valid concerns, stressing that the notion of a life worth living involves a value judgment made by humans rather than being an assessment made by the animals themselves. The concept of life worth living has however a much greater importance in philosophy, not so much regarding the question of ending life, but rather regarding that of creating a life. It raises the key question of whether life is better than nonexistence. As we will see repeatedly in this book, this concept is central in the economic theory of animal welfare. In a nutshell, this is because when individuals or regulators decide how many animals to consume or to save (think about laws that protect endangered species), a nonanthropocentric approach must compare different scenarios where animals exist in some scenarios and do not exist in others.

In the food domain, the concept of life worth living is strongly linked to the "logic of the larder" argument (Salt 1917). This argument stipulates that we would do animals a favor by eating them because they would otherwise not exist. In this view, meat consumption should be encouraged because animal farming would generate a positive externality on animals as it simply enables them to live. However, this argument hinges on whether the life experienced by these animals is indeed worth living. This argument has generated a long-standing philosophical debate; see for instance Matheny and Chan (2005) and Višak (2013).

In Espinosa and Treich (2021), we modestly contribute to this debate using survey data. We presented survey participants with the rearing conditions of broilers in France under different husbandry systems. We specifically focus on broilers as they constitute approximately 80 percent of terrestrial animals slaughtered for meat production in the country. Through the survey, we provided participants with information about the living conditions of broilers in several husbandry systems. We asked participants whether they believe the lives of broilers under the presented husbandry systems are worth living. Our data collection involves four distinct groups of participants: students, experts in animal ethics, experts in farmed animals (encompassing poultry, bovine, and porcine farming), and animal activists. The findings from our study are compelling, as nearly all respondents express the belief that the lives of broilers are not worth living, particularly under the most common husbandry systems prevalent in France (see Table 4.3 in which each of the four columns represents a farming system).

In a very original study, Bruers (2023) conducts a representative survey of 301 Flemish-speaking Belgians. Participants are asked to imagine the state of nonexistence as analogous to a deep sleep without any experiences. Bruers then explores how much money participants would be willing to pay (or accept) to experience the lives of different animals (chicken, pig, or cow) during an hypothetical state of deep sleep, as opposed to having no experiences at all. Most precisely, the questionnaire states to participants that "you have a lifelike experience that you are an animal that really exists. You experience everything just as that animal experiences things in

Table 4.3 *Assessment of whether a broiler's life is worth living according to four farming systems*

Characteristics	Broiler farming systems (indoor rearing)			
Density (chickens/m2)	20	14	14	8
Natural light	No	Yes	Yes	Yes
Perches	No	Yes	Yes	Yes
Pecking objects	No	Yes	Yes	Yes
Outdoor access	No	No	No	Yes
Stunning before slaughter	No	Yes	Yes	Yes
Age at slaughter (days)	40	40	60	80
Transport time to slaughterhouse (hours)	8	6	3	3
Participants	**Share of belief that life is worth living (%)**			
Activists	0	0	0	1.6
Animal ethics experts	0	0	0	0
Farm animals experts	5.3	10.5	15.8	63.2
Students	0.8	2.5	4.9	25.6

Source: Espinosa and Treich (2021)

reality. You feel everything the animal feels during its life, from birth to death. You only think about the things that the animal actually thinks." The resulting monetary values indicate that most participants believe that farm animals have lives not worth living.

In a simpler follow-up study, Bruers (2024) surveys 112 Flemish-speaking Belgians, asking them to rate the lifetime welfare of conventional broilers and wild birds on a scale from −10 ("the worst suffering") to +10 ("the highest happiness") where a "value of 0 corresponds to a neutral life, for example a life without positive and negative experiences or with equally strong positive and negative experiences." Using this direct approach, Bruers finds that participants assign a median score of −2 to conventional broilers, indicating a belief that these animals have negative lifetime welfare.

In contrast, wild birds receive a median score of zero, suggesting that participants believe that these animals have a neutral life.

To conclude this section, let me add a remark about suicidal behavior among animals. Can animals decide whether their own life is worth living? If animals are conscious and their lives are mostly filled with suffering, why don't they commit suicide? Only a minority of researchers defend the possibility of suicide among animals (Peña-Guzmán 2017). It is not clear indeed that animals possess the cognitive mechanisms necessary for suicide. There is also the question of their lack of knowledge and technique about how to commit suicide. Additionally, it is commonly said that to commit suicide, a person must intend to bring about his own death, which animals cannot do because they cannot conceptualize death. However, note that many animals such as cats, chimpanzees, dogs, foxes, horses, rabbits, as well as some birds experience feelings of bereavement, melancholia, and grief when relatives or companions die, suggesting that survivors understand the difference between life and death (King 2013, Monsó 2024). Moreover, there is some evidence of self-destructive behavior among animals. Experts in dolphin cognition such as Lori Marino believe that dolphin suicide is possible for instance (Peña-Guzmán 2017).

4.4 WILD ANIMAL WELFARE

The body of research on assessing animal welfare has predominantly centered on farmed animals. While wild animals represent a larger population than farmed animals, their welfare has received comparatively much less attention. This neglect is often emphasized by the effective altruism movement to shift the focus on wild animal welfare. The ecological literature has largely overlooked animal welfare aspects, focusing mostly on populations rather than individuals within species. This literature has primarily aimed to enhance our understanding of ecosystem functionality and assessed ecosystem services to humans. Conservation research has also typically ignored the differentiation between sentient and non-sentient beings (such as plants versus animals) and studied the quantity of life rather than its quality.

Michael Soulé (1985, page 731), one of the pioneers of the field of conservation biology, writes: "Although disease and suffering in animals are unpleasant and, perhaps, regrettable, biologists recognize that conservation is engaged in the protection of the integrity and continuity of natural processes, not the welfare of individuals. ... Conservation and animal welfare ... are conceptually distinct, and they should remain politically separate." Along this line, the influential papers by Callicott (1980) and Sagoff (1984) argue that it is neither possible nor desirable to combine animal ethics and environmental ethics.

One general problem with the literature in conservation biology is the frequent lack of a clearly defined normative criterion. Striving to revert ecosystems to a pristine state is not only impractical but also fails to serve as a sound moral guideline. Moreover, a significant portion of the conservation and biodiversity literatures actually maintain an anthropocentric perspective, primarily geared toward evaluating and managing ecosystems services to humans. This is exemplified by the Millenium Assessment Report (2005) "Ecosystems and human well-being" or the highly cited synthesis paper by Cardinale and coauthors (2012) "Biodiversity loss and its impact on humanity," where the objective with biodiversity preservation is ultimately human welfare. Biodiversity metrics systematically capture a certain quantity of life rather than its quality, and are thus not well suited for studying animal welfare. Hence, an important line of research concerns the integration of animal welfare in conservation policies (Webb et al. 2019, Sekar and Shiller 2020, Owens et al. 2024).

The issue of wild animal welfare is not only little studied, it is also highly controversial, leading to diverse perspectives among scholars. One central controversy concerns the question of policy intervention in the wild. While some argue for non-interference with nature (Donaldson and Kymlicka 2011), others hold differing opinions. This matter has sparked intense intellectual debates within the field of animal ethics and has given rise to the Reducing-Wild-Animal-Suffering (RWAS) movement in animal advocacy. The RWAS movement is based on the premise that there is a substantial amount of suffering occurring in the wild (Ng 1995, Horta 2010).

This viewpoint highlights the notion that natural selection prioritizes the maximization of offspring quantity over the well-being of individual offspring. Nature maximizes fitness, not welfare. A significant majority of animals in the wild are classified as r-selected species, namely species that produce many offspring, each of which has a relatively low probability of surviving to adulthood. A very high proportion of the individuals in those species perish shortly after birth or hatching. Often, their lives are marked by starvation or being preyed upon while still alive. Hence, it can be argued that on average the life of those r-selected species is not worth living. It is important to note though that these lives may also support the life of other sentient beings. Hence, unlike for farmed animals, the separate consideration of the welfare of a specific wild animal species may not be enough to inform policymaking with a broader perspective of maximizing global welfare.

In an early fascinating contribution, Ng proposed to create a new field coined "welfare biology" (Ng 1995), precisely with the aim to fill the absence of consideration of animal welfare in the biology literature. This approach proposed to use evolutionary economics to study animal sentience and its implications. According to Ng, the field could revolve around three key questions: "Which species are affective sentients capable of welfare? Do they enjoy positive or negative welfare? Can their welfare be dramatically increased?" Although these three questions were obviously worth exploring, Ng's proposals have generated limited attention from the scientific community.

Conversely, philosophers and animal activists have championed Ng's ideas in recent years. Veit and Browning (2021) argue that the exploration of those questions need not necessitate the establishment of a new discipline, but rather an expansion of existing frameworks and methodologies within animal welfare science to encompass wild animals. Notably, the central concept of sentience applies with equal relevance to both wild and farm animals. Hence, the priority is to extend the current tools of welfare science for the purpose of evaluating, and improving the welfare of wild animals.

One significant distinction however between the welfare of farm animals and that of wild animals lies in the direct dependence of the latter on their natural environment. Put differently, the welfare of wild animals is intricately shaped by the conditions of their natural habitats. It stands to reason, then, that the evolutionary dynamics governing the presence of suffering and enjoyment in nature continue to wield a pivotal influence over the well-being of wild animals.

Ng (1995), and later Groff and Ng (2019), crafted a conceptual model akin to a standard economic framework, in which nature determines the optimal balance of suffering and enjoyment. Ng (1995) suggests that individuals should experience neutral states most of the time, since maintaining positive or negative welfare states requires high energy expenditure. According to this perspective, the lived experience of animals would be close to a state of nonexistence or death in terms of utility level. Groff and Ng (2019) demonstrate that, depending on the specific form of the "cost function" governing suffering and enjoyment, suffering may or may not dominate enjoyment in nature. Interestingly, their illustration suggests that for organisms with more intense conscious experiences, the balance of enjoyment and suffering may tilt toward suffering. This aligns with the assertions made by some philosophers and animal activists that the lives of many wild animals may not be worth living. The link between animal welfare and conservation research and policy will be further discussed in Chapter 17.

REFERENCES

Adler MD (2011) *Well-Being and Fair Distribution: Beyond Cost-Benefit Analysis*. Oxford University Press.

Adler MD (2019) *Measuring Social Welfare*. Oxford University Press.

Adler MD, Hammitt JK, Treich N (2014) The social value of mortality risk reduction: VSL versus the social welfare function approach. *Journal of Health Economics*, 35, 82–93.

Ainslie G, Herrnstein RJ (1981) Preference reversal and delayed reinforcement. *Animal Learning and Behavior*, 9, 476–482.

Appleby MC, Sandøe P (2002) Philosophical debate on the nature of well-being: Implications for animal welfare. *Animal Welfare*, 11(3), 283–294.

Brambell FWR (1965) Report of the Technical Committee to Enquire into the Welfare of Animals kept under Intensive Livestock Husbandry Systems. https://archive.org/details/b3217276x.

Bronsteen J, Buccafusco C, Masur JS (2013) Well-being analysis vs. cost-benefit analysis. *Duke Law Journal*, 62(8), 1603–1689.

Broom DM (2014) *Sentience and Animal Welfare*. Cabi.

Browning H (2022) Assessing measures of animal welfare. *Biology and Philosophy*, 37(36), 1–24.

Bruers S (2023) The animal welfare cost of meat: Evidence from a survey of hypothetical scenarios among Belgian consumers. *Journal of Environmental Economics and Policy*, 12(3), 324–341.

Bruers S (2024) The suffering of a farmed animal is equal in size to the happiness of a human, according to a survey. Rethink Priorities. https://forum.effectivealtruism.org/posts/MP4rNBu6ftG4QE3nL/the-suffering-of-a-farmed-animal-is-equal-in-size-to-the.

Budolfson M, Fischer B, Scovronick N (2023) Animal welfare: Methods to improve policy and practice. *Science*, 381(6653), 32–34.

Callicott JB (1980) Animal liberation: A triangular affair. *Environmental Ethics*, 2(4), 311–338.

Cantlon JF, Piantadosi ST (2024) Uniquely human intelligence arose from expanded information capacity. *Nature Reviews Psychology*, 3(4), 275–293.

Cardinale BJ, Duffy JE, Gonzalez A (2012) Biodiversity loss and its impact on humanity. *Nature*, 486(7401), 59–67.

Clark AE (2015) Is happiness the best measure of well-being?. In *The Oxford Handbook of Well-being and Public Policy*, eds. MD Adler and M Fleurbaey, 518–552. Oxford University Press.

Dawkins MS (2004) Using behavior to assess animal welfare. *Animal Welfare*, 13, 3–7.

De Petrillo F, Caroli M, Gori E et al. (2019) Evolutionary origins of money categorization and exchange: An experimental investigation in tufted capuchin monkeys (Sapajus spp.). *Animal Cognition*, 22, 169–186.

De Petrillo F, Rosati, AG (2021) Decision-making in animals: Rational choices and adaptive strategies. In *Cambridge Handbook of Animal Cognition*, eds. A Kaufman, J Call, J Kaufman, 770–791. Cambridge University Press.

Donaldson W, Kymlicka S (2011) *Zoopolis: A Political Theory of Animal Rights*. Oxford University Press.

Dusel S, Wieck C (2024) Animal welfare in non-anthropocentric cost-benefit analysis and social welfare functions: A critical review to guide practical application, mimeo.

Espinosa R, Treich N (2021) Animal welfare: Antispeciesism, veganism and a "life worth living." *Social Choice and Welfare*, 56, 531–548.

Espinosa R, Treich N (2024) Beyond anthropocentrism in agricultural and resource economics. *Australian Journal of Agricultural and Resource Economics*, 68(3), 541–566.

FAWC (2010) *Annual Review 2009–2010*. Farm Animal Welfare Council.

Fleurbaey M, Hammitt JK (2024) The right numeraire or the just weights? How to make BCA rational and fair. *Journal of Benefit-Cost Analysis*, 15(S1), 6–25.

Fleurbaey M, Leppanen C (2021) Toward a theory of ecosystem well-being. *Journal of Bioeconomics*, 23(3), 257–295.

Groff Z, Ng YK (2019) Does suffering dominate enjoyment in the animal kingdom? An update to welfare biology. *Biology & Philosophy*, 34, 1–16.

Hackenberg TD (2009) Token reinforcement: A review and analysis. *Journal of the Experimental Analysis of Behavior*, 91(2), 257–286.

Horta O (2010) Debunking the idyllic view of natural processes: Population dynamics and suffering in the wild. *Telos*, 17(1), 73–90.

Kagel JH, Battalio RC, Green L (1995) *Economic Choice Theory: An Experimental Analysis of Animal Behavior*. Cambridge University Press.

Kahneman D, Wakker PP, Sarin R (1997) Back to Bentham? Explorations of experienced utility. *The Quarterly Journal of Economics*, 112(2), 375–406.

Keeler AG (2016) A modest proposal for the extension of nonmarket valuation methods. *Economic Inquiry*, 54(1), 719–724.

King BJ (2013) *How Animals Grieve*. University of Chicago Press.

Mason GJ, Cooper J, Clarebrough C (2001) Frustrations of fur-farmed mink. *Nature*, 410(6824), 35–36.

Matheny G, Chan KMA (2005) Human diets and animal welfare: The illogic of the larder. *Journal of Agricultural and Environmental Ethics*, 18, 579–594.

Matthews LR, Ladewig J (1994) Environmental requirements of pigs measured by demand functions. *Animal Behaviour*, 47, 713–719.

McCulloch SP (2013) A critique of FAWC's five freedoms as a framework for the analysis of animal welfare. *Journal of Agricultural and Environmental Ethics*, 26, 959–975.

Mellor DJ (2016) Updating animal welfare thinking: Moving beyond the "Five Freedoms" towards "A Life Worth Living." *Animals*, 6, 21.

Mellor DJ, Beausoleil NJ, Littlewood KE et al. (2020) The 2020 Five Domains Model: Including Human-Animal Interactions in Assessments of Animal Welfare. *Animals (Basel)*, 10(10), 1870.

Millenium Assessment Report (2005). *Ecosystems and Human Well-Being*. Island Press.

Monsó S (2024) *Playing Possum: How Animals Understand Death*. Princeton University Press.

Ng Y-K (1995) Towards welfare biology: Evolutionary economics of animal consciousness and suffering. *Biology and Philosophy*, 10(3), 255–285.

Owens KA, Bryja G, Bekoff M (2024) Wildlife conservation: The importance of individual personality traits and sentience. *Animal Sentience*, 9(34), 1.

Peña-Guzmán DM (2017) Can nonhuman animals commit suicide? *Animal Sentience*, 2(20), 1.

Sagoff M (1984) Animal liberation and environmental ethics: Bad marriage, quick divorce. *Osgoode Hall Law Journal*, 22(2), 297–307.

Salt HS (1917) The logic of the larder. www.animal-rights-library.com/texts-c/salt02.htm.

Schuck-Paim C, Pompilio L, Kacelnik A (2004) State-dependent decisions cause apparent violations of rationality in animal choice. *PLoS Biology*, 2(12), e402.

Sekar N, Shiller D (2020) Engage with animal welfare in conservation. *Science*, 369(6504), 629–630.

Soulé ME (1985) What is conservation biology? *BioScience*, 35, 727–734.

Veit W, Browning H (2021) Extending animal welfare science to include wild animals. *Animal Sentience*, 7(20). www.wellbeingintlstudiesrepository.org/animsent/vol1/iss7/20/.

Višak T (2013) *Killing Happy Animals*. Explorations in Utilitarian Ethics. Palgrave Macmillan.

Webb CE, Woodford P, Huchard E (2019) Animal ethics and behavioral science: An overdue discussion. *BioScience*, 69(10), 778–788.

Webster J (2016) Animal welfare: Freedoms, dominions and "A Life Worth Living." *Animals*, 6(6), 35.

5 Utility Potentials

5.1 INTERSPECIES COMPARISONS

Once equipped with a framework for evaluating animal welfare within a specific species, the next challenge lies in making comparisons across diverse animal species. While welfare science offers frameworks for assessing the well-being of individual animals (as discussed in the previous chapter), there is currently no standardized method for comparing these measures between different species. This is, however, a crucial step for making progress in the economics of animal welfare. This fundamental difficulty is often referred to as the "problem of interspecies welfare comparison." The critical challenge is to identify a robust measure capable of accommodating the divergent intensities with which animals feel pain and, more generally, experience the world.

This problem is well summarized by Browning (2023, page 532):

> We are certainly able to measure the welfare of individual animals. As mentioned, in animal welfare science, scientists use different indicators, such as changes in behaviour or physiological variables, to measure the changes in welfare under different conditions. When measuring the welfare of any individual animal, we're quantifying its welfare – in some sense defining the 'units' of welfare for that individual. We can establish both the full scale of welfare experience for an individual – its maximum and minimum levels and the associated indicator values – as well as where the individual sits along this scale at any particular time or under given conditions.
>
> The question for welfare comparisons is, do different individuals have different scales? And if they do, how can we convert the 'units' of welfare between the scales? Having different scales of measurement is not in itself a problem – think

> of scales like measurement of length (centimetres and inches) and temperature (Celsius and Fahrenheit). We're able to convert measurements between the scales because we have the appropriate formulas for doing so. In welfare comparisons what we lack is the appropriate conversion formulas. We may have the measurements of welfare of one animal and those of another animal – both of which quantify welfare in relation to the scale for that animal – but we don't know how to convert units between the scales of each individual and compare them on a common scale, to be able to say something about how many measured units of welfare for one animal are equivalent to a unit of welfare for another.

The notion of "utility potentials" is precisely providing the conversion tool we need for making interspecies welfare comparisons. It has been introduced to investigate the range of capacities for experiencing well-being across different beings. It essentially measures how good or bad life can be, and this may vary a lot across animal species. An initial discussion on this concept within economic theory was presented by Budolfson and Spears (2020). Building on Wong's (2016) work, these authors highlight that the key issue in interspecies comparisons lies in estimating the well-being capacity of nonhuman individuals relative to that of humans.

To derive the utility potentials of each species, Budolfson and Spears (2020) employ the ratio of the number of neurons in that species to the number of neurons in humans. Extending this methodology, Espinosa (2024) and Espinosa and Treich (2024) calculate a similar ratio but focus on cortical and pallial neurons, namely to neurons specifically related to the sensory parts of the brain in mammals and birds, respectively. This refers to types of neurons located in brain regions that are involved in higher-order functions such as cognition, perception, and decision-making. I will show how to use this ratio in a formal calibration model in Chapter 10, and how it can produce quantitative estimates. Introducing an alternative approach,

Fischer (2022) establishes a "welfare range" by assessing capacities per species, such as parental care, self-medication, or friendship-like behavior. The current chapter aims to scrutinize the computation of utility potentials and, more broadly, explore diverse methodologies to tackle the challenge of interspecies comparisons.

Before going further, I want to make a clarification point. It is about the distinction between the "empirical problem" and the "moral problem" (Browning 2023). The empirical problem is about comparing the measures of welfare between different species and obtaining an empirically founded rate of conversion. In essence, it involves making empirical assessments of how much welfare a given animal is experiencing and ranking this against the experiences of others. This is the focal point of discussion in this chapter. On the other hand, the moral problem pertains to assigning varying moral weights to different species or individuals. This is contingent upon our ethical framework. The moral problem will be discussed in the subsequent chapter when discussing the social welfare function.

5.2 SURVEY STUDIES

The primary objective of establishing a form of conversion rate across different species is to facilitate tradeoffs involving different species. A starting point would be to explore human decisions regarding these tradeoffs. This would be informative about how one species is valued against another. In line with the principles of empirical social choice (Gaertner and Schokkaert 2012), an avenue to explore is thus to assess how humans are inclined to make choices across various species. Let me present a few studies about humans' choices regarding interspecies tradeoffs.

Weathers et al. (2020) conducted a survey involving residents in the United States (n = 502) using the online platform Mechanical Turk. Participants were tasked with comparing the suffering of cows, pigs, and chickens through a series of tradeoff questions. For instance, in a typical comparison scenario, respondents were asked to compare two hypothetical programs: the first "prevented

1,000 cows in perfect health from getting an illness that causes rapid death" and the second program "prevented X chickens in perfect health from getting the same illness." Participants were asked to indicate the lowest value of X for which they would say that the second program produced the greater overall reduction in suffering. Overall, the results showed that approximately 40 percent of participants placed higher value on cattle compared to chickens, with a similar proportion valuing pigs more than chickens. Additionally, nearly half of the participants perceived cattle and pigs to have similar capacities for experiencing suffering.

Another preliminary (and unpublished) study, reported on the Rethink Priorities website, conducted a survey of the general public regarding specific interspecies tradeoffs. In March 2019, Scott Alexander used the Tumblr platform to fill in a small survey ($n = 50$), asking respondents to estimate the relative value of animal lives in comparison to a human life. The median respondent in this survey approximated that a human is deemed as valuable as 4,000 lobsters, 500 chickens, 50 cows, 35 pigs, 7 elephants, or 5 chimpanzees. Interestingly, the author correlated these results with the number of neurons in each animal, revealing some notable similarities. For instance, 50 cows would possess approximately the same total number of neurons as a single human. In the next section, I will describe how one can use neurons to compute utility potentials.

In a 2007 phone survey of one thousand participants in the United States, Norwood and Lusk ask whether they agree with the following statement: "If a new technology were created that could either eliminate the suffering of 1 human or the suffering of X farm animals, it should be used to eliminate the suffering of the 1 human." The variable *X* was randomly set. Extrapolating from the results, Norwood and Lusk conclude that the average American believes that the suffering of one human is equivalent to the suffering of about 11,500 farmed animals (Schukraft 2020).

Obviously, the survey approach regarding interspecies' tradeoffs is not without limitations. The rationale for assuming that humans inherently make judicious decisions regarding animals, and that these decisions provide informative insights into the desired conversion rate, remains unclear. As will be detailed in Part III about the indirect approach, humans are susceptible to various biases when contemplating matters related to animals. Moreover, the act of making choices about tradeoffs across animals is unfamiliar to us. Such decisions are never or seldom encountered in our usual decision-making contexts. Hence, the scope for mistaken decisions is large.

5.3 NEURONS

The first question to ask here is: why neurons? The basic idea is simple. As I said, the scope of experienced welfare may vary across species. For instance, a frog might undergo welfare experiences within a narrower spectrum compared to a chimpanzee. The rationale then is that if welfare is primarily shaped by mental states (i.e., the subjective feelings of animals), those animals capable of a broader range and more intense emotional experiences are likely to encounter welfare across a more extensive spectrum (i.e., encompassing more extreme well-being states). It is likely that a chimpanzee, for example, can experience all (or most) of the emotions felt by frogs but possesses the added capacity for more intricate as well as more intense emotions that a frog can experience.

Hence, it seems plausible that more complex emotions demand higher levels of cognition. Mammals typically have more advanced emotional responses compared to simpler organisms (Panksepp 2005). Elephants show grief and bonding behavior that hints at their profound emotional memory, and dogs and wolves display unique personality traits that shape their social interactions (Bekoff 2024). However, this should only be seen as a hypothesis, and more research is clearly needed here. For instance, it seems also possible that evolutionary pressure to avoid pain must be higher for species with lower cognitive abilities because they need a stronger signal to learn to avoid pain.

In short, the hypothesis is that a cognition proxy is likely to exhibit a correlation with utility potentials. An idea then would be to use the number of neurons for this proxy. Note, however, that the total number of neurons may not be ideal, as neurons serve various functions and may not contribute exclusively to enhanced cognition. For instance, larger bodies tend to require greater numbers of neurons regardless of intelligence and sensory aspects. Recent progress in cognition research suggests that neurons in the sensory-associative structures can potentially act as a predictor of the capacity for subjective experiences. This specific subset of neurons, coined forebrain neurons, located in the cerebral cortex for mammals and in the pallium for birds, has shown a robust correlation with cognition measurements (Herculano-Houzel 2017). These neurons are essential for the functioning of the cerebral cortex and are involved in a wide range of brain functions, from basic sensory perception to higher-order cognitive processes.

As an example of relevant study, Padoa-Schioppa and Assad (2006) show that neurons in the orbitofrontal cortex (OFC, a subset of forebrain neurons) encode economic value in the sense that they encode the value of offered goods when animals have to make a choice among those goods (e.g., raisin versus apple). The researchers trained monkeys to choose between different types and amounts of juice. By recording brain activity, they found that OFC neurons fire based on how much the monkey prefers one juice over another. This study suggests that when making choices, the OFC converts different options into a common "value currency," allowing the decision-maker to compare and choose between them, even when they are very different (e.g., choosing between more of a less-preferred drink versus less of a favorite one).

In Table 5.1, I present data about those cortical or pallial neurons replicated from Espinosa (2024), who himself used information from Herculano-Houzel (2017) and Olkowicz et al. (2016). I also present proxies for the utility potential for a specific species as estimated by the ratio of the number of forebrain neurons of that species over

Table 5.1 *Estimates of the number of cortical/pallial neurons by animal species*

Animal species	Forebrain neurons	Utility potential
Human	24.52 billion	1
Elephant	5.50 billion	0.224
Baboon	2.99 billion	0.121
Dolphin	2.36 billion	0.096
Hippo	1.31 billion	0.053
Cow	0.79 billion	0.032
Pig	0.55 billion	0.022
Dog	0.52 billion	0.021
Cat	0.19 billion	0.007
Chicken	0.08 billion	0.003
Rat	0.04 billion	0.001

Source: Olkowicz et al. (2016), Herculano-Houzel (2017) and Espinosa (2024)

the number of human forebrain neurons. This estimate for the utility potential using this ratio will be used later on when we calibrate the model of animal welfare assessment. Note that we could imagine a more complex function than a ratio, as is discussed in Budolfson and Spears (2020) and Espinosa (2024). In this chapter and in the rest of the book, I will stick to the simple ratio expression.

Forebrain neurons likely represent one of the most effective proxies for utility potentials presently available. An important advantage of forebrain neurons as a proxy lies in their easy quantifiability and measurability, with a substantial amount of existing data available. This proxy is consistent with a basic dimension of sentientism, a moral perspective that attributes no moral weight to plants, as plants lack neurons. However, it is essential to acknowledge several limitations (Shriver 2022). Notably, this proxy does not entirely determine the brain's processing power. Other factors, such as the firing rate of neurons, the number and properties of connections between neurons, and the spatial density of neurons, also play a role in influencing how much information can be processed within a given timeframe. The criticism also includes the lack of correlation of neuron number to many indicators of welfare experience. At this early stage in the effort to assess and compare welfare across species, I believe that the number of forebrain neurons can serve as a useful starting point.

5.4 WELFARE RANGE

Utility potentials are conversion factors that allow us to compare animal welfare across different species. Beyond neurons, alternative measures are emerging. A notable instance comes from the Moral Weight Project, conducted by Rethink Priorities. Specifically, a research team at Rethink Priorities initiated an extensive project aimed at estimating utility potentials (Fischer 2024). In this undertaking, researchers identified empirical proxies for welfare, encompassing hedonic and cognitive indicators. Across a range of perspectives, some key aspects seem relevant for determining the capacity for welfare. These aspects include the intensity of valenced experiences, self-awareness, general intelligence, autonomy, long-term planning, communicative abilities, affective complexity, self-governance, abstract thought, creativity, sociability, and the capacity for normative evaluation (Schukraft 2020).

Hence, the team meticulously examined the literature to discern evidence of proxies for these aspects across 11 farmed species, including pigs, chickens, shrimp, and bees. The capacities studied encompass parental care, self-medication, concept of death, shame-like behavior, depression-like behavior, and emotional contagion, among others (Fischer 2022). Results for the hedonic proxies are displayed in Figure 5.1 in which 47 capacities are scrutinized. The study shows that some animals like pigs or chickens display an important number of hedonic proxies. However, research is still scarce for many species so that much work is needed in animal sciences.

This approach then estimates a "welfare range," which corresponds to the difference between the welfare level associated with the

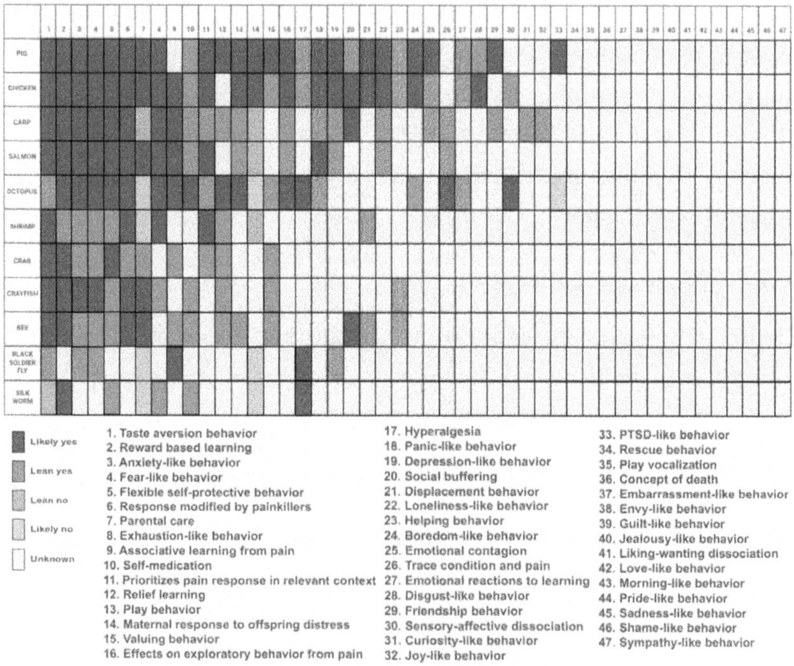

FIGURE 5.1 Hedonic proxies for animal welfare.
Source: Rethink Priorities and Fischer (2022, 2024)

most intense positively valenced state and the welfare level associated with the most intense negatively valenced state that the individual can realize. This range is estimated by counting and possibly adjusting the number of capacities (Figure 5.1). I refer to the Rethink Priorities website and Fischer (2024) for more detailed information. See in particular Duffy (2022) for explanations about how the estimation has been done and how uncertainty has been accounted for in this approach. Overall, using the welfare range approach applied to a 0–1 range metric, estimated utility potentials lie around 0.6 for pigs and 0.4 for chickens (Duffy 2022). These values are thus more than one hundred times higher than the utility potentials estimated using the neuron approach over the same range metric (see Table 5.1). Hence, the neuron approach seems a priori much more conservative than the welfare range approach.

The welfare range approach is a notable and valuable contribution that significantly advances both the methodology and the conceptual reflection on utility potentials. As with any ambitious endeavor, it serves as a foundational step that is likely to be refined and improved in the coming years. However, there are several issues that warrant further exploration. Before addressing the conceptual difficulties, note that a fundamental challenge lies in the practicality of the approach: investigating dozens of capacities across a wide range of animal species demands an immense research effort.

A basic conceptual issue concerns the selection of relevant capacities, which may appear somewhat arbitrary, given the potentially vast and subjective range of distinct capacities. It is unclear (at least to me) which abilities should be included, and which should be excluded. A related issue involves the differences in how various abilities impact welfare. It does not seem plausible, for instance, that solitary animals suffer because they do not engage in social behaviors. Therefore, the absence or presence of social abilities may not hold significant relevance for assessing the welfare of these animals. More generally, abilities may matter very differently in their contribution to welfare depending on the animals. Hence, it is unclear whether, for instance, parental care, play behavior, and rescue-like behavior should be given similar weight to all animals, and how the weights should be calculated (Schukraft 2020).

Relatedly, the "cognitive tradeoff hypothesis" suggests that species have developed enhanced cognitive abilities in some areas at the expense of others. For example, humans have evolved complex language abilities, possibly at the cost of certain memory capabilities that are more prominent in other primates. This hypothesis suggests that cognitive abilities have evolved to achieve a balance, which should be considered when assessing welfare based on specific capacities. Another issue with the welfare range approach is its binary perspective on capacities: Either a species possesses a capacity or it does not. Two species might exhibit anxiety-like behavior or the concept of death, but the intensity of the associated emotions could vary significantly. This variation should also be taken into account. Let me also add a point about the terminology. Note that in this book I do not talk about "moral weight" to mean the same thing as utility potential. This distinction is important and justified in the next chapter, when I discuss the normative properties of the social welfare function. In any case, the Moral Weight project conducted by Rethink Priorities promises to be an exciting and stimulating endeavor for the years ahead.

In conclusion, I want to emphasize a key point for empirical applications: the inclusion of humans in the analysis. As discussed in the introduction, our ultimate goal is to make tradeoffs not only among animals but also between humans and animals. This would allow for the development of sentientist benefit-cost analyses that incorporate and monetize the welfare of all sentient beings. To understand why this integration is possible, the key point is to recognize that humans also possess utility potentials. For example, as shown in Table 5.1, humans as a species achieve the maximum value for utility potential when using their forebrain neurons. Utility potential thus can serve as a critical parameter for estimating animal welfare. It can be used to translate human quantitative utility measurements from the economic literature into comparable measures for animals. That is, the utility potential parameter enables the conversion of animal welfare units into human welfare units, and vice versa. Furthermore, since utility potentials can differ significantly across species, they will be a major source of variation in welfare estimates, as we will see in Chapter 10.

REFERENCES

Bekoff M (2024) *The Emotional Lives of Animals: A Leading Scientist Explores Animal Joy, Sorrow, and Empathy – and Why They Matter*. New World Library.

Browning H (2023) Welfare comparisons within and across species. *Philosophical Studies*, 180(2), 529–551.

Budolfson M, Spears D (2020) Public policy, consequentialism, the environment, and nonhuman animals. In *The Oxford Handbook of Consequentialism*, ed. DW Portmore, 592–615. Oxford University Press.

Duffy L (2022) Welfare range and probability of sentience distributions, Rethink Priorities.

Espinosa R (2024) Animals and social welfare. *Social Choice and Welfare*, 62(3), 465–504.

Espinosa R, Treich N (2024) The animal welfare levy. *Journal of the European Economic Association*, in press.

Fischer B (2022) The welfare range table. https://rethinkpriorities.org/publications/the-welfare-range-table.

Fischer B (ed.) (2024) *Weighing Animal Welfare: Comparing Well-Being Across Species*. Oxford University Press.

Gaertner W, Schokkaert E (2012) *Empirical Social Choice: Questionnaire Experimental Studies on Distributive Justice*. Cambridge University Press.

Herculano-Houzel S (2017) Numbers of neurons as biological correlates of cognitive capability. *Current Opinion in Behavioral Sciences*, 16, 1–7.

Olkowicz S, Kocourek M, Lučan RK et al. (2016) Birds have primate-like numbers of neurons in the forebrain. *Proceedings of the National Academy of Sciences*, 113(26), 7255–7260.

Padoa-Schioppa C, Assad JA (2006) Neurons in the orbitofrontal cortex encode economic value. *Nature*, 441(7090), 223–226.

Panksepp J (2005) Affective consciousness: Core emotional feelings in animals and humans. *Consciousness and Cognition*, 14(1), 30–80.

Schukraft J (2020) How to measure capacity for welfare and moral status. Rethink Priorities. https://rethinkpriorities.org/research-area/how-to-measure-capacity-for-welfare-and-moral-status/.

Shriver A (2022) Why neuron counts shouldn't be used as a proxy for moral weight? Rethink Priorities. https://rethinkpriorities.org/research-area/why-neuron-counts-shouldnt-be-used-as-proxies-for-moral-weight/.

Weathers ST, Caviola L, Scherer L et al. (2020) Quantifying the valuation of animal welfare among Americans. *Journal of Agricultural and Environmental Ethics*, 33, 261–282.

Wong K (2016) Counting animals: On effective altruism and the prospect of interspecies commensurability (Doctoral dissertation, PhD thesis, Princeton University).

6 The Social Welfare Function

6.1 THE SWF APPROACH

The core objective of public economics revolves around the maximization of social welfare, which entails evaluating the well-being of individuals under various policies. Economists commonly use a social welfare function (SWF) to assess social welfare across different policies. The SWF is carefully constructed to adhere to specific normative properties, including for instance Pareto efficiency, anonymity, and separability. In the framework of utilitarian economics, social welfare is defined as the aggregate of individual utilities, often subject to certain transformations of individual utilities. The choice of normative assumptions within the SWF drives the ranking of different policies. Consequently, a critical step in advancing a sentientist approach within public economics involves thorough deliberation and examination of the normative criteria that should govern the SWF.

The SWF approach is widely used, for instance in the literature on optimal taxation or in the economics of climate change. However, before going further, it is crucial to acknowledge that the SWF approach itself is a subject of controversy, even within economics. Arrow's impossibility theorem highlights the challenges associated with the SWF. While the SWF generally upholds universality, nondictatorship, and monotonicity, it fails to satisfy another axiom, namely the independence of irrelevant alternative property. This last property implies that the social preference between two policies, say x and y, should solely rely on the individual preferences between x and y. However, the SWF approach necessitates additional information beyond individual preferences between x and y. It typically requires information about interpersonal welfare comparisons, namely how much an individual prefers x to y (or y to x) compared to another individual.

The problem of interpersonal welfare comparison is a fundamental issue in welfare theory, and various conceptual schemes have been proposed to address it. The main schemes, such as the extended preferences approach, involve a process of "empathetic identification." This process relies on the idea of putting oneself in others' shoes to compare different individuals' well-being. Detailed discussions of the extended preferences approach and interpersonal welfare comparisons can be found in Adler (2012, 2019) and Weymark (2016). While these schemes have been criticized, it is not clear to me whether they make sense when considering a multispecies setting. In particular, there is the challenge of empathetic identification with distant species. While this book will not explore further this issue, it is somewhat addressed (or perhaps bypassed) through the use of utility potentials that permit welfare comparisons of utilities across individuals from different species (see the Chapters 5 and 10).

Another central issue with the SWF approach is an empirical one: How to estimate individual welfare? As I already said, the standard approach in economics consists in adopting a revealed preference approach where welfare (change) is estimated through the observation of individual choices. But this approach has also been criticized, in particular because human choices may be inconsistent, and thus a poor indicator of welfare. This raises strong concerns regarding animal welfare. Indeed, as we have seen before, several works have shown that animals' choices seem to follow similar inconsistencies as those observed in humans (Ainslie and Herrnstein 1981, MacDonald et al. 1991).

Further, it seems plausible that in many contexts animals might display even more choice inconsistencies than humans due to limited cognitive abilities. Therefore, one may wonder if the observation of the choices of animals may be a useful guide for estimating their welfare. The second reason is that it may be difficult to interpret the decisions of animals. For humans, we can naturally reason by introspection, but the same reasoning seems much more elusive for animals, in particular for those which are evolutionarily distant from us (note that this is a problem for hedonism too). Last, the opportunities to learn to improve choices, for instance by repetition or by teaching, may be lower for animals. As said before, I will thus not follow the standard revealed preferences approach in this book, and instead adopt the SWF approach.

At this point, it is also important to recall that I adhere in this book to the prevailing tradition in economics by adopting a consequentialist approach. I acknowledge that this choice is also subject to debate, particularly considering that a substantial body of research in animal ethics has favored alternative approaches, such as deontological principles. It is indeed perfectly conceivable to envision a deontological (i.e., non-welfarist) but sentientist approach, where a set of principles or rights is defined to guide interactions among all sentient beings. For instance, Newman et al. (2017, Chapter 8) distinguishes "utilitiarian sentientism" (Singer 2011) from "rights-based (deontological) sentientism" (Regan 1983). Exploring these alternative perspectives represents an essential and valuable research direction for the future. Nevertheless, the incorporation of these non-welfarist approaches would present significant challenges in terms of relating the analysis to existing economic theory and ultimately deriving quantitative estimations, as I will do later on.

6.2 SENTIENTIST SWF

Two distinct possibilities emerge for incorporating animals into the SWF. The first approach involves the SWF that considers only human welfare. However, even in this case, animal welfare can still influence the SWF and the prioritization of policies if humans care about animals, for instance because they possess altruistic preferences toward animals. This is the common approach in economics, yet it remains anthropocentric, with human welfare serving as the basis for social welfare. I will pursue the indirect approach in Part III.

The second approach entails the SWF directly incorporating the welfare of all sentient beings. Under this direct approach, animal welfare holds intrinsic value and is considered independently of human preferences. By adopting this nonanthropocentric approach, one recognizes the inherent worth of animals themselves. Throughout the remainder of this part, I adopt this direct approach. It is worth noting that while these two approaches can potentially be combined, doing so raises significant conceptual issues, such as the risk of double counting animal welfare. Exploring the complexities of combining these approaches falls beyond the scope of this book.

What properties should a sentientist SWF have? A few works have started to explore this question, but the literature is still scarce. The inclusion of animals in the SWF raises significant normative considerations, as highlighted by Fleurbaey and Leppanen (2021). The seminal paper by Blackorby and Donaldson (1992) proposes a critical-level SWF, which grants equal consideration to the interests of both humans and animals. Zuber et al. (2024) have made substantial progress in this area by providing the first axiomatic characterization of a multispecies SWF that I am aware of. They establish various representation theorems based on separability and anonymity axioms, culminating in an additively separable utilitarian SWF for several species. Despite these valuable contributions, the literature on this topic remains limited, leaving ample room for further exploration and research.

A central question concerns the "moral weight" attributed to each species in the SWF. To be more precise, let me introduce some basic formalities. Let u_{is} be the utility of individual i in species s, with a_s being the moral weight of species s. Under the most standard normative approach used in economics, namely total utilitarianism, the SWF would simply take this form:

$$\Sigma_s\, a_s \left(\Sigma_i\, u_{is}\right) \tag{6.1}$$

This formulation permits to emphasize two polar cases:

- Anthropocentrism: a_s equals zero for all species except for humans $s = h$ where $a_h > 0$, and
- Antispeciesism: a_s is the same for all species s (this could also be called "egalitarian antispeciesism").

Moreover, any situation in between, that is, such that $0 < a_s < a_h$ for all $s \neq h$, can be viewed as "partial speciesism." This intermediate situation is related to what Kagan (2019) calls the "hierarchical approach," where animals count morally, but count in a lesser way than humans.

Note that antispeciesism corresponds to the standard anonymity axiom in a multispecies context. This axiom simply formalizes the ethical attitude of impartiality (Adler 2019). It means that each individual's well-being is given an equal moral weight in the social objective. It also formally captures the fundamental principle of "equal consideration of similar interests" as proposed by Peter Singer. Going further back in time, this also refers to Bentham's famous dictum: "Each to count for one and none for more than one" and also to Sidgwick's "The good of any one individual is of no more importance, from the point of view (if I may say so) of the Universe than the good of any other" (Singer 1975). The key point for economic modeling here is the following: If we interpret "similar interests" as an equal amount of utility change Δ for a representative individual in any species, then such a change would have exactly the same impact on social welfare no matter which individual benefits from it if and only if the moral weight a_s is the same for all species.

Note that focusing on species s introduces a degree of arbitrariness. Why aggregate over species rather than other biological taxa, such as classes or orders? How can we justify summing over species specifically? This approach somehow parallels economists' construct of a social welfare function, where a single or a few representative agents stand in for specific population segments. There are two main reasons for this focus on species. First, philosophical literature has historically emphasized the concept of species, introducing notions such as speciesism or antispeciesism. Hence, this approach, inspired by that literature, can be viewed as a formal representation of those concepts. Second, and more importantly, species provide a practical framework for defining specific levels of capacities that are shared within a given group. That is, a species can be viewed as a representative group of animals that are sufficiently homogeneous, particularly in terms of their levels and kinds of sentience. That said, this approach is not conceptually bound to species as the most relevant taxonomic level. While species may serve as a convenient unit of analysis, it remains open to critique, and alternative groupings at other taxonomic levels could be considered in the future.

Now, a key question emerges: how to choose the moral weights a_s? So far, I have relied on the existing literature in philosophy. Another possibility is to resort to the views of citizens. Sometimes the two approaches may be combined in the sense that we may explore whether citizens adhere to philosophers' views. Obviously, the citizens' view method presents challenges as it essentially reintroduces human judgments into the assessment of animal welfare, which could be viewed as anthropocentric and thus not aligned with Part I. But how to avoid relying on human judgment? The basic idea here is that citizens engaging in the evaluation may strive to be "impartial spectators." While imperfect, this approach merits consideration and may be refined in the future.

Johansson-Stenman (2018) conducted a survey study on Swedish citizens focused on moral weights, specifically examining how individuals perceive the significance of suffering in animals compared to suffering in humans within public decision-making. Participants were asked to express their view on the extent to which animal suffering should be taken into account relative to "an equal amount of suffering" in humans. Several response options were provided, including: animal suffering should not be considered; it should be considered indirectly through human preferences; it should be taken into account to some extent, to a fairly high degree, to the same degree as human suffering, or to a very high degree. The findings, presented in Table 6.1, reveal an interesting trend: The dominant view among participants aligns with an antispeciesist perspective, advocating for equal consideration of suffering reduction. Approximately half of the participants expressed support for this viewpoint. Together with Romain Espinosa, we conducted the same survey in France (Espinosa and Treich 2025), and found similar results as in Johansson-Stenman (2018).

Table 6.1 *Survey studies on moral weights in Sweden (N = 1,072) and in France (N = 1,526)*

Society can reduce animal as well as human suffering through various, usually costly, measures. To be able to prioritize, we need to know how great a weight society should place on reducing suffering in an animal (such as a cow) compared with reducing an equal amount of suffering in a human. Which of the following statements is most in accordance with your opinion regarding the weight that should be given to animal suffering in public decisions?

Possible answers:	Sweden (%)	France (%)
Animal suffering should not count at all in public decisions.	0.8	3.4
Animal suffering should not count per se. However, some people suffer when knowing that animals suffer, and this should be taken into account in public decisions.	3.2	3.6
Animal suffering should be taken into account to a certain extent in public decisions, even when no human beings suffer when knowing that animals suffer. However, animal suffering should be given much less weight than human suffering.	13.2	12.3
Animal suffering should be taken into account to a fairly high degree in public decisions, even when no human beings suffer when knowing that animals suffer. However, animal suffering should be given somewhat less weight than human suffering.	30.3	17.6
Animal suffering should be taken into account to a degree equal to human suffering in public decisions, even when no humans suffer when knowing that animals suffer.	49.3	41.6
Animal suffering should be taken into account to a very high degree in public decisions, even when no human beings suffer when knowing that animals suffer. Animal suffering should be given more weight than human suffering.	3.2	21.6

Source: Johansson-Stenman (2018) and Espinosa and Treich (2025)

A notable difference between the two samples concerns the category of "reverted speciesism" (Espinosa and Treich 2025): Our respondents are significantly more likely to believe that animal suffering should be given greater consideration than an equivalent amount of human suffering (21.6 percent) compared to the Swedish sample in Johansson-Stenman (2018) (3.2 percent). This surprisingly high proportion raises questions about the factors driving this result. One possible explanation is that participants use this response to signal strong concern for animal welfare. Alternatively, the interpretation of the question may play a role. For instance, respondents might perceive animal suffering as more severe than human suffering in today's world, leading them to prioritize it. Other common behavioral factors, such as experimenter demand effects or social desirability biases, may also be at play.

6.3 MORAL WEIGHTS VERSUS UTILITY POTENTIALS

In this section, I briefly discuss the distinction between moral weights and utility potentials (see Chapter 5). This distinction is key. The moral weight is a normative parameter that tells us how much individual utilities are comparatively weighted in the social objective. Under equal moral weights, a utility change Δ will have the same social impact no matter who is concerned by the change. But we need a way to compare utilities across species, which is precisely what the utility potential parameter does. Indeed, a level of standardized utility of 0.4 for a chicken may not be the same as 0.4 for a pig. The utility potential parameter allows us to weight standardized utility levels across different animal species to make them comparable in the SWF.

This distinction between moral weights and utility potentials relates to the distinction between the moral problem and the empirical problem (Browning 2023) already discussed in Chapter 5. The moral problem concerns the choice of moral weight, determining the ethical importance assigned to different sentient beings. In contrast, the empirical problem involves comparing measures of welfare between different species to obtain an empirically founded rate of conversion. Essentially, this requires making empirical assessments of how much welfare a given animal is experiencing and ranking this against the experiences of others.

Formally, this distinction concerns the difference between the moral weight a_s and utilities u_{is} in (6.1). As we will see later, one can conceive utilities as $u_{is} = \phi_s q_i$ where ϕ_s is the utility potential of species s, and q_i represents the standardized utility (or animal welfare score) mentioned in Chapter 4 for a specific individual i. Hence, the moral weight a_s and the utility potential ϕ_s of species s are both scaling parameters defined at the species level that play a similar mathematical role in the SWF. Blackorby and Donaldson (1992) already observe that assigning different weights to species in the SWF is mathematically equivalent to assuming different utility functions for each species during the measurement phase. However, my point is that the interpretation and estimation of each parameter differ significantly.

This distinction also drives the choice of the wording in the questionnaire. We follow Johansson-Stenman (2018) and refer to "suffering," specifically to an "equal amount of suffering." Our objective here is precisely to capture the notion of the same utility level or utility change Δ of different animal species. By focusing on suffering, we consider a welfare aspect, which is presumably comparable across species. One may argue that a unit of pain is a unit of pain, regardless of the individual experiencing it. This argument does have some backing, particularly from the public's perspective (Bruers 2024). Hence, we want to neutralize possible utility differences across species to make them directly comparable and equal so that we can concentrate on moral weights. In short, we are interested in this chapter in the moral problem, not the empirical problem. The discussion in Chapter 10 should further clarify the difference between moral weights and utility potentials since both concepts correspond to a different parameter in the social objective.

I conclude this section by a comment regarding the normative framework proposed by Kagan (2019) already mentioned in this chapter. Kagan's hierarchical approach justifies the use of different moral weights for different species based on their varying capacities. Species have different cognitive abilities and different capacities to feel pain, and he argues that these differences may induce different moral status. However, I want to stress one thing here: It is crucial not to blur the distinction between moral weights and utility potentials. Once it is clear that differences in species' capacities are captured through utility potentials, it is not evident that these differences should also affect moral weights. Doing so would amount to a double counting of the differences in abilities in the social objective.

6.4 ANIMAL POPULATION ETHICS

A fundamental characteristic of human choices concerning animals is its potential impact on the population size of animals. This is particularly evident in contexts such as meat consumption or biodiversity conservation where human actions directly affect the number of animals. In that case, we are in the realm of variable population. When evaluating these choices using SWFs, such as total utilitarianism, ethical dilemmas can arise. The implications of such SWFs can be morally troublesome.

The most famous implication of using a utilitarian perspective under a variable population is the repugnant conclusion (Parfit 1984). This conclusion arises in situations where a large population experiencing a very low level of well-being can be considered superior to a smaller population with a significantly higher level of well-being per person. Total utilitarianism is subject to the repugnant conclusion. This matters in our context. For example, there are critical discussions about whether a world inhabited by a vast population of very small animals with lives barely worth living (such as tiny mice) might constitute a better world (Posner 2004).

Should we escape the repugnant conclusion then, and how can we? The common way to address this moral problem is by considering alternative normative settings. For instance, average utilitarianism or critical-level utilitarianism (Blackorby et al. 2005) do not imply the repugnant conclusion. However, these alternative normative settings have other undesirable normative implications. Considering various arguments, about thirty philosophers and economists argue that the repugnant conclusion is not a reason to reject total utilitarianism (Zuber et al. 2021).

Various other notions in population ethics are relevant. I already discussed the notion of life worth living. This notion also relates to the "Procreation Asymmetry," originally introduced by McMahan (1981, page 100): "the fact that a person's life would be worse than no life at all (or 'worth not living') constitutes a strong moral reason for not bringing him into existence; the fact that a person's life would be worth living provides no (or only a relatively weak) moral reason for bringing him into existence." The intuition underlying this principle is that the moral imperative to avoid misery is stronger than that to generate happiness. Let me also mention the "replaceability argument" (Singer 2011, Višak 2013), which holds that animals can be killed and replaced by new animals who will experience lives of equal value. Applied to farming, this argument suggests that humanely raised animals, leading pleasant lives and being painlessly killed, can be replaced without any loss, thereby offsetting the good that is prevented by their killing.

Since the topic of population ethics is central, I will discuss more precisely, and more formally, some of these questions in Chapter 9, which is entirely devoted to population ethics aspects. But the key message here is that the choice of the SWF will have strong implications regarding the ethics of animal populations. This means that future economic research on animal welfare will have to carefully explore how a multispecies SWF addresses animal population ethics issues.

REFERENCES

Adler MD (2012) *Well-Being and Fair Distribution: Beyond Cost Benefit Analysis*. Oxford University Press.

Adler MD (2019) *Measuring Social Welfare*. Oxford University Press.

Ainslie G, Herrnstein RJ (1981) Preference reversal and delayed reinforcement. *Animal Learning and Behavior*, 9, 476–482.

Blackorby C, Bossert W, Donaldson DJ (2005) *Population Issues in Social Choice Theory, Welfare Economics, and Ethics* (No. 39). Cambridge University Press.

Blackorby C, Donaldson D (1992) Pigs and guinea pigs: A note on the ethics of animal exploitation. *Economic Journal*, 102, 1345–1369.

Browning H (2023) Welfare comparisons within and across species. *Philosophical Studies*, 180(2), 529–551.

Bruers S (2024) The suffering of a farmed animal is equal in size to the happiness of a human, according to a survey. Rethink Priorities. https://forum.effectivealtruism.org/posts/MP4rNBu6ftG4QE3nL/the-suffering-of-a-farmed-animal-is-equal-in-size-to-the.

Espinosa R, Treich N (2025) Fairness judgments about animals. *Journal of Economic Inequality*, in press.

Fleurbaey M, Leppanen C (2021) Toward a theory of ecosystem well-being. *Journal of Bioeconomics*, 23, 257–295.

Johansson-Stenman O (2018) Animal welfare and social decisions: Is it time to take Bentham seriously? *Ecological Economics*, 145(C), 90–103.

Kagan S (2019) *How to Count Animals, More or Less*. Oxford University Press.

MacDonald DN, Kagel JH, Battalio RC (1991) Animals' choices over uncertain outcomes: Further experimental results. *The Economic Journal*, 101, 1067–1084.

McMahan J (1981) Problems of population theory. *Ethics*, 92(1), 96–127.

Newman JA, Varner J, Linquist S (2017) *Defending Biodiversity*. Cambridge University Press.

Parfit D (1984) *Reasons and Persons*. Oxford University Press.

Posner RA (2004) Animal rights: Legal, philosophical, and pragmatic perspectives. In *Animal Rights: Current Debates and New Directions*, eds. CR Sunstein and MC Nussbaum, 51–66. Oxford University Press.

Regan T (1983) *The Case for Animal Rights*. Routledge.

Singer P (1975) *Animal Liberation: A New Ethics of Our Treatment of Animals*. Random House.

Singer P (2011) *Practical Ethics*. 3rd edition. Cambridge University Press.

Višak T (2013) *Killing Happy Animals: Explorations in Utilitarian Ethics*. Springer.

Weymark JA (2016) Social welfare functions. In *The Oxford Handbook of Well-Being and Public Policy*, eds. MD Adler and M Fleurbaey, 126–159. Oxford University Press.

Zuber S, Venkatesh N, Tännsjö T et al. (2021) What should we agree on about the repugnant conclusion? *Utilitas*, 33(4), 379–383.

Zuber S, Spears D, Budolfson MB (2024) Separable social welfare evaluation for multispecies populations, mimeo.

7 A Simple Consumption Model

7.1 THE CANONICAL MODEL

This chapter, and especially this section, is a central component of this book. This is because it introduces the canonical model of consumption of animals used as a reference case in this book, and from which I will make several adaptations. The primary application of this model is the consumption of meat. However, it can represent more generally various forms of animal use. This model builds on Blackorby and Donaldson (1992) and especially on Espinosa and Treich (2024a, 2024b).

The model is purposely very simple. I basically take the simplest possible model to study the implications of meat consumption for animal welfare. The idea is to focus on what is new with the direct integration of animal welfare in economic models, not on other aspects already treated in usual economic models, such as distortionary taxation or market power, for instance. In this model, there is one representative human agent. He derives utility from the consumption of animals, $u(n)$, which is assumed to be increasing and concave in the number of (identical) animals n, with $u(0) \geq 0$. The animal production cost function is equal to $c(n)$, which is assumed to be increasing and convex, with $c(0) = 0$. (Note to non-economists: These are standard assumptions for utility and cost functions made in economic theory.)

I first want to examine what is the socially optimal level of animal consumption in this simple economy. By "socially," I mean accounting for the welfare of both humans and animals. Hence, the approach is nonanthropocentric and I first need to precisely define the SWF. For now, and in most parts of this book, I consider total utilitarianism, a natural interpretation of "the greatest good for the greatest number," extended to all sentient species. I also assume antispeciesism, that is, the same moral weight for every individual, be they human or animal, in that society. Denoting v the level of utility of a farm animal, the social objective can simply be written:

$$U(n) \equiv u(n) - c(n) + nv, \tag{7.1}$$

which corresponds to the maximization of the representative consumer's utility derived from meat consumption, $u(n) - c(n)$, plus that of the n consumed animals, nv.

Framed in the usual economics language, this is a model with quasi-linear preferences over two goods: meat and money. For simplicity, the budget constraint is directly integrated into the objective. Since initial wealth plays no role due to the linearity assumption, it is simply ignored in the objective (or set to zero). I will keep that presentation in the rest of the book for various versions of this model. The key novelty of this model compared to conventional economics is the last term, nv, which captures the welfare of animals. That is, as announced, animal welfare is directly accounted for in the SWF. Hence, this is indeed a nonanthropocentric model.

For the sake of simplicity, I only focus on interior solutions. The first order condition (FOC) characterizing the socially optimal consumption $n^\star$ is thus given by:

$$u'(n^\star) = c'(n^\star) - v. \tag{7.2}$$

This condition simply states that the marginal benefit of consuming an animal, that is, $u'(n)$, is equal to its marginal cost, that is, $c'(n)$, minus the term v. This last term v corresponds to the extra social cost (or benefit) of producing an extra animal in this economy. Indeed, by consuming and thus producing an extra animal, one creates an additional life. The contribution of this life to social welfare is simply the utility of the animal, namely v, hence the additional term that can be seen as an extra social cost (or benefit).

Crucially, note that the social contribution linked to the production of an additional animal is positive when $v > 0$ and negative if $v < 0$. This simple analysis is consistent with earlier observations, highlighting the concept of a life being worth living or not, namely whether life is better than nonexistence, formally whether $v > 0$ or not here. Hence, the presence or absence of this positive value, v, serves as a crucial determinant in evaluating the societal implications and ethical considerations surrounding animal welfare.

I now explore the equilibrium in that economy. Let p be the price of meat. Producers maximize over n their profits $pn - c(n)$ while consumers maximize over n their utility $u(n) - pn$. This gives the standard condition characterizing the equilibrium price p_e and equilibrium quantity n_e:

$$u'(n_e) = c'(n_e) = p_e. \qquad (7.3)$$

This last condition is a standard optimality condition in economics. It simply states that marginal utility equals marginal cost and they both equal the equilibrium price. If animals did not have any intrinsic value, this condition would characterize efficient allocations, providing a simple illustration to the First Welfare Theorem in this basic economy. However, optimality condition (7.3) differs from condition (7.2). Indeed, the equilibrium condition (7.3) characterizes efficiency from the viewpoint of consumers and producers, while condition (7.2) characterizes efficiency from a social viewpoint, accounting for the welfare of both humans and animals.

This simple result illustrates a "market failure." This failure is due to the fact that the consumers and producers do not take into account the impact of their choices on the animals. Hence, this market failure may be viewed as an externality on animals. That is, human activities lead animals to exist, and this induces positive externalities if the animals' lives that are created are worth living and negative externalities otherwise. This last result is akin to the "logic of the larder" argument (see Chapter 4), according to which eating animals is good for them because otherwise they would not exist. In this view, meat consumption generates positive externalities. Consequently, this result underscores, again, the crucial aspect that determines the validity of the logic of the larder: whether the lives of the animals in question are worth living or not.

7.2 THE ANIMAL WELFARE LEVY

Given that the equilibrium outcome fails to maximize social efficiency, it is logical to consider policy interventions within society. The literature in economics often discusses various forms of intervention. Note first that one commonly mentioned approach to overcoming externalities is Coasian bargaining. Indeed, in a seminal contribution, Coase (1960) argued that if parties can costlessly bargain and property rights are well defined, a socially efficient level of externality could be reached without resorting to governmental intervention such as Pigouvian taxation. However, in our context, this Coasian approach appears elusive, as animals may lack the necessary capacities to engage in a bargaining process with the relevant property holders. Moreover, animals do not possess the freedom and awareness to relocate, and in turn evade the externality.

In the case of externalities, the most common approach in economics is to follow the Pigouvian logic, namely to "price" the externality. The idea is to use fiscal instruments to lead polluters to internalize the externalities, that is, the "polluter pays" principle. Hence, suppose there is a levy t applied to meat consumption, and that the revenue of the taxation is given back to consumers in the form of a lump sum transfer. (Similarly, the tax could be applied to meat production, and the result would also follow in this simple model). The FOC characterizing the choices of the consumers and producers now simply writes:

$$u'(n(t)) = c'(n(t)) + t, \tag{7.4}$$

where $n(t)$ denotes the number of animals consumed at the equilibrium as a function of the levy t. Maximizing over t social welfare

$$u(n(t)) - c(n(t)) + n(t)v \tag{7.5}$$

yields the following FOC

$$u'(n(t)) - c'(n(t)) + v = 0. \tag{7.6}$$

Note that the differentiation of (7.5) with respect to t equals the left-hand side of (7.6) multiplied by the term $n'(t)$, a term that can be eliminated from the FOC since it is strictly negative by (7.4) and by strict concavity of the utility. Hence, by combining (7.4) and (7.6), we can derive the optimal levy:

$$t = -v. \tag{7.7}$$

This simple equality, $t = -v$, constitutes a benchmark result in this book. The animal welfare levy is equal to the opposite of the utility level of an animal. As we saw earlier, it corresponds to the marginal cost (or benefit) to produce an animal. The implementation of this levy hence allows us to align incentives with the marginal social value of consuming an additional animal, effectively internalizing the externality imposed on animals by the consumer. It operates akin to a Pigouvian fee, taking into account the externalities associated with animals bred for meat production. Given the absence of other distortions in the economy, this levy allows for the maximization of social welfare. Indeed, (7.6) corresponds to the socially optimal solution characterized in (7.2). In essence, the implementation of the animal welfare levy allows us to reach the nonanthropocentric first-best outcome.

This analysis clarifies the real purpose of the fiscal instrument. Its purpose is not to compensate animals for their suffering nor to raise money for improving their rearing conditions. Rather, its goal is simply to encourage or discourage the production of animals for meat, contingent upon whether their lives are deemed worth living or not. As usual with Pigouvian fees, the levy serves to signal the externality through the price, and its purpose is to induce the internalization of the externalities in the choices of the decision-makers, here the human consumers and producers of animals.

Figure 7.1 represents the welfare impact of the levy when it is a tax, that is, $t = -v > 0$. The hatched areas represent the classical deadweight loss resulting from taxation, reflecting the decline in welfare for both consumers and producers. This decline is represented by the famous triangular shapes representing the loss in consumer and

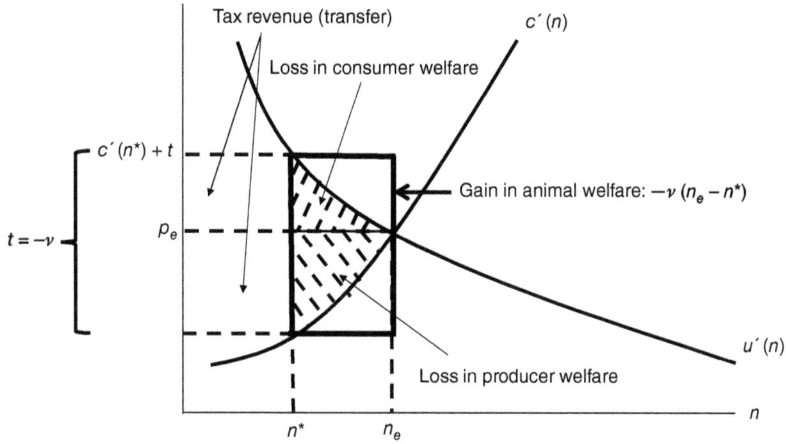

FIGURE 7.1 Welfare impacts of the animal welfare levy.
Source: Espinosa and Treich (2024a)

producer surpluses. Note that the rectangle area $-vn^*$ corresponds to the revenue from the tax, which has a neutral impact on welfare, since it is a simple transfer that can be given back to consumers and producers without any distortionary effects in this simple model.

The novelty in this figure, as compared to the economic textbook presentation of Pigouvian taxation, is the interpretation of the black rectangle. Indeed, this rectangle represents the gain in animal welfare: $-v(n_e - n^*)$. This gain stems from preventing the existence of animals whose lives are not worth living, induced by the reduction in meat consumption. As depicted in the figure, the animal welfare levy thus generates a "shift" of welfare from humans to animals, thereby enhancing overall welfare within society. This gain is due to the animal lives not worth living that are avoided as a result of lower meat consumption. Note however that this is an unusual welfare "shift," since the beneficiaries are nonexisting animals that would have existed without the policy.

As a final comment, let me stress that this analysis challenges the usual Kaldor-Hicks principle. This principle forms the basis for benefit-cost analysis, indicating that a policy passes the benefit-cost analysis test if the winners could "potentially" compensate the losers to make the policy a Pareto improvement. The point is that this principle does not appear immediately applicable here for two reasons.

First, it necessitates a compensation scheme going from animals to humans, but the practical (and political) implementation of such a compensation remains unclear. Suppose for instance that the policy would have been a subsidy on meat, namely a case with $v > 0$; how can we in practice organize transfers from the farmed animals that are born thanks to the policy to humans who are adversely affected by the policy? Second, in the context of the animal welfare tax, $v < 0$, the beneficiaries are animals that do not exist but could have existed without the policy. In that case, the application of the Kaldor-Hicks principle seems even more elusive. How to design transfers with non-existing individuals? Overall, this suggests that the potential Pareto improvement underlying benefit-cost analysis is hardly achievable in this context.

7.3 SPECIES' CONSERVATION POLICY

I will now make slight adjustments to the canonical model discussed earlier to illustrate its wider applicability. I consider in this section the problems of the conservation of species and preservation of biodiversity. In this model, humans derive benefits from ecosystems. They have the capacity to conserve certain species, albeit at a cost, which may involve forgoing production benefits associated with exploiting a resource upon which the species depend. As I will illustrate, if the welfare of certain animals holds intrinsic value, this provides justification for implementing targeted conservation policies. The concepts presented in this section bear relevance to the literature on "compassionate conservation" that I will briefly discuss again in Chapter 17.

The social objective is given by:

$$b(n) - c(n) + nv, \tag{7.8}$$

where $b(n)$ is the ecosystem benefit and $c(n)$ is the conservation cost. As before, n is the number of individuals in the targeted species. Here I have in mind wild animal species, not farmed animal species. The FOC for optimal conservation is simply given by:

$$b'(n) - c'(n) + v = 0. \tag{7.9}$$

This condition shows the existence of a "sentience premium," denoted as v, in addition to anthropocentric conservation considerations represented by the standard marginal benefits and costs of conservation, $b'(n)$ and $c'(n)$. The presence of this premium signifies the extra conservation benefits associated with sentient species. This premium may result for instance in prioritizing the preservation of animal species over plant species, recognizing the intrinsic value and welfare considerations associated with sentient beings.

Drawing upon the insights gained from the preceding sections, it becomes evident that relying solely on the market for the management of species populations is generally socially inefficient. This remains true even when ecosystem benefits are adequately addressed through optimal environmental policies. The rationale behind this inefficiency lies in the presence of an additional market failure beyond the environmental externality, specifically, the externality concerning the life of sentient species. Consequently, this underscores the need for targeted policies, such as the implementation of a levy that accurately reflects the sentience premium, in order to address and rectify these market failures and promote social welfare.

It is crucial to recognize that the sentience premium is contingent upon the welfare of individuals within a particular species, rather than the total population of that species. As a result, it diverges from conventional conservation strategies that focus on preserving specific species (e.g., endangered species) by prioritizing population levels over individual welfare. Additionally, the sentience premium can create inconsistencies with the eradication of invasive species, which are believed to harm ecosystems (i.e., $b'(.) < 0$).

It could indeed be justifiable to allocate resources toward the conservation (and not the eradication) of invasive species if the average individual welfare v within that species is sufficiently high. It is worth noting that, from a conservation perspective, invasive species often display a strong ecological compatibility with the affected ecosystem, which may imply high welfare levels of those species in that ecosystem. This highlights the delicate balance that must be found between conservation objectives and their potential impacts on overall well-being. See Chapter 10 for additional thoughts about this. Note also that, following the discussion earlier in this chapter, if life is not worth living, that is, $v < 0$, less, and not more, conservation effort is justified.

The model discussed earlier is very simple, and very limited, in particular because it does not take into account population dynamics and species interactions. Clarke and Ng (2006) conducted an early pioneering study that explores nonanthropocentric intertemporal welfare maximization under various assumptions regarding animal population growth. Their research was motivated by the culling of kangaroos at the Puckapunyal Army base in Australia. In their section on competing populations, they employ the well-known Lotka-Volterra model to demonstrate that maximizing offspring is significantly different from maximizing welfare. As Clarke and Ng (2006, page 407) argue, "welfare could be much higher at lower birth rates without even reducing numbers (at equilibrium)." This analysis suggests that, based on animal welfare considerations alone, there may be a justifiable rationale for human intervention in nature and the design of specific animal population control strategies. It is also worth noting that Eichner and Pethig (2006) have conducted a theoretical study on the broader nonanthropocentric context of nature protection, providing further insights into this subject matter.

7.4 THE ANIMAL WELFARE LEVY WITH WILD ANIMALS

This section extends the canonical model. This extension is motivated by two remarks. First, adjusting meat consumption also affects wild animal populations (Matheny and Chan 2005). Animal farming is indeed widely recognized as a major threat to biodiversity; for example, it contributes to approximately 85 percent of Amazonian deforestation (a biodiversity hotspot critical for wild animal habitats) (De Sy et al. 2015). Second, if the welfare of wild animals matters (as it should), this consideration should affect the animal welfare levy. Meat consumption indeed affects the welfare of farmed animals directly but also that of wild animals indirectly.

As before, I am going to consider the simplest model to study such an extension. In particular I assume a homogenous population of wild animals (as for farmed animals). I extend the model by adding two constraints. The first constraint is a "resource constraint." Formally, it states:

$$g + ng_a + wg_w = G. \tag{7.10}$$

This constraint stipulates that the total resources (such as grain or land) available per human, that is, G, can be consumed either directly by humans through g, or by farmed animals or wild animals. Here, w represents the number of wild animals and g_h and g_w the respective resource consumption per farmed and wild animal.

The second constraint is a "calorie constraint." Formally, it states:

$$g + nz = C. \tag{7.11}$$

This constraint stipulates that humans need a given amount of calories C. These calories can be provided either by the consumption of the resource g, or by meat through the consumption of animals in quantity n. The parameter z determines the conversion factor from animals into calories for human consumption (this factor is normalized to 1 for the resource).

The study of this model can then be summarized as follows. The consumption of animals in quantity n follows from the analysis described in the canonical model in Section 7.1. Through the calorie constraint this automatically determines the amount of resource consumed by humans g. Given the values of G and g_a, this determines the total resources left per wild animals, that is, wg_w. Given the value of g_w, this determines the number of wild animals w.

We are thus now in a position to explore the optimal animal welfare levy when the welfare of wild animals is also accounted for through the resource and calories constraints. Let us explore this step by step. First, using (7.10) and (7.11), the number of wild animals thus equals:

$$w = \frac{G - C + n(z - g_a)}{g_w}. \tag{7.12}$$

Now, the social objective is equal to

$$U(n) \equiv u(n) - c(n) + nv + wv_w, \tag{7.13}$$

where v_w is the welfare of wild animals. Replace w in (7.13) by its expression in (7.12). As before, the social objective depends on the number of farmed animals n. The difference is that there is an additional term representing the welfare impact of consuming meat on wild animals.

Using the same reasoning as in Section 7.1, it is then easy to show the optimal animal welfare levy is equal to

$$t = -v - \lambda v_w, \tag{7.14}$$

where $\lambda = \frac{z - g_a}{g_w}$ is a "technical factor" representing how a change in the number of farmed animals affects the number of wild animals. The key point to observe is that the sign of the levy now depends on the relative welfare of farmed and wild animals, up to the technical factor. In particular, if one assumes that farmed animals and wild animals are substitutes (as expected), that is, $\lambda < 0$, accounting for wild animals increases the animal welfare levy when $v_w > 0$. The intuition is simple: Consuming an extra-farmed animal decreases the number of wild animals, which is a social cost when the life of wild animals is worth living.

Note that λ decreases when the conversion factor of farmed animals into calories for humans (z) decreases, and when the amount of resources needed per farmed animal (g_a) increases. These two parameters measure how efficient meat consumption is in terms of converting resources into calories through animals for human consumption. Note also that when g_w is larger λ is smaller, so that the indirect impact is also smaller, other things being equal. This is intuitive: If wild animals require a lot of resources to live, the impact in terms of the number of wild animals from consuming more farmed animals is limited.

REFERENCES

Blackorby C, Donaldson D (1992) Pigs and guinea pigs: A note on the ethics of animal exploitation. *Economic Journal*, 102, 1345–1369.

Clarke M, Ng Y-K (2006) Population dynamics and animal welfare: Issues raised by the culling of kangaroos in Puckapunyal. *Social Choice and Welfare*, 27, 407–422.

Coase RH (1960) The problem of social cost. *Journal of Law and Economics*, 3, 1–44.

De Sy V, Herold M, Achard F et al. (2015) Land use patterns and related carbon losses following deforestation in South America. *Environmental Research Letters*, 10(12), 124004.

Eichner T, Pethig R (2006) Efficient nonanthropocentric nature protection. *Social Choice and Welfare*, 26, 47–74.

Espinosa R, Treich N (2024a) The animal welfare levy. *Journal of the European Economic Association*, in press.

Espinosa R, Treich N (2024b) Beyond anthropocentrism in resource and agricultural economics. *Australian Journal of Agricultural and Resource Economics*, 68(3), 541–566.

Matheny G, Chan K (2005) Human diets and animal welfare: The illogic of the larder. *Journal of Agricultural and Environmental Ethics*, 18(6), 579–594.

8 Animal Welfare Standards

8.1 OPTIMAL QUANTITY/QUALITY CHOICES

In Chapter 7, the canonical model operates under the assumption that the level of animal well-being is fixed. Consequently, the canonical model only encompasses a choice regarding the quantity of animals, while neglecting the consideration of the quality of their lives. In other words, I assumed that the animal production technology is fixed. In this chapter, I extend the previous model to consider both a quantity and a quality choice.

There are several compelling reasons to explore the choice of quality in the canonical model. First, quality means the quality of animal lives, or the level of animal welfare, which is of course central to the economics of animal welfare. Second, this focus on quality aligns with what most people and policymakers consider when discussing animal welfare policies, namely improving the well-being of animals directly. A major policy instrument in this context is an "animal welfare standard," namely a mandatory norm defining the rearing conditions of animals regarding housing, shelter, food, water, transport, slaughter, and so on. Third, studying quality helps distinguish it from quantity. As I said in the introduction, this distinction is a crucial contribution of this book. I will demonstrate how these two components – quality and quantity – have a very different impact and can interact in ways that yield unexpected results.

Before going into the formal details, let me make a remark about the canonical model. Recall that I assumed only one animal species. But it is easy to show that the result can be generalized to multiple animal species (Espinosa and Treich 2024). In that case, the levy per animal should simply be such that $t_s = -v_s$ where v_s is the utility of an animal in species s. Furthermore, s can, without loss of generality, be interpreted as representing an animal species under specific farming conditions. For instance, $s = 1$ can be "standard chicken" and $s = 2$ can be "organic chicken." This implies that the taxation scheme can accommodate for various quality levels associated with different farming practices. However, the point is that these levels are given, not chosen.

To explore the quality choice, I am going to adapt the canonical model in the simplest way. Suppose now that a regulator can change the technology by imposing a mandatory "animal welfare standard" $d \geq 0$ that affects animal well-being, now denoted $v(d)$, which is assumed to be increasing and concave. For simplicity, I assume in this chapter that the production cost per animal is equal to the baseline cost of production plus the cost of the improvement in animal welfare, that is, $c + d$.

As before, I first want to study the socially optimal choices in this economy. I keep assuming total utilitarianism. By summing up human and animal welfare, this amounts to maximizing over n and d the social welfare which is now given by: $u(n) - (c + d)n + nv(d)$. This leads to the following optimality conditions:

$$u'(n^*) - (c + d^*) + v(d^*) = 0, \tag{8.1}$$

$$-1 + v'(d^*) = 0. \tag{8.2}$$

The first equation is similar as in the canonical model: The marginal benefit of consuming an animal should be equal to its marginal cost plus the social value of adding an extra animal. The second equation states that the marginal cost of quality is equal to its marginal benefit. Note that, due to our assumption regarding the linearity of the cost function in n, optimal quality is independent from n. This is an important simplifying assumption.

Let me now turn to the consumer's problem. He maximizes over n his individual private objective: $u(n) - (c + d)n$. As before, the consumer does not internalize the impact of her consumption on animal well-being. Hence, there is a suboptimal consumption of meat. Following the logic presented in the canonical model, the immediate corollary of this observation is that the first-best outcome can be implemented if a tax $t = -v(d^*)$ is applied to meat consumption. The value of the socially optimal levy is thus, again, the opposite of the utility level, as in the canonical model. The only difference is that the animal utility level is now endogenous and determined by the animal welfare standard defined in (8.2).

The previous observation indicates that when the regulator has at her disposal two instruments, that is, meat taxation and an animal welfare standard, then first-best efficiency can easily be achieved. One instrument concerns the optimal quantity and the other the optimal quality. This is not surprising regarding, for instance, the literature in environmental economics, which indicates that multiple instruments are usually required to reach the first-best. But let me investigate this issue more formally: What happens if only one of both instruments is available?

Suppose first that only the quality instrument is available. Define $n(d)$ as the optimal consumer's meat consumption for a given animal welfare standard d, by the following FOC: $u'(n(d)) = (c + d)$. The regulator then optimizes over quality d the social welfare $u(n(d)) - (c + d)n(d) + n(d)v(d)$, which, using the previous equality, yields the optimality condition:

$$\frac{n'(d)v(d)}{n(d)} + \left(v'(d) - 1\right) = 0. \qquad (8.3)$$

Hence, the first-best outcome can be reached when the decisions $n(d)$ and d in the FOC (8.3) are the same as in the first-best as defined in (8.1) and (8.2). From the last condition, this is the case when we have $v'(d) = 1$ and $v(d) = 0$. Hence, this holds when the optimal animal welfare standard is exactly such that the life of an animal is "morally neutral." Yet, it is obvious that this is not generally true and would hold only for a very specific shape of $v(.)$, such as $v(d) = log(d)$.

I now consider the case where only a quantity instrument is available to the regulator. If the consumer can choose quality $d \geq 0$, she would set it to zero since d induces an additional private cost for the consumer without any benefit. Therefore, the regulator's problem simply amounts to maximizing over quantity n the objective $u(n) - cn + nv(0)$. Obviously, this can never reach the first-best except if it is socially optimal to choose $d = 0$, a corner solution. I conclude that, in general, the use of both a quantity instrument (i.e., the animal welfare levy) and a quality instrument (i.e., the animal welfare standard) are thus needed to retrieve efficiency. See Espinosa and Treich (2024), and see also Eichner and Runkel (2024) for a similar observation in a different model.

These results emphasize the need for both quality and quantity regulatory instruments. This yields an important policy implication. Currently, in most countries, animal welfare regulations primarily rely on legislative tools such as norms and guidelines. These measures aim to establish a practical minimum standard of animal welfare without unduly burdening the meat industry. Essentially, these are quality-focused instruments. However, the research presented earlier brings to light the critical role of incorporating meat taxation as an integral component of a comprehensive animal welfare framework. By imposing a levy on meat, externalities on farm animals can be mitigated by influencing animal population levels. Therefore, policymakers should include meat taxation into the package of animal welfare regulations.

8.2 THE EFFECT OF ANTISPECIESISM

In the canonical model, as well as its extension in this previous section, I assume antispeciesism. That is, I assume an equal moral weight in the SWF for all individuals: humans and animals. Now, I want to study the specific effect of the level of antispeciesism on the optimal choices affecting animal welfare. This is one advantage of formally defining antispeciesism in the sense that I can formally explore the impact of the level of antispeciesism.

Formally, I consider a minimal extension of the previous section's model. Suppose that the regulator maximizes over n and d the following social objective $u(n) - (c + d)n + anv(d)$, where the parameter a captures the level of antispeciesism (see Chapter 6). The optimal level of quality is now given by:

$$-1 + av'(d^*) = 0. \tag{8.4}$$

Given that $v(d)$ is concave, this implies that d^* is always increasing in a. Hence "more antispeciesism" in the sense of a greater weight a to animals in the SWF always increases the animal welfare standard, and thus animal well-being. This is intuitive.

After exploring the quality choice, let me now explore the quantity choice. The optimal level of quantity is given by:

$$u'(n^*) - (c + d^*) + av(d^*) = 0, \tag{8.5}$$

where d^* is given by (8.4). It is immediate then from the envelope theorem that more antispeciesism increases (resp. decreases) the number of animals consumed n^* if the utility of farm animals is positive (resp. negative), that is, $v(d^*) \geq 0$ (resp. ≤ 0).

Hence, this result shows an interesting U-shaped property, as illustrated in Figure 8.1. While quality always increases with

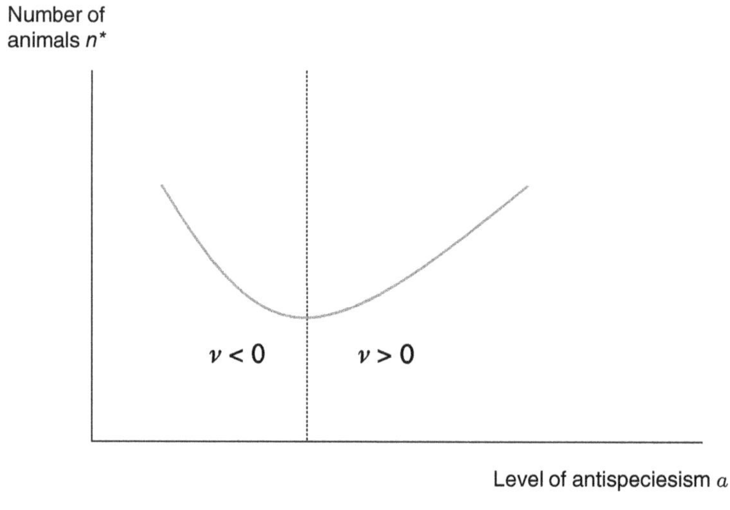

FIGURE 8.1 Animal consumption and antispeciesism.
Source: Espinosa and Treich (2021)

antispeciesism, quantity first decreases with antispeciesism when life is not worth living and then increases with it when life is worth living. The intuition is the following. As antispeciesism increases, investment in quality increases up to the point where life becomes worth living and where an increase in antispeciesism leads to increased animal consumption since it is socially beneficial to bring new animal lives into existence. This leads to a counterintuitive result that putting more weight on the welfare of animals increases their consumption. However, this result is not difficult to understand as it is a logical consequence of the assumptions of our model. Note though that one might argue that reducing speciesism should also lead to granting animals more rights, such as the right to freedom and protection from slaughter for food. In this sense, the result may also highlight a limitation of the model.

8.3 THE EFFECT OF THE SIZE OF ANIMALS

I conclude the chapter with a digression. What is the impact of the size of animals on the optimal consumption choices? If animal welfare counts, this may matter intuitively: It may be worse to consume smaller animals – e.g. chickens rather than pigs – as this would increase the number of animals killed per unit of meat (assuming equal capacity to suffer for instance).

To make things simple and meaningful, I focus solely on the effect of the size of animals. Hence, I consider that everything else is equal, such as the utility and price of meat, or the moral weight associated with chickens and pigs. The only difference is that one pig produces $k>1$ units of meat of chicken. Note that this is not very realistic since one may expect that animals of different sizes have different capacities to experience welfare in general.

The optimal number of chickens kn consumed is then simply given by:

$$u(n)-(c+d)n+aknv(d). \qquad (8.6)$$

This expresses the fact that utility and price of meat are the same for the consumer; only the number of animals differ. From this expression, it is immediate that the impact of animal size is equivalent to that of a change in the level of antispeciesism. Indeed, parameters a and k play formally an equivalent role in this model. I can now exploit previous results on the effect of a to understand the effect of k on optimal meat consumption n. Hence, this formal equivalence implies that there should be more investment in improving farm animal welfare when chickens are consumed instead of pigs: The societal returns resulting from investing in farm animal welfare are higher for chickens, as a larger number of animals would benefit from the improvements.

However, following previous results, the impact of animal size on the quantity of meat consumed is not clear, as it depends on whether the welfare of animals is positive or negative. Considering the prevailing modern industrial practices, it is likely that the welfare of both chickens and pigs is negative (as argued elsewhere in this book). Therefore, based on the nonanthropocentric perspective we have examined, it is socially more desirable to reduce meat consumption when smaller animals, such as chickens, are involved, rather than larger animals like pigs. However, let me stress again that I have assumed everything else is constant. In particular, one may question that the utility of a chicken and of a pig are similar. A pig has more cognitive capacities than a chicken, which should also matter in the decision-making process. I will specifically address this aspect in Chapter 10.

REFERENCES

Eichner T, Runkel M (2024) Animal welfare, moral consumers and the regulation of animal food production. *Ecological Economics*, 228, 108434.

Espinosa R, Treich N (2021) Animal welfare: Antispeciesism, veganism and a "life worth living." *Social Choice and Welfare*, 56, 531–548.

Espinosa R, Treich N (2024) The animal welfare levy. *Journal of the European Economic Association*, in press.

9 Animal Population Ethics

9.1 SOME IMPORTANT CONCEPTS

What is population ethics? It is essentially about how we must ethically act about the size or the composition of the population. In this chapter, my focus will be on the size of animal populations. As we have seen repeatedly, various decisions related to animals, such as meat consumption or biodiversity conservation, have an impact on the size of animal populations. Therefore, in evaluating these decisions, social choice must make comparisons between different scenarios that differ in terms of the number of individuals. This is the realm of population ethics.

The difficulty arises because animals as individuals have moral status, that is, animal lives matter intrinsically. To provide a concrete example, consider the following case. In the United States, over the course of a century, the number of cows has more than halved, yet each cow now produces about six times more milk. While the quantity of animal lives has decreased, the quality of these lives may also have declined due to intensified production practices. Is this trend good or bad for animal welfare? The answer is far from straightforward, as it hinges on how one balances the quantity of lives against their quality. This is one instance of the variable population case which is a central topic in population ethics.

Standard economic concepts, such as Pareto efficiency, typically focus on a given population. When comparing two social situations, it is usually assumed that the population remains constant in both situations. The variable population case raises various open questions, and it is not clear which normative setting can properly accommodate this case. The case has generated a lot of work in utilitarian philosophy in particular. The common approach in social choice and welfare theory involves examining and comparing various normative settings (such as total utilitarianism or average utilitarianism), each with its own normative advantages and disadvantages. See Parfit (1984) in philosophy and Blackorby et al. (2005) in economics for more insights into discussions surrounding the variable population case.

In this section, I will present a few important concepts that have been discussed in (animal) population ethics. See Table 9.1. But before, two quick warnings. First, while this chapter is versed into philosophy, please keep in mind that I am not a philosopher. I thus advise readers to study by themselves the philosophical sources for caution and clarity. Second, the perspective in population ethics that I am acquainted with is utilitarian. Consequently, the ethical discourse presented here is inherently constrained in its scope due to the specific utilitarian approach adopted.

We have already encountered the notion of life worth living in previous chapters. In essence, it means that life is better than

Table 9.1 *Some important concepts in (animal) population ethics*

Concept	Characterization
Preference for lives worth living	A world with an individual with a life worth living is better than a world without that individual
Avoidance of the repugnant conclusion	A world with a small population of individuals each with a high quality of life is better than a world with a very large population of individuals each with a life barely worth living
Replaceability argument	It is morally permissible to cause a happy individual to exist, and then painlessly kill it, as long as you replace that individual with an equally happy individual
Procreation asymmetry	The act of bringing new individuals with lives worth living into existence and the act of not bringing new individuals with lives not worth living into existence are not equivalent

nonexistence. The concept of preference for lives worth living states that a world with an individual with a life worth living is deemed better than a world without that individual, everything else being equal. This principle is similar to the "mere addition" principle (Parfit 1984) that adding more individuals to a population, provided these new individuals have lives worth living, should not make the outcome worse. In other words, if adding more people results in a larger total population where everyone has a life worth living, then this addition should be seen as a positive or, at least, not a negative change. One prominent critique of this principle revolves around the idea of "neutrality," contending that the mere possibility of an individual experiencing a fulfilling life is not a sufficient rationale for bringing that person into existence. Narveson (1973) succinctly expressed this viewpoint by famously stating that "we are in favor of making people happy, but neutral about making happy people."

The repugnant conclusion is a term coined by philosopher Parfit (1984) to describe a counterintuitive and seemingly paradoxical result that can arise in ethical reasoning within the context of population ethics. The conclusion suggests that a situation where there is a very large population of individuals leading lives that are just barely worth living might be considered better or preferable than a situation with a smaller population of individuals leading happy lives. The rejection of the repugnant conclusion seems intuitive. However, it can be shown that any theory that respects the mere addition principle and the "weak inequality principle" leads to the repugnant conclusion (Arrhenius et al. 2022). The weak inequality principle states that an increase in total and average utility that creates perfect equality is viewed as an improvement, another morally intuitive concept. It is not a surprise, then, that the repugnant conclusion has been the subject of several proofs of incompatibility in the literature (Arrhenius 2000), and whether this conclusion is actually repugnant has been contested (Zuber et al. 2021).

The replaceability argument states that animals can be ethically killed and replaced with new animals that would lead lives of at least equal value. Applied to farming, this argument states that "humanely raised animals that live pleasant lives and can be killed without pain and distress can be replaced, without loss, by new humanely raised animals, which thus offset the good prevented by the killing" (Delon 2019, page 2131). The argument hence proposes a way of compensating the welfare loss that is implied by the killing of animals. If valid, this argument could rationalize the cycle of raising and slaughtering animals for food. Peter Singer acknowledges that this argument has been the most contentious in his seminal book *Practical Ethics* (Singer 2011). Critics of the replaceability argument such as Tom Regan contend that it oversimplifies the moral consideration of individual animals and that it fails to treat animals with respect as it violates their right to life. They underscore the unique and sentient nature of each creature, asserting that no individual can be truly interchangeable when considering their experiences, desires, or capacity for suffering.

The procreation asymmetry principle refers to the idea that there is a moral asymmetry between the act of bringing new individuals into existence and the act of not bringing new individuals into existence. McMahan (1981) formulates the asymmetry as follows: "while the fact that a person would have a life worth not living provides a reason not to conceive him, the fact that a person would have a life worth living does not provide a reason to conceive him." An underlying justification is that creating an individual with a bad life is ethically objectionable since that individual can complain about this decision. Conversely, refraining from creating a person with a good life may not be problematic since the nonexistent individual cannot complain about the decision.

9.2 COMMON NORMATIVE SETTINGS

I now discuss how different normative criteria address these concepts in population ethics. To do so, I will consider and compare three standard normative settings: total utilitarianism (TU), average utilitarianism (AU), and critical-level utilitarianism (CLU). See Table 9.2

Table 9.2 *Some normative settings and formal expressions with two individuals*

Normative setting	Formal expression with two individuals
Total utilitarianism	$u_1 + u_2$
Average utilitarianism	$\frac{u_1 + u_2}{2}$
Critical-level utilitarianism	$(u_1 - \gamma) + (u_2 - \gamma)$

for the formal expression of the associated SWFs for two individuals with respective utilities u_1 and u_2. Note that so far in the book we have only considered TU, namely the simple (unweighted) sum of individual utility functions. AU is the average utility, namely TU divided by the number of individuals. AU is the most common alternative to TU. In its simple form, CLU is the sum of the excess of individual utilities above a critical level $\gamma \geq 0$.

I now explore how each normative setting deals with the common population ethics concepts presented in the previous section. Under TU it is clear that there is always a preference for life worth living. Suppose that the life of an individual that may be created is worth living and equals $v \geq 0$. Then, under TU, adding this individual to the world simply yields a benefit $v \geq 0$, and is thus beneficial. Under AU, however, this is not always true. This depends on whether v is greater or lower than the average utility of already existing individuals. Similarly, preference for lives worth living may or may not hold under CLU since the benefit of adding this individual depends on whether v is greater or lower than γ. Hence TU satisfies the property of preference for lives worth living while AU and CLU do not in general satisfy that preference.

Regarding the repugnant conclusion, it is well known that TU leads to that conclusion, while both AU and CLU can avoid it. AU always prefers a population with individuals with a very high life quality than one with a low life quality, no matter the respective sizes of those populations. Hence it avoids the repugnant conclusion.

Regarding CLU, it also may avoid the repugnant conclusion provided that the critical level is located just above the level of a life barely worth living. In that case, the welfare of the large population of individuals with a life barely worth living is always negative, while that of the smaller population can still be positive. Since these results are well known in population ethics, I let the reader explore the formal proofs, generalizations and discussions elsewhere; see for instance Blackorby et al. (2005).

Let me now discuss the replaceability argument (RA). As far as I know, there is no economic interpretation of the RA to date, so what follows is a first pass. For the sake of simplicity, I explore the RA with a simple example (see also Višak 2013). Suppose that each living animal derives utility $v \geq 0$ for any given period of time lived (e.g., one year). Consider scenario 1 in which only one animal lives for two periods of time, and consider alternatively scenario 2 in which two animals live, one is replaced by another equally happy animal after one period of time. What is the welfare obtained in each scenario under our three normative settings?

Under TU, total welfare is simply equal to $2v$ in both scenarios 1 and 2. The RA logic is thus consistent with TU: creating a new animal perfectly compensates for death or killing of the first animal. In other words, killing (painlessly) one animal to create another is morally neutral. But the point is that this is not the case under AU and CLU. As it is shown in Table 9.3, both AU and CLU give a premium to scenario 1. That is, they favor scenario 1, the one where one animal has a longer life. This is enough to show that the RA is not in general valid under these alternative normative settings.

Note that the equivalence under TU between scenario 1 and 2 sounds a bit disturbing at first since it treats in a similar way two scenarios that seem intuitively very different: one with a single animal and another with two animals. One way to see this oddity is the following: At the end of the first period, it appears that the situation with a preexisting animal continuing to live and the birth of a new animal are profoundly distinct. In philosophy, much of the debate

Table 9.3 *The replaceability argument under different normative settings: An example*

Scenario	Total utilitarianism (TU)	Average utilitarianism (AU)	Critical-level utilitarianism (CLU)
Scenario 1: One animal lives for two periods	$2v$	$2v$	$2v-\gamma$
Scenario 2: Two animals each live for one period	$2v$	v	$2(v-\gamma)$

about the replaceability argument revolves around the question of whether the initial animal has an interest in prolonging its own existence, and whether that interest can be compensated by the interest in existence that the new animal has. Singer (2011) puts forth a widely debated argument, contending that some "merely sentient" animals lack continuity of identity across periods of consciousness due to their absence of memory or psychological connections. In that case, he argues that they are indeed replaceable.

The discussions surrounding the RA are related to those about the moral cost of killing. Here, I follow the consequentialist approach and assume that the loss associated with death simply corresponds to the loss of utility from v to 0. Hence, there is no moral cost of killing per se, that is, there is no additional cost beyond that loss in utility. This implies that, under TU, the death of an animal can be exactly compensated for by the birth of another animal with utility v. Although CLU does not explicitly account for a moral cost of killing, this normative setting captures the fact that a death cannot be fully "compensated" by the birth of another animal. In other words, this normative setting implicitly induces a moral cost of killing. Moreover, note the counterintuitive effect induced by egalitarian principles. Indeed, it may be argued that scenario 1 is less fair in the sense that only one animal has an opportunity to live with the other does not even have the opportunity to exist. In contrast, in scenario

2 two animals have this opportunity. Taking a prioritarian function over lifetime utility would in general favor scenario 2.

Finally, let me discuss the procreation asymmetry principle (PAP). Again, I explore the principle with the help of a simple example. Suppose that scenario 1 corresponds to bringing a new individual with a life worth living into existence, and that this individual would have a utility $v > 0$. Suppose alternatively that scenario 2 prevents an individual with a life not worth living from existing, and that individual would have had a utility $-v < 0$. What is the welfare gain associated with each scenario under different normative settings? Under TU, both scenarios generate a welfare gain equal to v. Hence, the two scenarios are equivalent, and TU fails APP. Similarly, both scenarios are equivalent under AU, which thus also fails PAP. However, under CLU, the benefit associated with scenario 1 is equal to $v - \gamma$, while it is equal to $v + \gamma$ for scenario 2. Hence, both scenarios are not equivalent. In particular, the moral imperative for refraining from creating an individual with a bad life seems more compelling than the one from creating an individual with a good life of equal magnitude in absolute value. This result under CLU seems consistent with some ideas put forward in the population ethics literature.

9.3 A SURVEY STUDY ABOUT MORAL BELIEFS

In Espinosa and Treich (2025), we design a simple survey questionnaire to study the beliefs of the general population about some normative questions related to animal population ethics. This survey was conducted using a representative sample of the French population (N = 1,526), with data collected online in July 2023. The questionnaire presented in this section was translated from French. Table 9.4 presents a few statements included in the questionnaire along with the corresponding answers reflecting agreement or disagreement with each statement.

The first two statements explore the population beliefs about whether a life worth living or not is socially desirable. We find that most participants (77.4 percent) agree that a life not worth living

Table 9.4 *General population beliefs about animal population ethics*

Statement	Agreement
"Imagine that society faces a situation where it has the possibility of avoiding the conception of an animal whose life would not be worth living given the very poor living conditions that this animal would experience if it were to exist. (Note: this animal does not even exist as a fetus yet, so it is not an abortion.) Some people say it is best to avoid the conception of this animal whose life would be very bad."	77.4 percent of participants agree with this statement ("yes, it is best to avoid this existence"). 22.6 percent of participants do not agree with this statement.
"Imagine now that society faces a situation where it can, on the contrary, bring into the world an animal whose life would be worth living given the very good living conditions that this animal would experience if it were to exist. We imagine that the happiness of this animal would be equivalent (in positive terms) to the unhappiness that the animal would have experienced in the previous question. Some people say that it is better to bring into existence this animal whose life would be very good."	81.3 percent of participants agree with this statement ("yes, it is best to bring this animal into existence"). 18.7 percent of participants do not agree with this statement.
"Imagine a society with several animals. Imagine that in this society we could give birth to a new animal, and that, if it were to be born, it would have a life made up mainly of happiness and pleasures. Over the entire duration of its life, it is estimated that the happiness of this new animal would be a little lower than that of animals that already exist, but that it is still positive. Do you consider that the birth of this animal would be desirable?"	49.9 percent of participants believe that the birth of this animal would be desirable. 42.7 percent of participants believe that the birth of this animal would be neither desirable nor undesirable. 7.4 percent of participants believe that the birth of this animal would not be desirable.

Source: Espinosa and Treich (2025)

is not socially desirable. Moreover, we find that most participants (81.3 percent) agree that a life worth living is socially desirable. This last result is consistent with the concept of preference for lives worth living presented earlier.

We also used the two previous questions to explore the procreation asymmetry principle. It is not clear a priori how to explore empirically this principle (see Spears [2020] for a recent attempt). One difficulty is that perceptions about how bad a bad life is and how good a good life is can vary. Hence, it may be of limited interest to notice an asymmetry in situations, which can be perceived as asymmetrical in the first place. To try to neutralize that possible perception effect, note that we asked the respondents to imagine that "the happiness of this animal would be equivalent (in positive terms) to the unhappiness that the animal would have experienced in the previous question."

Looking at the results, note that there is support for both (i) avoiding the birth of an animal with a life not worth living and (ii) bringing an animal with a life worth living into existence. Moreover, the level of support is very similar in both cases. Therefore, we cannot conclude from our survey data that people support the procreation asymmetry principle for animals. Hence, this result suggests that the justification for conceiving a person with a life worth living is as strong as the one for not conceiving a person with a life not worth living. Since TU and AU fail to respect the principle, this result may be viewed as consistent with both normative approaches.

However, it is important to distinguish between the idea that it may be better or worse to bring a life into existence and the notion that we are "required" to create or note to create a particular animal life. The procreation asymmetry principle typically suggests that we are not required to create animals with lives worth living, while we are required to avoid creating those with lives that are not. This subtle interpretive difference makes the wording crucial, and it is unclear whether our survey study correctly assesses support for that interpretation of the principle itself. More research is needed on this point.

Moreover, we asked participants whether they would believe that the birth of an animal is desirable if that animal has a life worth living, but "the happiness of this new animal would be a little lower than that of animals that already exist." About half of the participants (49.9 percent) support that belief or at least believe that the birth of this animal would be neither desirable nor undesirable (42.7 percent). Only a few participants (7.4 percent) believe that the birth of this animal would not be desirable. Since bringing that animal into existence would reduce average welfare, this result seems inconsistent with AU.

Finally, a few words about the survey study approach in general to study normative issues related to animal welfare. This approach offers valuable insights and serves as a useful complement to the general axiomatic approach to normative issues. However, it is important to exercise caution when interpreting these types of studies. Since the questions posed are hypothetical, participants have limited incentives to deeply reflect on them, potentially leading to less reliable answers. Also, these questions are likely very unfamiliar to the participants, which raises general concerns about the understanding of participants. These issues may be exacerbated here precisely because we talk about animals, not humans. Finally, it is also unclear whether normative conclusions follow from what people think.

Since the book is explicitly organized into direct and indirect approaches, it is worthwhile examining the relevance of a survey focused on human values within the direct section. One might indeed question whether this survey would be more appropriately placed in the part that deals with "The Indirect Approach." This concern ties back to a point made at the end of the introduction. However, it is important to differentiate here between surveys that assess "human valuations" and those that explore "human moral proxies" for the value of different animal lives. Questionnaires about human moral proxies aim at capturing how people believe animals should be valued in policymaking, not how they themselves value animals. Therefore,

I think it is consistent to include such a survey study in Part II. That said, the difference between the two can be subtle, and respondents may unintentionally conflate them when answering.

The use of surveys to reflect on animal ethics is fairly new. In terms of future research, it would be beneficial to examine whether the survey responses remain consistent when the framing of the questions is altered, and if there are systematic differences in responses when considering humans instead of animals. Finally, a research direction involves considering real choice tasks. While it is ethically challenging to study normative questions with real stakes involving humans, it is sometimes possible to do so with animals.

9.4 APPLICATION TO THE CANONICAL MODEL

In the variable population case, we have seen that TU has been criticized, in particular because it may induce the repugnant conclusion. In the canonical model studied in the previous chapters, I have assumed TU. In this section, I will show that alternative normative settings advocate for a reduced level of animal production, consequently necessitating a higher level of taxation. See Espinosa and Treich (2024).

Consider the canonical model (7.1). Under AU, the social objective is simply equal to:

$$\underline{U}(n) \equiv \frac{1}{1+n}\left(u(n) - c(n) + nv\right) \tag{9.1}$$

It is easy to show that the socially optimal consumption level is always lower under average utilitarianism than under TU. To show this, denote $\underline{n}$ the maximum of $\underline{U}(n)$, and as before, denote n^* the maximum of $U(n) \equiv u(n) - c(n) + nv$. Hence, by definition $\frac{U(\underline{n})}{1+\underline{n}} \geq \frac{U(n^*)}{1+n^*}$. Since $U(n^*) \geq 0$, this implies $\frac{1+n^*}{1+\underline{n}} \geq \frac{U(n^*)}{U(\underline{n})} \geq 1$, hence $n^* \geq \underline{n}$.

By the same logic as in Chapter 7, it is easy to show (and this is left as an exercise) that the optimal animal welfare levy under AU is equal to

$$\underline{t} = -v + \frac{u(n(t)) - c(n(t)) + n(t)v}{1 + n(t)} \tag{9.2}$$

$$= \frac{u(n(t)) - c(n(t)) - v}{1 + n(t)} \tag{9.3}$$

This closed form solution for the levy under average utilitarianism exhibits interesting properties. The expression (9.2) shows that a positive term is added to the tax under TU, indicating that either the tax increases or the subsidy decreases compared to TU: $\underline{t} > -v$. Observe that the animal welfare levy under AU corresponds to the sum of the levy under TU and average welfare in the society. Hence, the levy under AU not only depends on the utility of those who are directly affected (i.e., the animals), but also on everything else, including human welfare. Therefore the levy under AU is much more complex.

Now look at the expression (9.3). Observe that $\underline{t}$ is always positive if and only if $u(n(t)) - c(n(t)) \geq v$, namely if and only if human welfare is greater than animal welfare. Hence, under AU only taxes (not subsidies) are implemented under the plausible assumption that human welfare is greater than animal welfare. The intuition is simple: Taxing meat reduces the number of individuals with the lowest welfare in the society (i.e., animals), which always increases average welfare in the society. In other words, it is not possible under AU to subsidize the creation of individuals with the lowest welfare.

What about CLU? Under CLU, the social objective is simply equal to:

$$U^{CLU}(n) \equiv u(n) - c(n) - \gamma + n(v - \gamma) \tag{9.4}$$

It is obvious then that optimal consumption under CLU is always lower than under TU given $\gamma \geq 0$. It is also immediate to show that the optimal levy is then equal to:

$$t^{CLU} = -v + \gamma \tag{9.5}$$

This implies that the animal welfare levy is always greater under CLU than under TU. This is intuitive since parameter γ increases the threshold from which life is socially valuable.

Overall, this analysis shows that the use of alternative normative settings may require significant adjustments to the animal welfare levy. More fundamentally, this shows that the Pigouvian principle of increasing the marginal private cost/benefit by the exact amount generated by the negative externality (i.e., the marginal social damage principle prevalent in environmental economics) is no longer valid under alternative normative settings. This illustrates the importance of population ethics issues for the pricing of externalities.

Before concluding, let me make a digression. It can be argued that farmed animals need not be slaughtered, which may be a social benefit if their life is worth living. Let us explore what happens in that case. Let n be the number of animals bred and slaughtered (as in the canonical model) and b the number of animals bred (but not slaughtered). The social objective may then be written: $u(n) - c(n) + nv - c_b(b) + bv_b$ where $c_b(.)$ and v_b are respectively the cost of production and the utility of a bred animal. Hence, humans do not derive any benefit from bred animals, but they nevertheless pay a cost $c_b(.)$ for producing them. Note then that it is perfectly possible that we have an interior solution $b > 0$ when v_b is positive and high enough. Nevertheless, under the separability of cost productions of slaughtered and bred animals, the choice of n and b are independent. In terms of policy intervention, the first-best number of bred animals b may be reached by giving a per-animal subsidy v_b to animal farmers. This policy, under TU, is thus independent from the meat tax policy that concerns the animals raised for human consumption, namely the n slaughtered animals. In other words, the paper focuses on this policy issue regarding slaughtered animals and can ignore without loss of generality the policy issue regarding bred animals. Importantly, this separability argument does not hold under AU.

A general conclusion from this section is that the results are highly sensitive to the selected normative setting. Indeed, we have seen in the previous section that TU, AU and CLU exhibit divergent responses to distinct normative principles, such as the repugnant conclusion or the replaceability argument. Furthermore, we have seen that these normative settings yield varying implications for the consumption of animals and, consequently, for the stringency of policy interventions. It will thus be important in the following to remain mindful of these divergences among different normative settings when examining policies that impact the number of animals involved.

9.5 TOWARD MULTISPECIES POPULATION ETHICS?

I conclude this chapter with some reflections about future research. The literature on population ethics has primarily focused on humans, typically analyzing scenarios involving human populations. A smaller but notable subset extends this focus to animals, comparing scenarios involving animal populations, as I have done in this chapter. However, an important point to highlight is that scenarios considering both humans and animals together – or, more broadly, multiple species – remain largely unexamined. This gap presents a compelling opportunity for further exploration.

This is a significant gap because one could argue that, ultimately, we should aim to maximize overall welfare in the world. Achieving this requires determining the optimal population sizes for each species (including humans) to maximize total welfare within the constraints of available resources. O'Brien (2024) introduces the idea that species differ in their efficiency at converting resources into welfare. He suggests that certain animals, such as mice, may be more "efficient" in this regard than humans, raising profound normative questions. Similarly, Sebo (2023) argues that we might have reasons to favor a population consisting of more, smaller animals rather than one dominated by larger animals. He refers to this as "the rebugnant conclusion" (since he assumes insects, or bugs, are sentient).

To avoid the rebugnant conclusion, one might argue for introducing a critical level, as is commonly done in the single-species case to address the repugnant conclusion (see earlier in this chapter). At first glance, this intuition appears reasonable. After all, it seems plausible to consider that only certain types of lives are socially valuable, namely lives characterized, for instance, by abilities such as self-awareness over time, or even perhaps the capacity to tell stories or play music. That is, this favors lives with high utility potential. However, Williamson (2021) argues that this approach is "elitist" in the sense that it is inherently unfair to species with low utility potential, whose utilities could never meet the critical level. It seems deeply problematic indeed to suggest that the existence of such animals inherently worsens the world and that their lives should not exist rather than exist below this threshold.

Williamson (2021, page 406) advances another objection, which he calls the problem of "disproportionate disvalue." He presents it with the following example:

> Suppose the average human life contains up to 10,000,000 welfare units, the average insect life contains up to 100 welfare units, and the universal critical level is placed at 100,000 welfare units: combine these two facts and we discover that the critical value of an insect life is – 99,900 welfare units. That is, the creation of a single insect life offsets the creation of an entire human life containing 199,900 welfare units.

This implies that the birth of a group of low-utility animals could significantly harm overall welfare, potentially so much that it outweighs the positive impact of creating many humans living good lives.

Williamson (2021) argues that these problems are due to the use of a uniform critical level, namely the same critical level for all species. He then discusses the implication of adopting instead species-specific critical levels. He contends that such an approach avoids issues of elitism and disproportionate disvalue and can be grounded based on biological differences. For instance, humans typically have much longer lifespans than insects, meaning that lifetime well-being sums for different species naturally exist in distinct ranges. However,

Williamson also acknowledges that using species-specific critical levels introduces new challenges. One notable issue is the potential re-emergence of the rebugnant conclusion. For example, a very large population of insects with utilities just above their species-specific critical level would be considered preferable to any population of humans with lives equal to the human critical level.

We have seen that the extension of a critical-level utilitarian SWF to a multispecies context is not straightforward. To conclude, let me briefly discuss average utilitarianism. The result in Section 9.4 indicates that bringing animals into existence for meat purposes can reduce average welfare, even if those animals have lives that are worth living. However, few would probably argue against consuming animals because their welfare is lower than that of humans. This is one of the many problems of using a non-separable SWF in this context (Blackorby et al. 2005, Zuber et al. 2024). Another issue is that species diversity becomes inherently problematic: Average utilitarianism would favor eliminating species with lower welfare unless their existence contributes to higher-welfare species, even if all species have a life worth living. This brief discussion highlights the need for further research on multispecies SWFs, taking into account the complex dilemmas posed by animal population ethics.

REFERENCES

Arrhenius G (2000) An impossibility theorem for welfarist axiologies. *Economics and Philosophy* 16(2), 247–266.

Arrhenius G, Bykvist K, Campbell T, Finneron-Burns E (eds.) (2022) *The Oxford Handbook of Population Ethics*. New York: Oxford University Press.

Blackorby C, Bossert W, Donaldson DJ (2005) *Population Issues in Social Choice Theory, Welfare Economics, and Ethics* (No. 39). Cambridge University Press.

Delon N (2016) The replaceability argument in the ethics of animal husbandry. In *Encyclopedia of Food and Agricultural Ethics*, eds. P Thompson and D Kaplan, 2130–2136. Springer.

Espinosa R, Treich N (2024) The animal welfare levy. *Journal of the European Economic Association*, in press.

Espinosa R, Treich N (2025) Fairness judgments about animals. *Journal of Economic Inequality*, in press.

McMahan J (1981) Problems of population theory. *Ethics*, 92(1), 96–127.

Narveson J (1973) Moral problems of population. *The Monist*, 57(1), 62–86.

O'Brien GD (2024) Totalism, animals, and the Repugnant Conclusion. *Utilitas*, 36(3), 211–229.

Parfit D (1984) *Reason and Persons*. Oxford University Press.

Sebo J (2023) The rebugnant conclusion: Utilitarianism, insects, microbes, and AI systems. *Ethics, Policy & Environment*, 26(2), 249–264.

Singer P (2011) *Practical Ethics*. Cambridge University Press.

Spears D (2020) The asymmetry of population ethics: Experimental social choice and dual-process moral reasoning. *Economics and Philosophy*, 36(3), 435–454.

Višak T (2013) *Killing Happy Animals: Explorations in Utilitarian Ethics*. Springer.

Williamson P (2021) A new argument against critical-level utilitarianism. *Utilitas*, 33 (4), 399–416.

Zuber S, Venkatesh, N, Tännsjö, T et al. (2021) What should we agree on about the repugnant conclusion? *Utilitas*, 33(4), 379–383.

Zuber S, Spears D, Budolfson MB (2024) Separable social welfare evaluation for multispecies populations, mimeo.

10 Valuing Animal Welfare

10.1 A MASTER FORMULA

Ultimately, a key objective of animal welfare economics is to value animal welfare. In the previous theoretical discussions, a key parameter is the utility level of an animal v. As we have seen, this parameter drives the policy outcomes. Typically, it determines the animal welfare levy or the sentience premium. But, how to estimate v?

Encouragingly, methods for valuing animal welfare are emerging, as emphasized by Kuruc and McFadden (2023a,b) and Budolfson et al. (2024). In this chapter, I present one of these methods. It builds upon a formula introduced, and progressively elaborated by Wong (2016), Budolfson and Spears (2019), Espinosa (2024), and Espinosa and Treich (2024a,b). This master formula integrates all the components outlined earlier in Chapters 4, 5 and 6, and reads as follows:

$$v = m\phi_s \int_{t=0}^{t=T} q(t)\,dt \tag{10.1}$$

where:

$q(t)$ is the "animal welfare score" at a given time t between birth ($t = 0$) and death ($t = T$);

ϕ_s is the "utility potential" of species s (which allows for interspecies comparisons); and

m is the monetization parameter (which allows translating utility levels into monetary units).

The parameter $q(t)$ corresponds to the instantaneous level of utility of the animal at date t. It will be expressed on a normalized scale where $q(.) = 1$ indicates the highest possible level of utility and $q(.) = 0$ represents the point where positive and negative experiences are balanced so that the net utility is equal to zero. The welfare of the animal over its entire life is simply defined by the integral of instantaneous utility from birth ($t = 0$) to death ($t = T$). In its spirit, this method is aligned with Kahneman et al. (1997)'s concept of experienced utility assessed through the sum of instant utilities: "The measured primitive of experienced utility is instant utility, the hedonic value of a moment of experience as immediately reported or recorded. Significant outcomes last more than an instant, however, and the total utility of such outcomes must therefore be derived from a temporal profile of instant utility." Kahneman et al. (1997) provide an axiomatic support to this method (see also Fryxell 2024 for a more recent reference).

The parameter ϕ_s permits to translate animal welfare scores into comparable utility points; see next section for more details about the calibration and normalization. Finally, the parameter m transforms utility points at a given time (i.e., $\phi_s q(t)$) into monetary equivalents. Hence, the parameter v in the formula corresponds to the monetary equivalent of the lifetime well-being of an animal. This monetization is consistent with the assumption in the canonical model of a quasi-linear utility function where v is expressed in the unit of the tax, namely money. It is also central if one wants ultimately to include animal welfare into benefit-cost analysis.

This method shares similarities with the one employed in the quality-adjusted life years (QALYs) literature within health economics. Here, animal welfare scores $q(.)$ can be assimilated to "animal QALYs" or AQALYs. Both QALYs and AQALYs range between 0 and 1, with 1 representing the highest possible score and 0 a score equivalent to death (or nonexistence), while values below 0 indicate a life deemed not worth living. These scores are then aggregated over the lifespan of an individual. This method also aligns with certain existing scores for animal welfare, such as those advocated by the

World Society for the Protection of Animals (WSPA 2003), the Welfare Footprint Project (https://welfarefootprint.org/) or the Animal Ask modeling approach (Animal Ask 2024), where the welfare magnitude is typically calculated as the product of severity, duration, and the number of animals affected.

The central novelty compared to the QALY literature concerns the introduction of the utility potential parameter ϕ_S. This is the key parameter in the multispecies setting since it permits us to make utilities comparable across species. In other words, the quantity $\phi_S q(t)$ corresponds to the utility of species s at any point in time t evaluated in a comparable unit to other species' utilities. One way to understand the concept is through the following basic example. Imagine choosing between the lives of two animals, say a frog and a pig, each with a maximum welfare level of 1. Should we be indifferent simply because both are sentient animals with maximal welfare? In other words, should they count equally for social welfare? One could argue that pigs, with their broader range of emotions and higher cognitive abilities, can experience a greater intensity and variety of welfare states than frogs. This would imply that a pig has a higher utility potential parameter, meaning its capacity for welfare is greater. In other words, a pig with maximal welfare would generate "more social welfare" than a frog with maximal welfare, and thus should be given priority.

Formally, to further understand the mathematical role of ϕ_S, consider two animal species $s = 1,2$ where species 2 has a higher utility potential than species 1, $\phi_2 > \phi_1$. To make things simple, suppose again that each animal species has exactly the same animal welfare score $q(t)$ at any point in time t over their whole lifetime. The point, as shown on Figure 10.1, is that species 2 then always reaches higher utility levels in absolute value than species 1. Again, this is consistent with the idea that a species with a higher utility potential can experience more intense emotions, both positive and negative.

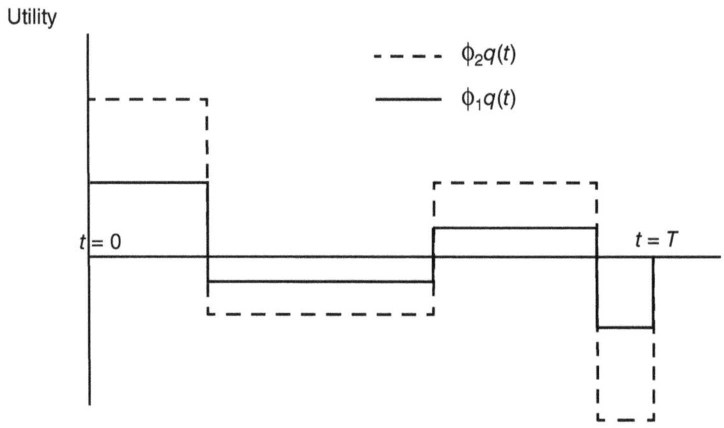

FIGURE 10.1 Utilities of two species with the same animal welfare score $q(t)$ and different utility potentials: $\phi_2 > \phi_1$.

10.2 CALIBRATING THE MASTER FORMULA

In this section, I outline a step-by-step process for calibrating the three key parameters in the master formula. This calibration will serve as the basis for the applications presented in the next section. However, it is important to note that this calibration method is in its early stages and should be considered as a preliminary exploration. My basic aim here is to complete the calibration exercise and generate some initial figures, as in Espinosa (2024) and Espinosa and Treich (2024a). While this helps initiate discussions and demonstrates the feasibility of the exercise, it necessitates numerous assumptions, some of which are quite "heroic." Therefore, I want to stress once again that this calibration exercise is a starting point and will certainly be subject to extensive revisions, if not a complete overhaul. Therefore, I urge the readers to approach the estimated values in the next section with a lot of caution.

The estimation of animal welfare first requires calibrating the animal welfare score $q(t)$, namely the level of welfare at any point in time t. As a first pass, Espinosa (2024) estimates it using the Five Freedom framework; see Chapter 4. We also build on this approach in our recent paper Espinosa and Treich (2024a). (Note that Romain

Espinosa, Heather Browning, and I are currently working with the more comprehensive Five Domains framework to construct an AQALY score; but in this book I will be using the more widespread Five Freedom framework throughout.) We consider that each of the five freedoms can be violated to different extents (no violation, mild, moderate, severe, very severe violations). We note $W(t)$ the total number of violation points that the animal endures in the living conditions at date t. We then consider the following linear parametric form for the animal welfare score:

$$q(t) = \frac{W_0 - W(t)}{W_0} \qquad (10.2)$$

Hence, as expected, the animal welfare score decreases in the number of violations $W(t)$. It takes the maximum value 1 with no violations $W(t) = 0$, and the value 0 when $W(t) = W_0$. That is, W_0 defines the threshold where life becomes (not) worth living. Conceptually, if the animal has a utility associated with $W(t) = W_0$ for its entire life, then its life is morally neutral and equivalent to death or nonexistence.

Let me now explain how $W(t)$ can be calibrated. Again, this is based on Espinosa (2024) and Espinosa and Treich (2024a). Consider a standard chicken raised in France, for instance. The idea is to evaluate each stage of a chicken's life by computing the number of freedoms violated in each stage. A standard factory-farmed chicken has a typical lifespan of 40 days. Dividing this lifespan into three stages – farm, transport, and slaughterhouse – the respective durations are 38 days, 1 day, and 1 day.

Drawing from the insights provided in Chapter 2 regarding intensive farming practices in France, the violations on animal freedoms at each stage of a chicken's existence are assessed as follows. First, despite regular, albeit monotonous, feeding (mild violation), the high density of chickens induces significant psychological distress (severe violation) and physical discomfort (very severe violation) at the farm. Additionally, practices like debeaking, rapid growth, and exposure to ammonia lead to substantial pain and further restrict natural behaviors (very severe violations). During transportation and slaughter, we anticipate maximal freedom violations due to heightened psychological distress and the inability to exhibit natural behaviors (very severe violations). Moreover, there are high violations of freedom from pain (very severe violation). Table 10.1 provides a breakdown of the violations for each stage and freedom category (refer to numbers in the parentheses).

Once the number of violations is determined for each stage, the master formula for a specific W_0 can be computed. For most calculations hereafter, I will assume the following threshold $W_0 = 10$, which means that the threshold is reached when there is a moderate level of violations for each of the five freedoms. Using the calculations presented in Table 10.1, it is then possible to compute the animal welfare score over the whole lifetime of the chicken, namely

$$\int_{t=0}^{t=40} q(t)dt = -22.8 - 0.7 - 0.7 = -24.2 \tag{10.2}$$

Note the life stage on the farm overwhelmingly dominates the calculation in equation (10.2). This makes sense since this stage represents almost all of the animal's lifespan. But this also points to a potential limitation of the method. The approach of aggregating severity and time linearly may inadvertently downplay instances of very intense pain with short durations, such as those experienced during transport and at the slaughterhouse. This suggests that this calculation may not fully capture the acute suffering experienced in brief yet intense episodes.

The next step concerns the calibration of the utility potential parameter ϕ_s, namely the utility potential of species s. Following the pioneering idea of Budolfson and Spears (2019) and Espinosa (2024), I use the number of forebrain neurons to compute this utility potential parameter; see Chapter 5. That is, I consider that ϕ_s is equal to the ratio of the number of forebrain neurons of the species s over the number of forebrain neurons of humans.

At this juncture, it is thus possible to compute the utility of a standard chicken raised in France expressed in terms of utility. For chickens, I use $\phi_s = \dfrac{0.08}{24.52}$ from the data presented in Chapter 5,

Table 10.1 *Steps to estimate the lifetime animal welfare score with* $W_0 = 10$ *based on the Five Freedom framework*

Freedom	Farm	Transport	Slaughterhouse
Freedom from hunger, malnutrition and thirst	Mild (1)	Moderate (2)	Moderate (2)
Freedom from fear and distress	Severe (3)	Very severe (4)	Very severe (4)
Freedom from heat stress and physical discomfort	Very severe (4)	Very severe (4)	Very severe (4)
Freedom from pain, injury, and disease	Very severe (4)	Severe (3)	Severe (3)
Freedom to express normal patterns of behavior	Very severe (4)	Very severe (4)	Very severe (4)
$W(t)$ (= total number of violations)	16	17	17
$q(t) = \frac{10 - W(t)}{10}$	–0.6	–0.7	–0.7
Number of days	38	1	1
$\int_t q(t)dt$	$38(-0.6) = -22.8$	$(-0.7) = -0.7$	$1(-0.7) = -0.7$

Source: Espinosa (2024) and Espinosa and Treich (2024a)

yielding $\phi_s \int_{t=0}^{t=40} q(t)dt = \phi_s \times (-24.2) \simeq -0.08$. This step in the evaluation is important since, thanks to the utility potential parameter, it makes the obtained utils comparable across all animal species. Note that utilities are comparable because we employ a uniform evaluation method based on the Five Freedom approach for all animals. The scores then translate into utilities through ϕ_s, so that animal utilities are comparable by construction. We could stop the analysis here, which would be useful to develop some cost-efficiency analysis of animal welfare policies.

However, the next step for a full economic evaluation is to convert utils into monetary units. This is undoubtedly a very difficult step. As a benchmark, the basic idea is to consider humans in the master formula (10.1) (because humans are animals too). Now consider this: If one can get a monetary value equivalent to one day with maximal welfare for a human, then this value is equal to $m\phi_s q(t)$. Given that $\phi_s = 1$ for humans, and $q(t) = 1$ (maximal welfare), the value of one day with maximal welfare precisely equals m. Hence, we have a way to calibrate m. Using a WTP per QALY approach estimated from data on the value of statistical life (Baumstark et al. 2013), the value of one year of human life in France has been estimated to be about 147,000 euros (Téhard et al. 2020). Dividing this figure by 365 yields a daily value, and we have $m \simeq 400$. See Espinosa (2024), Espinosa and Treich (2024a), and Budolfson et al. (2024) for a discussion of this method.

We thus have obtained a value for each of the three key parameters, $q(t)$, ϕ_s and m. It is thus finally possible to compute the social value associated with the life of a standard broiler chicken in France. Using the master formula, it is equal to $v = m\phi_s \int_{t=0}^{t=40} q(t)dt = 400 \times (-0.08) \simeq -32$ euros.

Allow me to reframe the rationale behind this estimate. Drawing from research on human WTP per QALYs, we can derive an estimate of the monetary valuation for a day of maximal welfare for a human. Next, we use the utility potential parameter to calculate the equivalent for a day of maximal welfare for a particular animal, such as a chicken. Subsequently, we factor in the animal welfare score to adjust downward this value, reflecting the specific living conditions of the animal in question. We then do this for any day of the life of that animal and arrive at a total to obtain the monetary equivalent value of the lifetime utility of an animal.

Note finally that it is not clearcut whether the comparability of animals' utility with that of humans is a priori. It is ensured here due to the "high/low scaling" method (Adler 2019; page 190). The low scaling point corresponds to the zero-utility level, namely the level of utility equivalent to nonexistence or death for both animals and humans. The high scaling point corresponds to the maximal possible instantaneous welfare, i.e., $q(.) = 1$ for animals and the maximal QALY (= 1) for humans. It is worth noting however that when using QALYs for humans, we solely consider perfect health as this benchmark value, not perfect welfare. Consequently, the estimates should in general be understood as a lower bound in our valuation of animal welfare.

10.3 APPLICATIONS

10.3.1 Application 1: Animal Welfare Levies

In this first example, I use the calibration method just presented to compute animal welfare levies as described in previous chapters. I refer in particular to the canonical model in Chapter 7, and again to Espinosa and Treich (2024a) where this application is described in more detail.

First, remember from Chapter 7 that the expression for the animal welfare levy in the simplest total utilitarian setting was: $t = -v$. Therefore, I can immediately derive the tax per chicken, which is equal to about 32 euros from the calculations in the previous section. Considering that a chicken contains about 2.5 kg of meat, I thus obtain a tax of about 13 euros per kg of chicken meat. I can now repeat the same exercise for the most common types of meats, namely pork and cow meat that is differentiated between meat from a dairy herd and from a beef herd. The main differences across animals are reported on Figure 10.2.

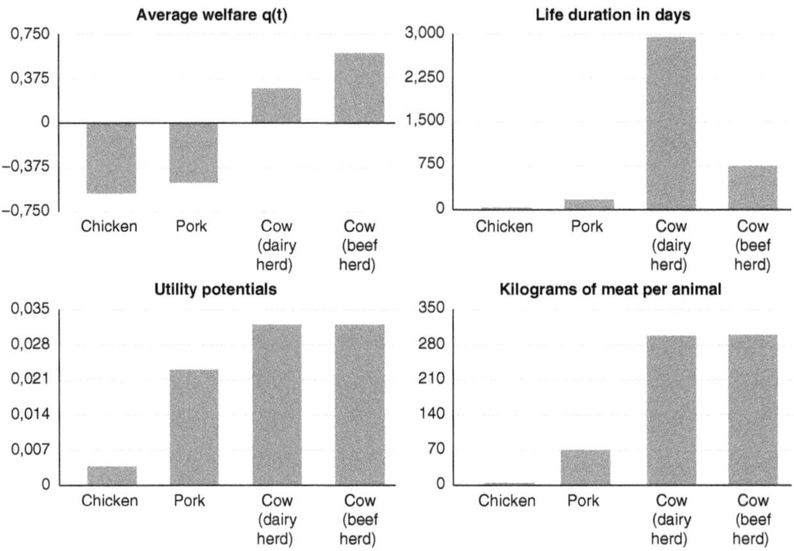

FIGURE 10.2 Key parameters' values for four animal species (chicken, pork, cow [dairy herd], cow [beef herd]) for $W_0 = 10$.
Source: Espinosa and Treich (2024a)

It is thus possible to obtain animal welfare levies for those four categories of animals. To check for robustness, we consider two values of the threshold value W_0, namely $W_0 = 10$ and $W_0 = 7$. The levies per kg of meat are reported on Figure 10.3 along with retail prices and environmental taxes associated with each type of meat.

Let me offer a few insights drawn from Figure 10.3. First, this figure highlights first-order importance of animal welfare considerations. Most significantly, the high values for the animal welfare levies would likely render intensive animal production methods, such as chicken and pig farming, economically unviable. Second, the impact on animal welfare largely overshadows environmental concerns, including here greenhouse gas emissions, as well as air and water pollution.

These two observations echo the initial claim in the introduction of this book that animal welfare matters a lot in terms of welfare impacts overall. Besides, it is worth noting that our estimates tend to

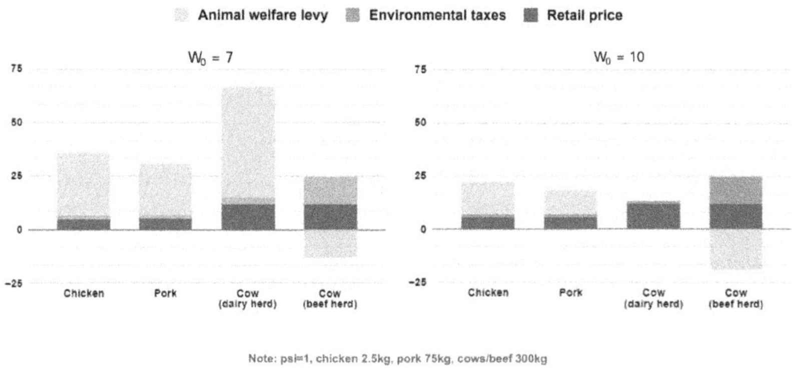

FIGURE 10.3 Retail prices, environmental taxes and animal welfare levies for $W_0 = 10$ and $W_0 = 7$.
Source: Espinosa and Treich (2024a)

err on the side of conservatism, likely providing a lower bound of the potential magnitude of these effects: As I said in the previous section, the monetization parameter considers "maximal health" (while the loss of a day of life with "maximal happiness" should be even higher). Moreover, I assume total utilitarianism, which provides the lowest level of tax compared to utilitarian alternatives (see Chapter 9). Additionally, the findings reveal a notable sensitivity to the threshold value W_0. Even a fairly modest shift from $W_0 = 10$ to $W_0 = 7$ yields a substantial increase in the magnitude of the taxes (see, e.g., the huge shift in the levy on dairy cows, which is explained by the long life duration of these animals). This calls for more research on this specific parameter W_0.

Finally, note that retail prices and environmental externalities are much higher for beef compared to pork or chicken. However, animal welfare levies work typically in the opposite direction since pork and chicken meat should be highly taxed while beef should even be subsidized (this is because cows produced for meat are estimated to have a life worth living). This observation puts forward another key policy dilemma: A climate policy centered primarily on a "methane tax" on meat, predominantly targeting beef, could inadvertently impact animal welfare negatively. This tension between environmental concerns and animal welfare is not unexpected (Mathur 2022, Kuruc and McFadden 2023a), but it highlights a fundamental tradeoff. If we prioritize animal welfare and allocate more resources to livestock, such as land and food, it is likely to result in a heightened environmental impact. This fundamental tradeoff between environmental and animal welfare impacts may be viewed as highly regrettable, signifying a key tension that our societies may inevitably confront in the future.

10.3.2 Application 2: Global Animal Welfare Trends

The second application is a simple follow-up to the first. It was developed during the spring of 2024 together with my intern, Elisabeth Klages. (And I am currently working on related issues with Maya Eden and Jojo Lee.) The objective of this section is to provide background information for Figure 1.1 presented in the Introduction. As can be seen on Figure 10.4, the aggregate curve already plotted on Figure 1.1 is simply the sum of welfare of three major categories of farmed land animals, namely cows, chickens, and pigs. Data about the total number of these animals come from the Food and Agriculture

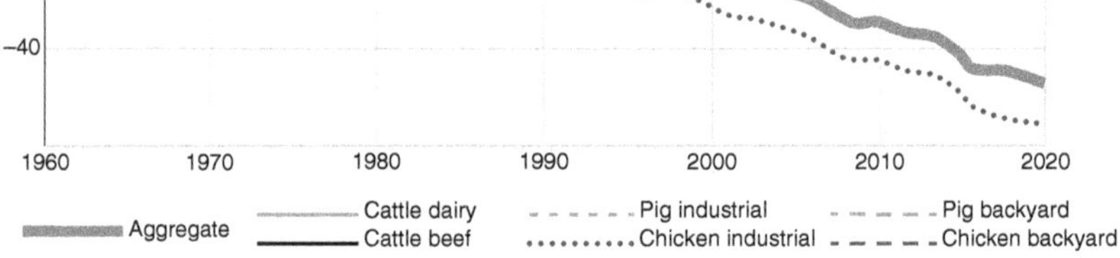

FIGURE 10.4 Global welfare of cows, pigs, and chickens over time under different farming systems.
Source: Food and Agriculture Organization of the United Nations and Espinosa and Treich (2024a)

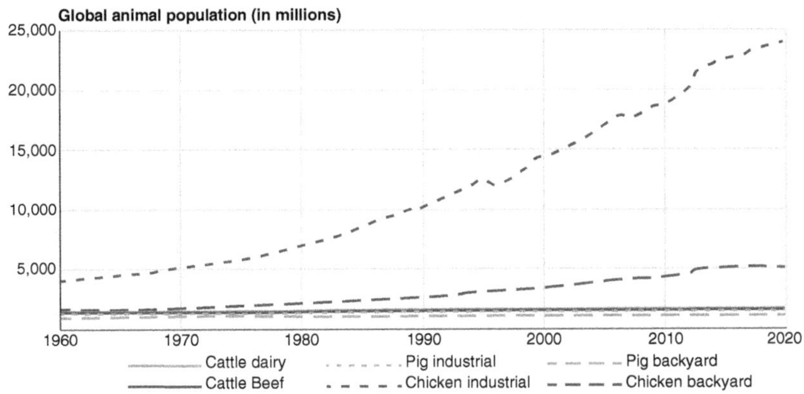

FIGURE 10.5 Global population of cows, pigs, and chickens over time under different farming systems.
Source: Food and Agriculture Organization of the United Nations and Espinosa and Treich (2024a)

Organization of the United Nations; see Figure 10.5. In particular, the data about the shares associated with different farming systems for each animal species (i.e., industrial versus backyard chickens and pigs, and dairy versus beef cows) are taken from the GLEAM dashboard for the year 2015 (https://foodandagricultureorganization.shinyapps.io/GLEAMV3_Public/).

Building on the master formula (10.1), total welfare of a given species in a given year is equal to the population of that species (at any point during a given year) multiplied by the utility potential multiplied by the species' average welfare score over their lifetimes.

The specific numbers used are detailed in Table 10.2. For the animal welfare scores, we use the method proposed by Espinosa and Treich (2024a, see previous section), with $W_0 = 10$. We also estimate the number of freedom violations for each category of animals based on Espinosa and Treich (2024a) as well as scientific articles for backyard production systems. As usual, we aim to be conservative and probably overestimate the level of animal welfare. For instance, the average welfare of dairy cows is estimated to be close to zero, as is the case in France (see previous section). This may be an optimistic view,

Table 10.2 *Data used for Figures 10.4 and 1.1*

Species	Farming conditions	Lifespan in days	Lifetime welfare	Average daily welfare	Share (%)	Utility potential
Chickens	Intensive	40	-24.2	-0.605	54	0.003
Chickens	Backyard	81	-1.6	-0.020	16	0.003
Chickens	Hens	720	-432.2	-0.600	30	0.003
Cows	For dairy	1,825	-1.6	0.001	47	0.032
Cows	For beef	730	435.3	0.596	53	0.032
Pigs	Intensive	150	-75.6	-0.504	77	0.022
Pigs	Backyard	300	28.2	0.094	23	0.022

as dairy cows in France are often raised more extensively, likely resulting in better welfare compared to dairy cows worldwide. Since China and Brazil emerged as major producers of meat recently, keeping the same (current French) animal welfare score is likely to overestimate animal welfare. Developing countries face challenges in the adoption of intensive animal production (different climate/temperate zones that typical high-production breeds are not adapted to withstand, lack of infrastructure between farms and slaughterhouses, and lack of monitoring…), which impact animal welfare negatively, and which is not reflected if the same welfare score is used for all time periods (Von Keyserlingk and Hötzel 2015).

For utility potentials, we use the same values as in the previous application (see also Table 5.1). Due to a lack of detailed historical data, the shares of the farming systems are assumed to be constant over time, corresponding to the proportions observed in 2015. This assumption might lead to an underestimation of animal welfare levels prior to 2015, as the prevalence of less intensive farming methods was likely higher in the past. Conversely, it could also underestimate the rate at which animal welfare conditions have deteriorated, given the expansion of industrial farming practices in the last decades. Note that the units of Figure 10.4 are utility levels, as explained before. But since the animal populations are in the millions or billions in case of the chickens, "total welfare" is divided by a million, to make the scaling of the y-axis more visually appealing.

As shown in Figure 10.4, animal welfare trends vary significantly across and within animal species. While the welfare of pigs raised under intensive conditions has been decreasing, the welfare of suckler cows has remained significantly positive and is increasing. However, the welfare of chickens in intensive farming has decreased drastically due to their much larger and rapidly increasing population. In absolute terms, the negative welfare of chickens surpasses that of cows, even though cows have ten times the utility potential of chickens. In 1961, there were four times as many chickens as cattle, whereas by 2022, there were seventeen times as many chickens as cattle. This dramatic increase in the chicken population explains why the total welfare of chickens largely dominates all other trends and drives the aggregate animal welfare as we have seen in Figure 1.1. Before the chicken population surged, the positive welfare of cows almost balanced the negative welfare of pigs and chickens. Population effects have shifted this balance, resulting in an overall sharp decrease in animal welfare.

10.3.3 Application 3: Project Isabela

Project Isabela was a large-scale conservation initiative launched in 1997 aimed at eradicating invasive species, particularly feral cattle, from the Galápagos Islands to restore and protect the unique ecosystems of the archipelago. This initiative was primarily motivated by the preservation of giant tortoises, which suffered significantly from habitat degradation (Márquez et al. 2013). Project Isabela is considered one of the largest and most successful eradication efforts globally and serves as a model for similar conservation projects, demonstrating the feasibility and importance of removing invasive species to protect and restore natural ecosystems.

However, the motivation here is that discussions about eradication policies usually overlook the cost in terms of animal welfare. This holds true for Project Isabela, but this holds true almost universally, such as for conservation projects that have led to rodent eradication operations on hundreds of islands across the world (Amos et al. 2016). As I will show, integrating animal welfare considerations into the evaluation of a "successful" program such as Project Isabela would present a different perspective, highlighting the ethical complexities and potential tradeoffs involved in conservation efforts.

Overall, Project Isabela has removed more than 140,000 goats for a cost of US$10.5 million (Carrion et al. 2011). Various eradication methods were employed, including aerial hunting using helicopters, ground hunting, and the use of specially trained dogs to locate goats. Radio-collared "Judas goats" were also used to locate the remaining goat populations, as these goats would lead hunters to other goats. It is also estimated that more than 18,000 pigs and 1,000 donkeys were eradicated (Donlan et al. 2011). Let me now apply the method described in the previous section to provide an initial estimate of the cost of Project Isabela in terms of animal welfare. As before, this is a very rough estimation intended only to provide an application of the method and a general sense of scale. Therefore, this exercise is purely illustrative and has very limited scientific value.

In the wild, I estimate conservatively that goats, pigs, and donkeys have life expectancies of at least 12, 8, and 20 years, respectively. Therefore, I estimate that killing a goat, pig, or donkey reduces their life expectancies by approximately 6, 4, and 10 years, on average. These invasive populations thrived on the islands due to abundant food and the absence of natural predators, leading me to assume their animal welfare scores were at a maximum level, equal to one. Critically, it is important to note that this perspective is somewhat "static," as it overlooks potential changes in population dynamics over time and the risks of reduced welfare and starvation as populations approach their carrying capacity in the long term.

The calculation of the animal welfare costs may be presented as follows. The loss of one day of life of a goat is equal to the loss of one day of life of a human (about 400 euros, see earlier in this section), multiplied by the utility potential of goats (0.02), namely 8 euros.

Table 10.3 *Data used for calculating the animal welfare cost of Project Isabela*

Animals	Number of individuals killed	Average life expectancy loss in years	Animal welfare score	Utility potential	Average utility loss in euros	Cost per species in million euros
Goats	140,000	6	1	0.020	17,520	2,452.8
Pigs	18,000	4	1	0.022	12,848	231.2
Donkeys	1,000	10	1	0.032	46,720	46.7

Multiplying this figure by the number of days lost on average due to the eradication policy (6 multiplied by 365, or 2,190 days) gives an average money-equivalent utility loss per goat equal to 17,520 euros. Multiplying this figure again by the numbers of goats killed (140,000), I arrive at a figure of 2.452 billion euros for the cost associated with the eradication of goats. This corresponds to the total sentience premium of the eradication policy of goats, as described in Chapter 7. The calculation proceeds similarly for pigs and donkeys. For further details, including utility potentials and additional data, see Table 10.3.

Overall, Project Isabela had a short-term estimated animal welfare cost of more than 2.7 billion euros. Once again, this initial (and admittedly, very exploratory) calculation shows that animal welfare impacts far surpass any other considerations such as the project's financial costs by several orders of magnitude. Let me emphasize again that Project Isabela has certainly contributed to the flourishing of other species, including the iconic Galápagos tortoises. Ideally, the welfare impacts on these other species should also be weighed alongside the benefits to humans in terms of (e.g.) increased touristic activities. However, considering the estimated multi-billion-euro costs of the eradication policy, it remains to be demonstrated that the project was truly successful in terms of what I believe should matter morally: the welfare of all sentient species involved, including humans, tortoises, and … goats.

REFERENCES

Adler M. D (2019) *Measuring Social Welfare*. Oxford University Press.

Amos W, Nichols HJ, Churchyard T, Brooke MDL (2016) Rat eradication comes within a whisker! A case study of a failed project from the South Pacific. *Royal Society Open Science*, 3(4), 160110.

Animal Ask (2024) Modeling the outcomes of animal welfare interventions: One possible approach to the trade-offs between subjective experiences. www.animalask.org/post/modelling-the-outcomes-of-animal-welfare-interventions-one-possible-approach-to-the-trade-offs-betw.

Baumstark L, Dervaux B, Treich N (2013) Eléments pour une révision de la valeur statistique de la vie humaine (No. halshs-00958423).

Budolfson M, Espinosa R, Fischer B, Treich N (2024) Monetizing animal welfare impacts for benefit–cost analysis. *Journal of Benefit-Cost Analysis*, 15(S1), 1–18.

Budolfson M, Spears D (2019) Quantifying animal well-being and overcoming the challenge of interspecies comparisons. In *The Routledge Handbook of Animal Ethics*, ed. B Fischer, 92–101. Routledge.

Carrion V, Donlan CJ, Campbell KJ, Lavoie C, Cruz F (2011) Archipelago-wide island restoration in the Galápagos Islands: Reducing costs of invasive mammal eradication programs and reinvasion risk. *PloS One*, 6(5), e18835.

Donlan JC, Carrion V, Campbell KJ, Lavoie C, Cruz F (2011). Biodiversity conservation in the Galapagos Islands, Ecuador: Experiences, lessons learned, and policy implications. Biodiversity conservation in the Americas: Lessons and Policy Recommendations, 221–240.

Espinosa R (2024) Animals and social welfare. *Social Choice and Welfare*, 62(3), 465–504.

Espinosa R, Browning H, Treich N (2025) Animal quality-adjusted life year - AQALY, mimeo.

Espinosa R, Treich N (2024a) The animal welfare levy. *Journal of the European Economic Association*, in press.

Espinosa R, Treich N (2024b) Beyond anthropocentrism in agricultural and resource economics. *Australian Journal of Agricultural and Resource Economics*, 68(3), 541–566.

Fryxell, L (2024) XU, mimeo.

Kahneman D, Wakker PP, Sarin R (1997) Back to Bentham? Explorations of experienced utility. *The Quarterly Journal of Economics*, 112(2), 375–406.

Kuruc K, McFadden J. (2023a) Monetizing the externalities of animal agriculture: Insights from an inclusive welfare function. *Social Choice and Welfare*, 1–24.

Kuruc K, McFadden J (2023b) Animal welfare in economic analyses of food production. *Nature Food*, 4(5), 355–356.

Márquez C, Gibbs JP, Carrión V, Naranjo S, Llerena A (2013) Population response of giant Galápagos tortoises to feral goat removal. *Restoration Ecology*, 21(2), 181–185.

Mathur MB (2022) Ethical drawbacks of sustainable meat choices. *Science*, 375(6587), 1362–1362.

Téhard B, Detournay B, Borget I, Roze S, De Pouvourville G (2020) Value of a QALY for France: A new approach to propose acceptable reference values. *Value in Health*, 23(8), 985–993.

Von Keyserlingk MA, Hötzel MJ (2015) The ticking clock: Addressing farm animal welfare in emerging countries. *Journal of Agricultural and Environmental Ethics*, *28*, 179–195.

Wong K (2016) Counting animals: On effective altruism and the prospect of interspecies commensurability (Doctoral dissertation, PhD thesis, Princeton University).

WSPA (World Society for the Protection of Animals) (2003) Concepts in animal welfare. An animal welfare syllabus [CD ROM format]. University of Bristol and WSPA.

PART III The Indirect Approach

As explained in the introductory chapter, the indirect (anthropocentric) approach is about studying the proanimal concerns of citizens or consumers, and exploring the implications of these concerns for individual, collective, policy, and political decision-making. This part mostly concerns the fields of behavioral economics and psychology, and to some extent political economy. I first present various empirical studies about proanimal concerns including survey and WTP studies (Chapter 11), before briefly summarizing the literature in behavioral sciences about the relations between humans and animals, anthropomorphism as well as the meat paradox (Chapter 12).

I then adapt the canonical model introduced in Part II to present economic models on animal welfare as a public good, merit good, the meat paradox, and decision-making related to pets (Chapters 13–15). Lastly, I discuss broader market-related issues such as the morality of markets and corporate social responsibility (Chapter 16), along with additional explorations, particularly regarding social, informational, and political aspects (Chapter 17). The final chapter offers a brief conclusion for the book by outlining some overlooked topics (Chapter 18).

Overall, this part is strongly behavioral in the sense that it hinges on the nature of the behavioral assumptions describing how humans care about animals. While the initial chapters in this part present various empirical results in economics and other fields, chapters 13 to 15 are theoretical and follow fairly standard economic theory. In those chapters, along with the presentation of the technicalities, I try to discuss the main hypotheses and results in simple terms. The last chapters discuss informally more exploratory topics that build on the existing literature developed in specific fields in economics such as behavioral, environmental, or agricultural economics.

11 Proanimal Concerns

Empirical Studies

11.1 SURVEY STUDIES

There is an important recognition among the general public that the welfare of animals matters and should be considered in policymaking. This recognition is documented in multiple surveys developed over the years in various countries. For instance, a large majority of Europeans (91 percent) agree that it is important to protect the welfare of farmed animals, and 84 percent agree that the welfare of farmed animals should be better protected (Eurobarometer 2023, see Figure 11.1).

Similar results are observed in the United States. According to the Faunalytics animal tracker survey, the public support for the overarching goal of the animal protection movement ("to minimize and eventually eliminate all forms of animal cruelty and suffering") was quite strong in 2019, at 68 percent for adults. However, the survey also revealed that most individuals do not feel knowledgeable about issues impacting animal welfare, except when it comes to pets. According to a 2018 Gallup survey, the percentage of United States

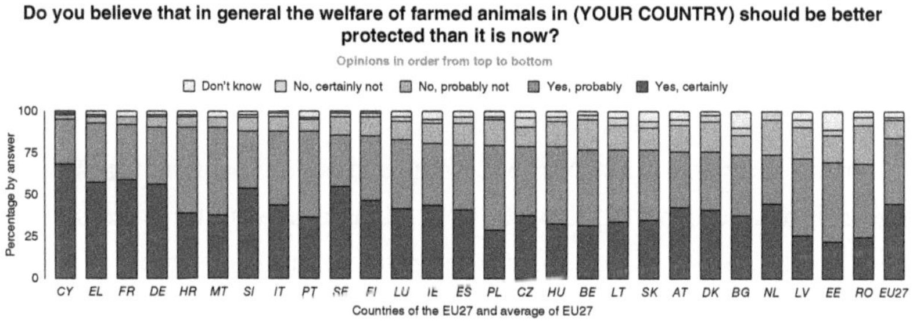

FIGURE 11.1 European attitudes toward animal welfare protection. Source: Eurobarometer (2023)

citizens who support the idea that animals' rights should be equal to those of humans increased across all major demographic groups. Women remain more likely to support this view than men, but there is little difference between younger and older Americans. Democrats are also more supportive of this view than republicans.

Ladak and Anthis (2022) examined the views of approximately 1,500 adults in the United States on the animal agriculture industry. A notable finding is that a significant majority of respondents (74.6 percent) express discomfort with the current state of the industry, indicating a widespread concern about its practices. The study also identifies surprisingly strong support for seemingly radical policy changes aimed at improving animal welfare. Nearly half of the participants (49.1 percent) favor the idea of banning slaughterhouses, while over half (52.7 percent) support the cessation of factory farming. Impressively, a substantial portion (38.8 percent) advocate for the elimination of animal farming altogether, showcasing a growing interest in alternative approaches to food production.

Should we trust this data based on hypothetical survey studies? To reflect on this question, it is useful to compare survey data with voting outcomes. In November 2024, Berkeley, California, became the first United States city to ban factory farming through Measure DD, a citizen-initiated ballot measure. However, survey data generally appears to be at odds with other voting outcomes: Denver's initiative to ban slaughterhouses received only 36 percent support, while Sonoma County's attempt to ban factory farming garnered just 15 percent. Switzerland, a leading country in animal welfare, also had a failed ballot initiative for banning factory farming in 2022. Overall, votes highlight the varying regional perspectives on animal farming practices, with some areas advocating for stricter regulations and others opting to uphold current standards. In survey studies, the West North Central region, commonly known as the nation's "Agricultural Heartland," displays the least opposition to animal farming, suggesting that economic and political aspects play an important role in shaping attitudes toward animal farming.

How much do people actually know about animal farming practices? In a discussion about the California egg paradox, Norwood and Lusk (2011) point out that while the average consumer believes only 37 percent of eggs sold in grocery stores come from caged production systems, the actual figure is closer to 80–90 percent. This suggests an overall underestimation of animal suffering by the public. Bryant and colleagues surveyed a representative sample of 1,000 Brits to study what they think of common practices involved in farming cows, chickens, and pigs. As shown on Figure 11.2, the vast majority of the British public find common animal farming practices to be unacceptable. These results raise questions about how knowledgeable people are about common practices in the animal farming industry.

Sinclair et al. (2022) survey thousands of members of the general public on their perceptions of animals and animal welfare across fourteen geographically and culturally diverse countries, including China and India. Most participants across all countries agree that the welfare of both farmed animals and companion animals is important to them. There is also a notable agreement on the significance of laws safeguarding animal welfare. Remarkably, a substantial majority of respondents acknowledge that both chickens and fish can experience pain, indicating a growing awareness of animal sentience across the surveyed nations. In some countries, the welfare of dogs is considered more important than human welfare, and in others (predominantly Muslim nations) it is considered of minimal importance. A compelling conclusion drawn from the research is that the perception of animal welfare as a significant concern is not solely confined to highly developed nations. The authors propose that a key explanation for these varying perspectives is proximity and exposure to animals.

Sinclair and Philipps (2017) explore the connections between the importance of global social issues and attitudes toward animal protection. Their study surveys over 3,000 university students from 11 Eurasian countries, examining views on 13 global issues, including animal protection, environmental conservation, sustainable development, racial equality, women's rights, LGBT equality, human euthanasia, and

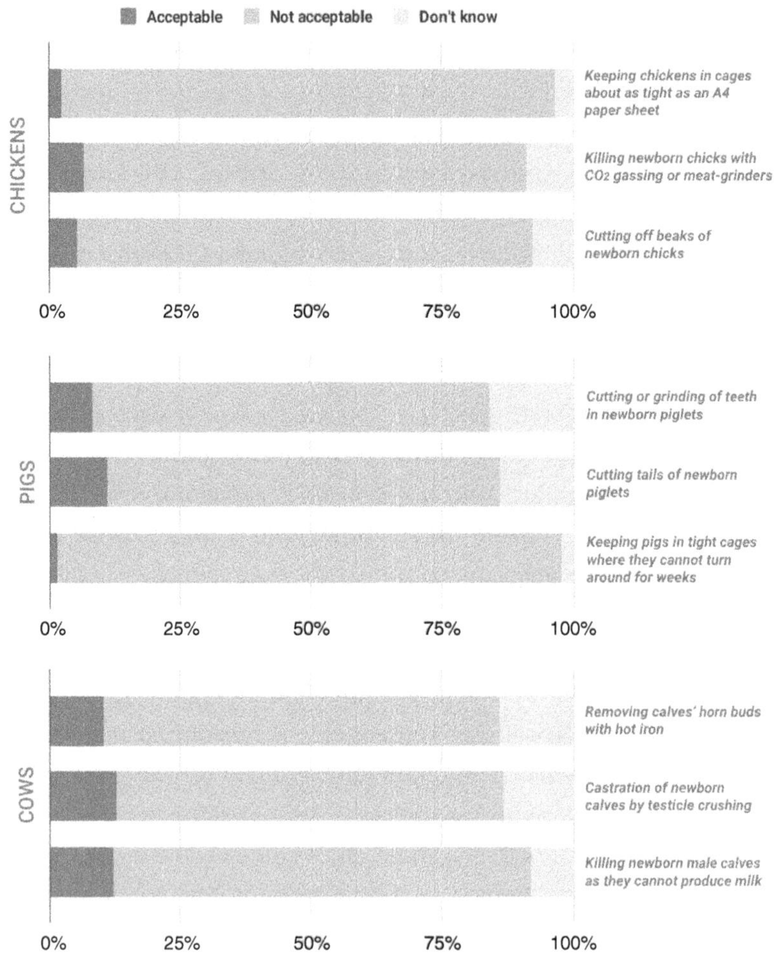

FIGURE 11.2 Acceptability of common farming practices in the United Kingdom.
Source: Data collected by Bryant Research Ltd in July 2022

capital punishment. They find that environmental protection received the highest importance rating across the countries, followed closely by sustainable development and then animal protection – a grouping they refer to as the "nature trifecta." Additionally, the study reveals that the perceived importance of each issue varied more significantly between countries than across other demographic factors.

11.2 WTP STUDIES

In the economics literature, most of the literature about animal welfare consists of WTP studies. There actually exists quite a number of WTP studies on animal welfare. Let me start by presenting two meta-analyses about farmed animals' welfare. First, Lagerkvist and Hess (2011) examine 24 studies reporting 106 estimates of consumers' WTP for animal welfare. They consider four criteria for capturing animal welfare: good feeding, good housing, good health, and appropriate behavior. They emphasize a large amount of heterogeneity in WTP. Consumers' income and age as well as information provision significantly affect WTP. Second, Clark et al. (2017) examine fifty-four studies with a focus on production diseases that arise in intensive systems. They find that WTP estimates are usually quite small. Sociodemographic characteristics account for the largest amount of variation within the data. WTP decreases with age, increases with income, and is higher for females. WTP for laying hens, broiler chickens, and pigs are not significantly different from one another. For more information about individual WTP studies, see Norwood and Lusk (2011, chapter 9 appendix) where more than thirty WTP studies are presented.

An important limitation of most WTP studies is that they are hypothetical. Participants express their WTP for certain goods or services, but they do not have to actually pay or purchase the items they claim they are willing to pay for. As a result, the answers may not be thoughtful and truthful. There has been a longstanding concern about the existence of a hypothetical bias in survey studies (Loomis 2011), which suggests that reported WTP values tend to be higher than what people would actually pay in real buying decisions. The discrepancy between hypothetical results and real buying decisions can be attributed, at least in part, to the fact that it is easier for individuals to state that they care about a particular cause, such as animal welfare, when there are no actual costs or consequences involved. In hypothetical situations, people might feel inclined to express higher values for WTP, as there are no immediate financial implications or obligations.

Lusk and Norwood (2012) provide an early example of a non-hypothetical WTP study on animal welfare. In their study, subjects (N = 288) received about $75 for participation. They were shown two farm systems that differed systematically by a number of attributes related to animal well-being (e.g., space, group sizes). They could pay real money for moving animals from one production system to another. The study uses the familiar Becker–DeGroot–Marschak (BDM) mechanism, which provides incentives (under minimum rationality conditions) for participants to submit bids equal to their maximum WTP. The authors find that the average WTP is equal to $57 for moving 1,000 hens to a free-range system (resp. $23 for 1,000 pigs). This represents a very high WTP, incommensurable with market data. Note that the study finds however small median WTP values, about $1–$2, and 1/3 of WTP equal to zero. This emphasizes, again, a wide heterogeneity among subjects indicating that the "the average value of animal welfare is profoundly impacted by a few unique individuals." Interestingly, the authors vary the number of animals that can be affected by subjects' decisions. Although the average total WTP is increasing in the number of animals, the per-animal WTP declined as the number of animals affected increased significantly, indicating scope insensitivity.

Albrecht et al. (2017) also elicit concerns for animal welfare using a non-hypothetical setup. They use an incentivized environment to elicit subjects' WTP for transferring a hen to an environment that is better suited to its needs. They also find substantial heterogeneity: While 37 percent of subjects have a WTP of 25 Euros (the highest possible amount), 15 percent are not willing to pay anything. Most interestingly, the authors compare these WTP values with morally relevant dispositions in subjects, relying on well-established measures such as the Big 5 personality test (neuroticism, extraversion, openness to experience, agreeableness, and conscientiousness). The data confirm a strong, positive relation between WTP for animal welfare and moral dispositions. In a related study, Frey and

Pirscher (2018) find that different moral attitudes lead to different WTP for animal welfare improvement.

Lai et al. (2022) study the social desirability bias, which refers to the tendency of survey participants to provide responses that align with what they believe others would view favorably. This can create the incentive to portray a socially desirable image, rather than revealing "true" preferences. The social desirability bias can lead to inflated or skewed responses, particularly in sensitive topics where respondents may feel pressured to provide socially acceptable answers. For many people, the treatment of farm animals is indeed a sensitive issue with strong ethical implications. Animal welfare is thus potentially subject to that bias, which may lead to inflated WTP values for animal welfare improvement. To investigate this bias, Lai and coauthors employ a technique that allows survey participants to indicate the overall distribution of responses while maintaining anonymity regarding their actual responses. The findings of their study support the presence of social desirability bias, indicating that public support for animal welfare issues may have been consistently overestimated when assessed using conventional survey formats. More generally, this emphasizes the importance of social image in issues related to proanimal concerns.

There also exists a small amount of literature in environmental economics about WTP for wild animals. As far as I am aware, all of this literature is concerned with species' preservation. Hence it focuses on the quantity rather than quality of animal lives. Using the WTP approach, Pearce (1993) estimates a shadow price value for various species such as the bald eagle, the grizzly bear, or the blue whale. A key finding in this research is the prevalence of a strong preference for certain charismatic species, which has been revealed through meta-analyses of WTP studies for individual species (Metrick and Weitzman 1996, Loomis and White 1996, Moore et al. 2022). Albert et al. (2018) gathered data from various sources to identify the twenty most charismatic animal species. The majority are large, exotic, terrestrial mammals, with the top five being the tiger, lion, elephant, giraffe, and panther.

Charismatic species are those that possess immediate recognition and can be easily identified by name. These species often evoke emotional connections and garner widespread public support for their conservation efforts. Note however that this generates a sort of paradox since most charismatic animals nevertheless remain at high risk of extinction. Courchamp et al. (2018) argue that this may be attributed to these species being consistently featured in product marketing, potentially fostering an illusion of abundance that mitigates effective conservation efforts. The affinity toward charismatic species is often linked to their association with specific geographic locations or habitats, such as the African savannahs, Indian forests, or Chinese bamboo forests. Besides, there is also evidence that one or a few individuals within a species (e.g., Cecil the Lion, Fungie the Dolphin, Otis the Brown Bear) are orders of magnitude more valuable than the average animal in their respective species (Costello et al. 2023).

It is often argued that the preference for charismatic or emblematic species in conservation is problematic. For example, Clark and May (2002) highlight the disproportionate focus on vertebrates, especially mammals and birds, over invertebrates, plants, and lesser-known taxa. This bias in research can skew resource allocation, potentially overlooking species vital to ecosystems. While broadening conservation efforts is necessary, it is also worth noting that this preference may reflect genuine public concern for the life and welfare of some animals and possibly a sort of "sentience premium." Hence, this preference may capture a valid welfare aspect and need not be seen only as a drawback. In simple terms, when animal welfare enters the picture and conservation priorities must be set, it may make sense to focus on the protection of mammals and birds rather than insects or plants.

A notable study conducted by Kontoleon and Swanson (2003) examines the WTP of OECD citizens for the conservation of the Giant Panda. The study reveals that a significant portion of the

WTP can be attributed to the perceived "naturalness" of the species. This suggests that the symbolic nature of the panda, along with its unique attributes, serves as a potential instrument for motivating greater biodiversity conservation efforts. Beyond the specific case of the Giant Panda, the results show that people's motivations for animal conservation are multifaceted and diverse. People may value animals both as individuals and as species, and their preferences might extend to preserving entire populations or preventing species extinction. Additionally, people may recognize and appreciate ancillary benefits associated with the conservation of specific species, such as the positive impact on ecosystems and other environmental factors.

A casual observation is that environmental NGOs often use images of individual animals in need of assistance in their campaigns. This practice suggests that people do indeed care, to some extent, about the welfare of individual animals. The emotional appeal of these individual stories can resonate with the public, driving greater support and engagement in conservation initiatives. Consider for instance the case of Italy, where authorities attempted to eliminate a population of non-native squirrels. However, legal actions taken by animal advocacy organizations delayed the program long enough for the species to become too entrenched for eradication to remain feasible (Fraser 2010). Many citizens harbor concerns for both environmental conservation and animal welfare, often intertwining their passions for these important causes. This can be a strong political issue, as exemplified by the case of brumbies in Australia where conflict has been escalating over the years.

Regarding pets, Carlson et al. (2019) estimate through a survey study in the United States the human WTP for a reduction in the mortality risk for dogs. Following the standard approach in the economics literature, this allows them to calculate the value of statistical dog life (VSDL). Specifically, respondents were asked about their hypothetical WTP for a vaccine that would mitigate the risk of canine influenza. Based on their analysis and underlying assumptions, they arrive at a VSDL of about $10,000. Comparing this VSDL estimate to the value of statistical life (VSL) for humans, which is approximately $10 million in the United States, suggests a ratio of 1 to 1,000 between humans and dogs in terms of the perceived societal benefit of preventing their respective mortality risks.

The VSDL could potentially inform benefit-cost analyses related to policies aimed at reducing mortality risks for dogs, such as regulations on pet food or pet toys, as well as chemical regulations that have posed fatal risks to pets. For instance, if a policy is projected to save 100 dogs, the total benefit would amount to $1 million (i.e., 100 times $10,000), a figure that can be compared to the cost of the policy. The VSDL could also be used to determine compensation for the wrongful death of a pet. It is actually important to note that the estimated VSDL is orders of magnitude higher than the "replacement value" typically derived from the market for typical breed dogs. This disparity between the VSDL and the market value for acquiring new dogs sheds light on the monetary-equivalent value of the emotional bond that owners share with their dogs. It gives insights about the need to adjust the legal system of penalties for the wrongful death of a pet so that pets are not solely considered as purely replaceable properties.

Another important dimension of WTP is the willingness to donate. Donations play a pivotal role in animal advocacy, necessitating an understanding of their determinants. However, it is important to put things in perspective. Despite their significance, total donation amounts pale in comparison to other expenditures impacting animals. It remains uncertain whether the public significantly and effectively influence outcomes through their donation choices. Lewis Bollard, in his Open Philanthropy farm animal welfare research newsletter, indicates for instance that the entire global advocacy budget for farmed animals is less than the budget of the New York Metropolitan Museum of Art (Bollard 2023). Additionally, there is a strong disparity in donation allocation: As stressed in the introduction, people donate disproportionately to shelters rather than to farmed or wild animals, despite the latter groups being orders of magnitude more numerous and facing more pressing welfare concerns on average.

Given the challenges associated with the WTP method, such as hypothetical bias and scope insensitivity (Bateman et al. 2004), Chilton et al. (2006) employ the matching method to evaluate animal welfare. This approach assesses whether respondents prefer a specific welfare improvement policy for one species (e.g., cows) over another (e.g., pigs) during the same period, without requiring monetization. Their findings reveal significant discrepancies between the matching method and WTP-based valuations. These differences raise concerns, suggesting that behavioral effects play a crucial role and warrant further investigation into elicitation methods.

11.3 THE VOTE–BUY GAP

The "vote-buy gap" describes the discrepancy between how individuals vote on animal welfare issues and how they behave as consumers in the marketplace. This concept is one of the most discussed puzzles in the economics of animal welfare. A now classic example is the "California egg paradox" mentioned in the introduction, which was popularized by Jayson Lusk, particularly through his blog and research.

In the food demand survey (FooDS), Lusk (2015) asked this question to the general population:

> In 2008, 63% of voters in California voted to ban the use of small cages for egg-laying hens. However, at the time around 90 to 95% of the eggs Californians purchased came from small cages and only 5 to 10% were cage free. So, a majority of voters voted to ban a product that a majority of shoppers routinely bought. Why do you think there is such a gap between how people voted and how they shopped for different types of eggs?

This open-ended question reveals that many consumers were unaware they were purchasing eggs from caged hens. If they had been better informed, they said that they might have made different choices – a phenomenon Lusk termed the "information hypothesis."

Paul et al. (2019) carefully explore the vote-buy gap through real incentives in a lab setting. Participants first made choices among snack options, some of which contained eggs from caged hens, and then voted on a proposition to ban snacks containing such eggs. Their findings confirm the reproducibility of the vote-buy gap: About 80 percent of individuals who initially chose snacks with caged eggs later voted to ban them. While the study provides some support for the information hypothesis, it finds limited evidence for public goods or expressive voting as contributing factors. I would like to mention though that it is very difficult to test for the effect of public goods in the lab since one can only capture the impacts associated with the subjects participating in the experiment, namely only a tiny fraction of the set of people affected by the policy.

Another hypothesis to explain the vote-buy gap is that voters and consumers may not be exactly the same people. In the real world, not all voters consume eggs; for example, vegans may vote in favor of animal welfare measures like Proposition 2, despite not purchasing eggs themselves. Note that Paul et al.'s lab experiment uniquely compared each individual's purchasing decisions with their voting behavior. This study thus also suggests that the vote-buy gap is not simply due to different people making different choices but rather reflects a possible inconsistency within individuals themselves.

A plausible explanation for the vote-buy gap is salience. The idea would be that many people genuinely care about animal welfare but fail to consider it in various decision-making situations because they do not think about it. This disconnect could help explain the discrepancy between people's shopping habits and their voting behavior. Salience, or the prominence of certain information in decision-making, might be a key factor in explaining this gap. When shopping, individuals probably focus primarily on price, with animal welfare concerns being less visible on packaging. Consequently, shoppers may not consider the living conditions of hens when buying eggs.

In contrast, during a referendum, voters are more likely to focus on animal welfare due to the explicit information provided (e.g., on the voter's information leaflet). This disparity between everyday consumer behavior and voting patterns suggests that the prominence of information can drive seemingly inconsistent decision-making across different contexts.

This explanation aligns with Bordalo et al. (2022)'s economic theory of salience, which posits that a product's valuation is determined by a weighted sum of its attributes. The "weights" assigned to these attributes vary depending on their prominence in the decision-making context. For instance, in a market setting, the weight given to price may be high, while the weight on animal welfare is low. In a voting context, however, animal welfare might become more prominent, increasing its weight and decreasing the emphasis on price. This hypothesis suggests that voters might not fully consider the economic impacts of a reform that enhances animal welfare, as their focus in the voting booth shifts toward the more salient issue of animal welfare. The salience hypothesis also supports the information hypothesis, as better information could make animal welfare more prominent in consumers' minds, thereby reducing the vote-buy gap.

However, to fully understand the vote-buy gap, it is important to consider all possible mechanisms influencing decision-making in different contexts. There are clear differences between market and voting contexts, such as how the public goods problem is perceived and the impact of social norms. In markets, transactions often involve agreements between parties, which can reduce consumers' feelings of responsibility or guilt. This diminished sense of complicity might explain why people who vote for animal welfare reforms might still buy products that conflict with those reforms. Another potential factor is the shift in preferences when individuals act as consumers versus when they act as voters, as proposed by Nyborg (2000). As citizens, individuals may prioritize the public interest, such as animal welfare, because they are considering broader societal impacts. However, as consumers, they might focus more on self-interest, making decisions driven by factors like price and convenience rather than ethical considerations. Note finally that I will formally investigate the vote-buy gap in Chapter 13.

11.4 THE ORIGIN OF PROANIMAL CONCERNS

Animal welfare can be conceptualized as a public good, allowing us to leverage the extensive economic literature on prosocial behavior in public good scenarios to gain deeper insights into proanimal concerns. In doing so, we might naturally consider factors such as warm glow, self- and social image, which have been shown to play a major role in such contexts. However, a pivotal question arises: Can we simply apply these conventional notions to proanimal concerns, or is there something distinctive about them that sets them apart from more general prosocial considerations? At this point, this is largely an open question.

But this raises an even more basic question: Why would we care about animals in the first place? Interestingly, the evolutionary origin of proanimal concern is not clear. There is essentially no specific research about this aspect. Concerns for animal welfare present a puzzle from an evolutionary standpoint. As emphasized in Chapter 2, humans have historically benefited from exploiting animals for food, transport, labor, and other resources, often with little immediate benefit from treating them well. Hence, from a purely evolutionary perspective, it might even seem counterproductive to avoid exploiting animals or to invest resources in the welfare of animals, especially when they cannot later reciprocate such kindness. This paradox raises a fundamental question: Where do concerns for animal welfare come from?

One hypothesis is a sort of misapplied kinship theory, which suggests that humans have evolved to develop a sense of kinship toward certain animals due to their physical, behavioral, or cognitive similarities to humans (Batt 2009). This hypothesis suggests that preferences that evolved to be adaptive in specific contexts might sometimes be expressed in contexts where their original function is absent, a phenomenon sometimes coined "spillover" (Hoffman and Yoeli 2022). This seems consistent with an anthropomorphism bias that I will discuss in the next chapter: Species exhibiting physical, behavioral, or cognitive similarities, essentially species that are closer to us from an evolutionary perspective, evoke more positive emotions, such as greater compassion (Miralles et al. 2019). This may explain why people tend to favor certain animals, such as mammals, or those with baby faces (e.g., pandas) for instance. A simple explanation is that juvenile features may trigger instinctive nurturing behavior (Borgi and Cirulli 2016).

Another hypothesis for why humans care about animals is rooted in our evolutionary history of cooperation with certain species, such as dogs, cats, and horses. This cooperation has fostered a sense of empathy toward these animals, which benefits us through stronger bonds, better recognition of animal needs, and symbiotic activities like hunting (Phillips 2009). Moreover, humans may feel a sense of responsibility toward animals they have domesticated or interact with regularly, reinforcing this empathy. The concept of spillover may also play a role here. Humans have evolved to show concern for others, such as friends or romantic partners, where reciprocation of kindness and cooperation is expected. This concern can spill over into contexts where reciprocation is not possible, extending our empathy and protective instincts to animals that cannot directly return the favor. This spillover effect might explain why humans often extend their social and emotional responses to nonhuman animals, driven by the same mechanisms that foster human social bonds.

An informative starting point is to explore how empathy toward humans correlates with empathy toward animals. In an early study, Paul (2000) reports a significant but modest link between empathy for humans and empathy for animals based on self-reported measures of empathy. However, this research faces the difficulty of properly measuring empathy. Conversely, there is a lot of evidence on the link between inter-human and human–animal violence (Lockwood 1999, Ascione 2005). This suggests that a lack of empathy demonstrated by some individuals is a general deficit not simply restricted to its expression toward other human beings.

Human beings typically exhibit a tendency to identify with and attribute mental states to their conspecifics. These cognitive abilities are underpinned by the coordinated activity of several brain regions, with many of these areas engaged in processing emotions. Emotions play a crucial role in fostering social understanding, potentially serving as a cornerstone for the development of empathy and prosocial concerns. However, the bulk of previous research characterizing empathy-related responses have not distinctively delineated empathy toward humans or animals.

Interestingly, Westbury and Neumann (2008) exposed 73 participants to film stimuli featuring humans, primates, quadruped mammals, and birds in distressing situations. The findings validate the influence of phylogenetic similarity on both subjective self-report and psychophysiological indicators of empathy-related responses. Filippi et al. (2010) compared brain imaging data from 20 omnivore subjects, 19 vegetarians, and 21 vegans to investigate how the brain responds to conditions of suffering involving humans or animals among individuals with varying dietary habits. The findings of this study suggest that empathy may be represented differently in the neural activity of individuals with different feeding habits, potentially reflecting distinct motivational factors and beliefs. The main finding is the "demonstration of a common functional architecture of emotional processing in vegetarians and vegans."

Going back to the behavioral literature in economics (Bursztyn and Jensen 2017), it seems also important to better understand the role that self-image and social image concerns play in shaping behavior toward animals. Using an information experiment, Mechtenberg et al. (2024) suggest that people may vote in favor of animal welfare in order to boost their self-image. Also, people may be motivated to engage in behavior that is seen as socially desirable, such as purchasing animal-friendly products or donating to animal welfare organizations, in order to (consciously or unconsciously) signal their identity or values to others. This can sometimes lead to what is known as virtue signaling, a term used to describe the act of expressing a moral or ethical stance in order to enhance one's social image or reputation, rather than out of genuine concern for the cause. While proanimal actions may still have a positive impact, the desire to make actions that generate social rewards may reduce effectiveness in the actions in favor of animals (Burum et al. 2020).

In addition, social norms can play a pivotal role here, especially when it comes to behaviors like food choices, which are usually observable and tend to be intertwined with strong cultural effects (Nyborg et al. 2016, Dannenberg and Weingärtner 2023). I will come back to this issue in the Chapter 17. In sum, despite a few interesting recent contributions, the literature on proanimal concerns still remains very scarce.

REFERENCES

Albert C, Luque GM, Courchamp F (2018) The twenty most charismatic species. *PloS One*, 13(7), e0199149.

Albrecht K, Krämer F, Szech N (2017) Animal welfare and human ethics: A personality study, mimeo.

Ascione FR (2005) *Children and Animals: Exploring the Roots of Kindness and Cruelty*. Purdue University Press.

Bateman IJ, Cole M, Cooper P et al. (2004) On visible choice sets and scope sensitivity. *Journal of Environmental Economics and Management*, 47(1), 71–93.

Batt S (2009) Human attitudes towards animals in relation to species similarity to humans: A multivariate approach. *Bioscience Horizons*, 2(2), 180–190.

Bollard L (2023) A year of wins for farmed animals. Open Philanthropy farm animal welfare research newsletter.

Bordalo P, Gennaioli N, Shleifer A (2022) Salience. *Annual Review of Economics*, 14(1), 521–544.

Borgi M, Cirulli F (2016) Pet face: Mechanisms underlying human-animal relationships. *Frontiers in Psychology*, 7, 298.

Bursztyn L, Jensen R (2017) Social image and economic behavior in the field: Identifying, understanding, and shaping social pressure. *Annual Review of Economics*, 9(1), 131–153.

Burum B, Nowak MA, Hoffman M (2020) An evolutionary explanation for ineffective altruism. *Nature Human Behavior*, 4, 1245–1257.

Carlson D, Haeder S, Jenkins-Smith H et al. (2019) Monetizing bowser: A contingent valuation of the statistical value of dog life. *Journal of Benefit-Cost Analysis*, 11(1), 131–149.

Chilton SM, Burgess D, Hutchinson WG (2006) The relative value of farm animal welfare. *Ecological Economics*, 59(3), 353–363.

Clark B, Stewart GB, Panzone LA, Kyriazakis I, Frewer LJ (2017) Citizens, consumers and farm animal welfare: A meta-analysis of willingness-to-pay studies. *Food Policy*, 68, 112–127.

Clark JA, May RM (2002) Taxonomic bias in conservation research. *Science*, 297(5579), 191–192.

Costello C, Lewis L, Lynham J, Richardson L (2023) The charisma premium: Iconic individuals and wildlife values. *Journal of Environmental Economics and Management*, 122, 102872.

Courchamp F, Jaric I, Albert C et al. (2018) The paradoxical extinction of the most charismatic animals. *PLoS Biology*, 16(4), e2003997.

Dannenberg A, Weingärtner E (2023) The effects of observability and an information nudge on food choice. *Journal of Environmental Economics and Management*, 120, 102829.

Eurobarometer (2023) Attitudes of Europeans towards animal welfare. https://europa.eu/eurobarometer/surveys/detail/2996.

Filippi M, Riccitelli G, Falini A et al. (2010) The brain functional networks associated to human and animal suffering differ among omnivores, vegetarians and vegans. *PloS One*, 5(5), e10847.

Fraser D (2010) Toward a synthesis of conservation and animal welfare science. *Animal Welfare*, 19, 121–124.

Frey UJ, Pirscher F (2018) Willingness to pay and moral stance: The case of farm animal welfare in Germany. *PloS One*, 13(8), e0202193.

Hoffman M, Yoeli E (2022) *Hidden Games: The Surprising Power of Game Theory to Explain Irrational Human Behaviour*. Hachette UK.

Kontoleon A, Swanson T (2003) The willingness to pay for property rights for the giant panda: Can a charismatic species be an instrument for nature conservation? *Land Economics*, 79(4), 483–499.

Ladak A, Anthis JR (2022) Animals, Food, and Technology (AFT) Survey: 2021. www.sentienceinstitute.org/aft-survey-2021.

Lagerkvist CJ, Hess S (2011) A meta-analysis of consumer willingness to pay for farm animal welfare. *European Review of Agricultural Economics*, 38 (1), 55–78.

Lai Y, Boaitey A, Minegishi K (2022) Behind the veil: Social desirability bias and animal welfare ballot initiatives. *Food Policy*, 106, 102184.

Lockwood R (1999) Animal cruelty and violence against humans: Making the connection. *Animal Law*, 5, 81.

Loomis JB (2011) What's to know about hypothetical bias in stated preference valuation studies? *Journal of Economic Surveys*, 25, 363–370.

Loomis JB, White DS (1996) Economic benefits of rare and endangered species: summary and meta-analysis. *Ecological Economics*, 18(3), 197–206.

Lusk, JL (2015) Why don't people vote like they shop? https://jaysonlusk.com/blog/2015/3/12/why-dont-people-vote-like-they-shop.

Lusk JL, Norwood FB (2012) Speciesism, altruism and the economics of animal welfare. *European Review of Agricultural Economics*, 39(2), 189–212.

Mechtenberg L, Perino G, Treich N, Tyran JR, Wang S (2024) Self-signaling in voting. *Journal of Public Economics*, 231, 105070.

Metrick A, Weitzman M. (1996) Patterns of behavior in endangered species preservation. *Land Economics*, 71: 1–16.

Miralles A, Raymond M, Lecointre G (2019) Empathy and compassion toward other species decrease with evolutionary divergence time. *Scientific Reports*, 9(1), 19555.

Moore FC, Stokes A, Conte MN, Dong X (2022) Noah's Ark in a warming world: climate change, biodiversity loss, and public adaptation costs in the United States. *Journal of the Association of Environmental and Resource Economics*, 9(5), 981–1015.

Norwood FB, Lusk JL (2011) *Compassion, by the Pound: The Economics of Farm Animal Welfare*. Oxford University Press.

Nyborg K (2000) Homo economicus and homo politicus: Interpretation and aggregation of environmental values. *Journal of Economic Behavior & Organization*, 42(3), 305–322.

Nyborg K, Anderies JM, Dannenberg A et al. (2016) Social norms as solutions. *Science*, 354(6308), 42–43.

Paul ES (2000) Empathy with animals and with humans: Are they linked? *Anthrozoös*, 13, 194–202.

Paul AS, Lusk JL, Norwood FB, Tonsor GT (2019) An experiment on the vote-buy gap with application to cage-free eggs. *Journal of Behavioral and Experimental Economics*, 79, 102–109.

Pearce D (1993) *Economic Values and the Natural World*. Earthscan.

Phillips C (2009) Empathy towards animals. In *The Welfare of Animals*, ed. C Phillips. Animal Welfare, vol. 8, 47–54. Springer.

Sinclair M, Lee NYP, Hötzel MJ et al. (2022) International perceptions of animals and the importance of their welfare. *Frontiers in Animal Science*, 3, 960379.

Sinclair M, Phillips CJ (2017) The cross-cultural importance of animal protection and other world social issues. *Journal of Agricultural and Environmental Ethics*, 30, 439–455.

Westbury HR, Neumann DL (2008) Empathy-related responses to moving film stimuli depicting human and non-human animal targets in negative circumstances. *Biological Psychology*, 78(1), 66–74.

12 Behavioral Studies

12.1 HUMAN–ANIMAL RELATIONSHIPS

This chapter builds mostly on studies in psychology with the aim to better understand our behavior toward animals. However, its scope extends far beyond psychology, as our psychological relationship with animals is itself deeply rooted in evolutionary, social, cultural, and physiological processes (Beck 2014). For the vast majority of human history, our ancestors lived within hunter–gatherer communities, forging deep and intricate connections with the animal kingdom. These interactions have necessarily left a mark on the evolution of human responses to animals. This enduring bond is well illustrated through the artistry found within cave paintings and tombs. Historical evidence reveals that relationships between people and animals are deeply complex and emotional in nature (Serpell and Paul 1994).

This bond has also been vividly illustrated in literature for centuries. One of the earliest known literary classics, Homer's epic *The Odyssey*, composed around the 8th century BCE, provides a poignant example. In the epic, the story of Argos, Odysseus' faithful dog, stands out as one of its most touching moments. When Odysseus finally returns to Ithaca, disguised as an elderly beggar and hiding his true identity, the old Argos lay there, sick and covered with ticks. Despite the twenty-year separation, Argos recognizes Odysseus. He lifts his head and wags his tail, showing signs of recognition and joy, but lacks the strength to get up and go to his master. Odysseus sees him but turns his head to keep his identity secret, wiping away a tear. Having fulfilled his duty of waiting for his master's return, Argos dies shortly after the reunion. This moment underscores the deep bond between humans and their pets, highlighting themes of loyalty and love that transcend time. It also illustrates that nearly three millennia ago, people were already sensitive to the special relationship they could have with their pets.

There is significant literature in psychology about human–animal relationships. Amiot and Bastian (2015) discuss the different forms that our relationship with animals can take, mostly focusing on pets. Their exploration highlights the substantial health and welfare benefits that pets bring into our lives. One of the most renowned pieces of research showcasing the positive impact of animal companionship on human health is a seminal longitudinal study conducted by Friedmann and colleagues in 1980 showing that pet owners have a significantly greater life expectancy after a heart attack. This groundbreaking study ignited widespread interest in the potential health benefits of human–animal interactions, subsequently inspiring a succession of replications and extensions. Nonetheless, there is also evidence of potentially detrimental interactions with animals. Amiot and Bastian discuss various moderating factors that can explain why animals may sometimes have positive, negative, or neutral effects on human well-being. Life circumstances, stages, and the nature of our relationships with animals play significant roles in shaping these outcomes. Additionally, some studies highlight that animals, particularly dogs, also reap benefits from their interactions with humans.

Several factors play a role in predicting attitudes toward animals. Notably, research in psychology has consistently shown that individuals with higher levels of empathy tend to hold more positive attitudes toward animals (Taylor and Signal 2005, Caviola et al. 2019). This suggests that proanimal sentiments may align with broader prosocial or proenvironmental values. Gender also emerges as one of the main predictors of empathy toward animals, with being a woman found to be associated with higher levels of empathy. On average, women exhibit higher levels of positive behaviors and attitudes, such as favorable views on animal use and active involvement in animal protection. In contrast, men generally show higher levels of negative attitudes and behaviors, including hunting, animal abuse, and less favorable attitudes toward animal protection (Herzog 2007). Unsurprisingly, ideological beliefs that either support hierarchy or endorse social dominance orientation tend to be less favorable to animals: for instance, the less people believe that humans and animals are similar, the more they report using animals to their own end (Amiot and Bastian 2015).

Sevillano and Fiske (2016, page 277) explore the way people characterize specific animals, using as its conceptual framework the way people describe human groups. More precisely, they use "two basic and apparently universal dimensions of social perception, namely Warmth – perceived intent (What is the goal, good or bad, of another person/group?) and Competence – ability and general capacity (What resources, abilities, and power does a person/group have at their disposal to achieve their goal?)." As shown on Figure 12.1, the studies identify four clusters indicated by different shades of grey: high warmth/high competence animals (dog, elephant, horse), high warmth/low competence animals (cow, pig, rabbit), low warmth/high competence animals (bear, lion, whale) and low warmth/low competence animals (fish, rat, snake).

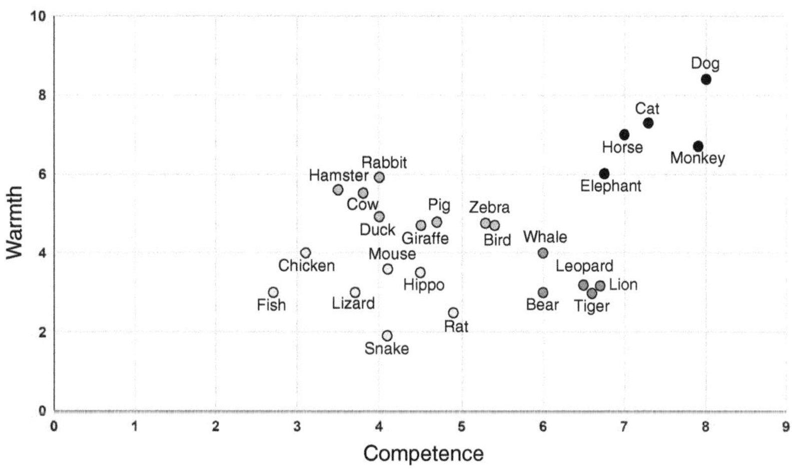

FIGURE 12.1 Perceptions of animals' warmth and competence.
Source: Sevillano and Fiske (2016)

Plous (1993) hypothesizes that animals could often be perceived as an outgroup, akin to how individuals from diverse cultures, religions, or nationalities are often viewed as outgroup members. Extensive psychological research has consistently demonstrated the inclination of ingroup members to regard outgroup members as inferior. This hypothesis also relates to the notion of speciesism that I have already discussed at length in this book (see, e.g., Jaquet 2021). However, it is likely that some animals, such as pets, are perceived as belonging to the ingroup. Many survey studies report that people consider their pets to be members of the family.

Caviola et al. (2019) have recently introduced a measure of speciesism as a stable construct, revealing significant interpersonal variations. They find positive correlations between speciesism and prejudicial attitudes, including racism, sexism, and homophobia. Additionally, they identify links between speciesism and ideological constructs associated with prejudice, such as social dominance orientation, system justification, and right-wing authoritarianism. They also show that speciesism can predict prosocial behaviors toward animals, both in terms of charitable donations and time investment. Relatedly, Gunnthorsdottir (2001) shows that an animal's attractiveness substantially increased support for its protection as a species. She finds more support for saving animal species larger in size and more similar to humans.

Dhont et al. (2019) survey the diversity of research paradigms and theoretical frameworks developed within the intergroup relations literature that are relevant to the study of human–animal relations. Their study notably underlines the distinctiveness of our attitudes toward various animal species. While individuals hold strong regard for the social connections they share with companion animals, they often devalue other animals, perceiving them merely as commodities intended to serve human interests and desires. Again, the nature of our relations with animals seems related to ingroup–outgroup patterns largely documented in humans' relationships.

Interestingly, Caviola et al. (2021) show, using hypothetical as well as real-life sacrificial moral dilemmas, that individuals seem to adopt a utilitarian approach when considering matters related to animals, while adopting a more deontological stance in their judgments involving humans. Their findings reveal that participants are more likely to deem it permissible to harm a few animals to save a greater number of animals than to harm a few humans to save a greater number of humans. This somehow supports a hybrid view in animal ethics, as coined by Robert Nozick as "Utilitarianism for animals, Kantianism for people" (Nozick 1974). Caviola et al. (2021) show that this deontological component appears to be the strongest for humans, followed by dogs, chimpanzees, pigs, and finally inanimate objects.

One might also question whether individuals adopt a hedonistic view of animal welfare, where an animal's well-being is ultimately reducible to its subjective experience. Hedonistic theories of welfare define it as a descriptive concept, meaning that assessing an animal's welfare involves accurately representing or describing its mental state. This approach is common in animal welfare science and was largely the perspective adopted in Part II, for instance through the Five Freedoms framework. However, Robbins et al. (2018) provide evidence that folk judgments of animal welfare are not entirely determined by animals' subjective experiences. In other words, people seem to believe that animal welfare is not reducible to experiencing certain mental states. Robbins and coauthors' findings suggest that welfare attributions are also influenced by normative considerations about the life the animal is living. For instance, they report that "a chimpanzee living a natural life with negative emotions was rated as having better welfare than a chimpanzee living an unnatural life with positive emotions" (page 1).

Trenkenschuh et al. (2024) show that personality traits are associated with people's attitudes toward specific animal welfare legislation. They consider Proposition 12, which was passed in California in 2018. This law requires in particular that animals such as veal calves, breeding pigs, and egg-laying hens are provided enough space. This study first shows that people largely endorse the law. Moreover, it examines how persuasive participants perceived specific arguments for or against the regulation. The study reveals that participants who are more open, agreeable, and prone to withdrawn negative emotions are more likely to support animal welfare policies and find various arguments in favor of such policies compelling. Notably, the study shows that associations between personality traits and attitudes toward animal rights are consistent regardless of political orientation, region, gender, or age. This suggests that personality plays a crucial role in shaping attitudes toward animal welfare independently of other demographic factors.

What about children? Anecdotal evidence regarding the emotional reactions of young individuals to animals, as seen in their responses to toys or cartoons, underlines the significance of animals in their lives. Scientific research largely supports this observation, indicating that this affinity may manifest from a very early age. For instance, just hours after birth, infants exhibit heightened stimulation in response to visual cues simulating animal movement, such as that of a domestic chicken, compared to non-biological animations (Simion et al. 2008). Children are more inclined to interact with animals than with toys (Lobue et al. 2013). College students exhibit greater interest in studying animals as opposed to plants, with a selective recall of more animal-related images (Schussler and Olzak 2008). Furthermore, research by Wilks et al. (2021) suggests that children display a less pronounced inclination than adults to prioritize humans over animals. This result suggests that the prevailing perspective that assigns significantly greater moral importance to humans in comparison to animals may emerge relatively late in the developmental process and is likely influenced by social factors.

12.2 ANTHROPOMORPHISM AND ANTHROPODENIAL

A crucial difference between proanimal and prosocial concerns lies in the complexity of understanding animals compared to humans.

While we have some understanding of what motivates human actions and contributes to human happiness, typically by introspection, identifying the sources of action and happiness in animals seems much more elusive. Animals and humans exhibit significant differences, making it challenging to understand the behavior of animals and assess their welfare.

Anthropomorphism, the tendency to attribute human traits to non-human entities, seems unavoidable here. This is because we have to interpret the world, including other animals, and we can only do this through our own perspective, that of humans. As David Hume (cited in Dacey 2017, page 1152) put it: "There is an universal tendency among mankind to conceive all beings like themselves ... We find faces in the moon, armies in the clouds." Anthropomorphism serves as a basic heuristic, a starting point to understand the world and others. It may help to understand and predict the behavior of animals and facilitate communication and cooperation with them, which historically has proven to be useful. It may also boost empathy and compassion. When people anthropomorphize animals, they are more likely to feel concern for their welfare and may be motivated to take action to protect them (Butterfield et al. 2012).

Anthropomorphism is prevalent. It is frequently used in marketing and design to make products more appealing and relatable to consumers. Companies often employ anthropomorphic characters and mascots to evoke positive emotions and create memorable brand associations. This technique has a rich history, often utilized by moralists to impart lessons and sometimes satirize human behavior, as exemplified by the timeless fables of Jean de la Fontaine. In the realm of children's literature, anthropomorphism is particularly pervasive, with animals frequently taking on human-like qualities. Picture books commonly depict animals wearing clothes, speaking, and even inhabiting human-like dwellings. A quintessential example of this phenomenon can be found in Disney cartoons, where animals such as dogs often embody benevolent characters, in contrast to portrayals of less favorable creatures like rats or bats (Stanton 2021).

However, although our inevitable anthropomorphic tendencies are prevalent and often useful, they have drawbacks. Typically, they induce systematic biases in the way we view animals. One such bias is akin to the "projection bias," a well-documented bias both in psychology and economics. It occurs when individuals assume that others share similar beliefs, values, or preferences as themselves, leading them to inaccurately predict others' behavior or decisions. This bias often stems from an inability to fully separate one's own perspective from that of others. People tend to project their own thoughts, feelings, and preferences onto others, assuming that others think or feel similarly to themselves. This can lead to misunderstandings, miscommunications, and erroneous judgments about others' intentions or motivations. Hence, the projection bias is likely to arise when considering other animals, with the potential for even more significant errors in judgment. This risk is exacerbated by the inherent "distance" between humans and animals, coupled with the typically limited depth of our knowledge about animal behaviors and motivations.

Dacey (2017) stresses the notion that our intuitive folk psychology likely evolved primarily to navigate social interactions with other humans, before being repurposed to interpret interactions with animals. However, our intuitive responses may be overly sensitive, often triggered by simple or even irrelevant cues. Common cues such as hands, eyes, faces, and movement can strongly influence our tendency to attribute conscious mental states. For instance, research has revealed a bias among humans to attribute conscious mental states to animals that move at approximately the same speed as humans (Morewedge et al. 2007). This highlights how our intuitive processes, shaped by social interactions, can influence our perceptions of animals, sometimes leading to unwarranted attributions of consciousness or mental states.

The perils of anthropomorphism have been widely acknowledged and extensively discussed, particularly within scientific circles. One of the most commonly advocated strategies for mitigating anthropomorphism is known as Morgan's canon, named after the 19th-century

British psychologist C. Lloyd Morgan. Put simply, this approach urges researchers to refrain from attributing complex mental processes or emotions to animals when simpler explanations suffice. It promotes a commitment to parsimony, encouraging scientists to interpret animal behavior in the most straightforward terms available. By emphasizing the importance of simplicity in explaining animal behavior, Morgan's canon acts as a barrier against anthropomorphism. It serves as a reminder to researchers to exercise caution when interpreting animal behavior and to refrain from projecting human-like attributes onto animals without robust empirical support.

However, as Karlsson (2012) emphasizes, efforts to avoid anthropomorphism may inadvertently lead to the creation of errors or "other morphisms." Most significantly, de Waal (1999) and others have argued that Morgan's canon raises the risk of anthropodenial. This corresponds to a systematic reluctance or refusal to acknowledge the similarities between humans and other animals, particularly in terms of cognitive abilities, emotions, and social behaviors. Hence, anthropodenial represents the opposite extreme of anthropomorphism, where instead of attributing human-like qualities to animals, individuals deny or downplay the shared characteristics between humans and other species.

The risk of anthropodenial is serious. As we have seen in Chapter 2, there is a historical tendency within scientific discourse to emphasize the differences between humans and animals, often to the exclusion of acknowledging commonalities. Think of Descartes' animal machine. For much of history, humans were considered to be fundamentally different from other animals, possessing unique cognitive abilities, emotions, and consciousness. This perspective, often rooted in religious or philosophical beliefs, led to the marginalization or dismissal of evidence suggesting similarities between humans and animals. However, with advancements in fields such as ethology and neuroscience, researchers have increasingly recognized the continuum of cognitive and behavioral abilities across species. Studies have demonstrated that many animals possess sophisticated cognitive skills, emotions, and social behaviors once thought to be exclusive to humans. This recent change in the attitude in science toward animals is sometimes coined the "animal turn" (Ritvo 2007).

Leach et al. (2023) explores the risks of both anthropomorphism and anthropodenial in the population. It examines biases in how people remember information about animal intelligence, thus providing an objective criterion to assess the accuracy of these judgments. The study finds that meat eaters tend to remember more anthropomorphic information about companion animals, like dogs, but not about food animals, like pigs. Meanwhile, vegetarians and vegans exhibit an anthropomorphic bias for both types of animals. Over time, both groups shift toward an anthropodenial bias. This research highlights that memories concerning animals' minds can systematically deviate from reality, leading to biased evaluations of their mental capacities.

Therefore, as always, the question is about where to draw the line, rather than an outright rejection of anthropomorphism. The appropriate approach is probably to harness anthropomorphism judiciously and to our benefit, exercising caution in its application. De Waal (1999, page 274) summarizes it well:

> Some forms of anthropomorphism fail to provide useful information or generate useful hypotheses, but the fact that we are animals ourselves also provides us with an immense advantage. The full exploitation of this advantage requires a tolerant attitude toward the borrowing of human concepts to explain animal behavior. After all, with respect to species close to us the most parsimonious explanation, from an evolutionary perspective, is that they share numerous emotional and cognitive processes with us. Thus, anthropomorphism ought to be a nonissue in the case of anthropoid apes. But even in the case of more distant species, anthropomorphic explanations deserve serious attention. We should never accept explanations without critical reflection, but there is nothing wrong with widening the workspace of permissible hypotheses while retaining high standards of replicability and scientific scrutiny.

12.3 THE MEAT PARADOX

I now discuss the meat paradox (Loughnan et al. 2010), which I believe to be a pivotal concept in understanding animal welfare concerns. In a nutshell, the meat paradox is the psychological conflict that occurs when people feel empathy for animals but still consume meat. This paradox possibly creates cognitive dissonance, where a person's values (caring about animals) clash with their actions (eating meat). In Chapter 14, I will present an economic model of the meat paradox. As an introduction, this section presents some psychological research on the meat paradox that has first shed light on its origins and implications. Although the expression "meat paradox" is relatively new, the concept has long been around. To illustrate, in the 1990 edition of his 1975 book *Animal Liberation*, Peter Singer already summarizes the key idea around the meat paradox: "Anyone who eats meat is an interested party. (...) For behind the mere momentary desire to eat meat on a particular occasion lie many years of habitual meat-eating which have conditioned our attitudes to animals" (Singer 1990).

The meat paradox builds on cognitive dissonance, a well-established concept in psychology. Cognitive dissonance occurs when individuals experience psychological tension between conflicting beliefs or actions. In our context, the tension may be simply sketched as follows: People like animals, but they also like meat. Indeed, people often express affection for animals or at minimum express a desire not to cause them harm, yet simultaneously most people derive enjoyment from consuming meat. That is, following Singer's quote, meat eaters have a conflict of interest.

It seems plausible that this inherent conflict, or meat paradox, generates a "psychological cost" (to use an economic terminology) that people may naturally want to reduce. One cost reduction strategy involves modifying behavior, such as reducing meat consumption or adopting a vegetarian or vegan lifestyle. However, if these actions prove to be too costly or too burdensome, another strategy is to (unconsciously) adjust beliefs. For example, individuals may attempt to downplay the suffering experienced by farmed animals as a means of reconciling their conflicting beliefs. Then, they would believe that it would not be too bad to eat farmed animals. This strategy leading to self-serving beliefs is the core implication of the meat paradox. The prevalence of omnivores as the predominant dietary choice worldwide suggests that this strategy is a commonly taken route: people keep consuming meat and thus adjust their beliefs to reduce cognitive dissonance.

There is substantial evidence that suggests that the meat paradox triggers cognitive dissonance, affecting people's beliefs regarding farmed animals and meat consumption. One line of evidence focuses on the correlation between meat consumption and belief systems. The hypothesis is that the incentive to alter beliefs is more pronounced when meat consumption is greater (i.e., when the psychological cost is higher). Supporting this hypothesis, Bilewicz et al. (2011) observe consistent differences in emotional attributions between vegetarians and omnivores. They note that omnivores tend to differentiate between the emotional capacities of meat-producing animals and non-meat-producing animals, a distinction less prevalent among vegetarians. Additionally, vegetarians are more inclined than omnivores to acknowledge the potential for suffering in animals raised for food (Bratanova et al. 2011).

In an unpublished study designed in 2017 with Nina Hestermann and Yves Le Yaouanq, we compare the responses of participants to the objective answer regarding animal-rearing conditions as given by the Ministry of Agriculture. We grouped participants in three categories, namely vegetarians, flexitarians (i.e., those who consume meat "a few times a month" or "a few times a year") and omnivores. We find that vegetarians are in general the most realistic category, and that omnivores and to a lesser extent flexitarians tend to underestimate animal suffering in the farming industry. For instance, omnivores and flexitarians significantly underestimate the proportion of male piglets castrated without anesthesia (which is about 85 percent); see Figure 12.2. We find similar perception biases about other aspects of pig farming such as the proportion of pigs without outdoor access

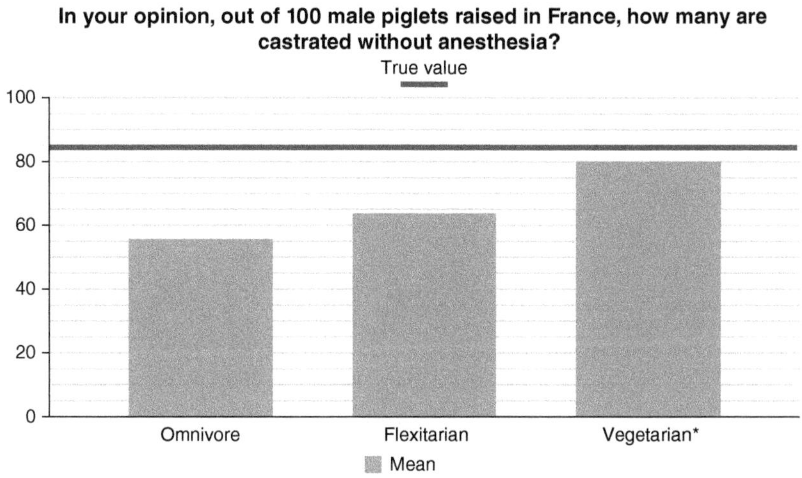

FIGURE 12.2 Perception of the proportion of piglets castrated without anesthesia.
Source: Hestermann et al. (2017) (*N = 3054 with only 66 vegetarians)

(95 percent) or other farmed animals' rearing conditions for hens and rabbits for instance.

Along this line, Rothgerber (2014) mentions a positive correlation between meat consumption and agreement with statements such as "animals don't really suffer when being raised and killed for meat" and "animals do not feel pain the same way humans do." Bastian et al. (2012) also identify a negative correlation between individuals' perceptions of animals' cognitive abilities and their edibility. Their findings are illustrated in Figure 12.3: Animals like dogs, cats, and horses, along with monkeys and lions, are perceived as having high cognitive abilities but low edibility. Interestingly, farmed animals, namely chickens, cows, goats, rabbits, and sheep are seen as highly edible but possessing low cognitive abilities. Hence, farmed animals are perceived as less intelligent, and the meat paradox provides an explanation. The explanation is that people are motivated to believe that farmed animals are less intelligent, because it reduces the psychological cost associated with eating them.

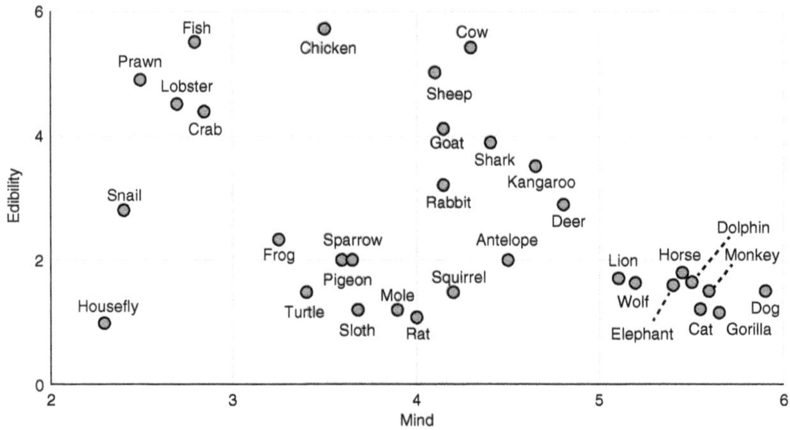

FIGURE 12.3 Perceptions of animals' edibility and cognitive ability. Source: Bastian et al. (2012)

However, the research outlined earlier in this chapter leaves open the question of causality: Do individuals alter their beliefs due to cognitive dissonance triggered by meat consumption, or conversely do individuals with different beliefs simply choose different levels of meat consumption as a response to their beliefs?

Bratanova et al. (2011) offer causal evidence supporting the cognitive dissonance hypothesis. They present participants with descriptions of an unfamiliar animal (a tree kangaroo) and manipulate whether the animal is depicted as "food" (i.e., whether the description specifies it as commonly consumed by humans), whether the narrative includes a reference to the animal's death, and whether hunting is responsible for it. Their findings indicate that labeling an animal as "food" diminishes its perceived capacity to suffer, consequently reducing individuals' moral concern for the animal. Similarly, Bastian et al. (2012) demonstrate that people attribute fewer mental capacities to animals (such as sheep or cows) when reminded of their intended use for meat consumption. Furthermore, Bastian et al. (2012) randomly assign participants to conditions where they are either served cold cuts of roast beef or slices of apple. Before consuming the food, participants are asked to rate the cognitive abilities of cows. Those anticipating the opportunity to eat beef imminently report diminished cognitive capacities for cows.

Relatedly, it has been suggested that individuals who consume meat often exhibit avoidance behaviors toward information concerning the practices within the meat industry and the cognitive abilities of animals. This avoidance of information provides meat eaters with a means to uphold their self-serving beliefs. Ioannidou et al. (2023) highlight surveys showing that respondents generally prefer not to think about animal suffering associated with factory farming. Furthermore, Leach et al. (2022) conduct research involving samples of adults and students from the United Kingdom and United States, revealing that individuals who displayed stronger commitments to meat consumption are more inclined to evade information regarding animal sentience. They also show diminished interest in engaging with articles discussing the intelligence of farmed animals compared to those with less commitment to meat consumption.

Another strategy omnivores may use to resolve the meat paradox is rationalization. Rationalization involves offering reasonable justifications for one's actions when they are questioned or criticized, or when those actions seem to conflict with one's perceived character. It plays a crucial role in preserving a positive self-image as a morally upright individual. According to Joy (2010), meat eaters typically rely on three main types of justification, collectively referred to as the "3Ns" theory, which asserts that eating meat is Necessary, Natural, and Normal. Piazza et al. (2015) provide empirical support for this theory and introduce a fourth "N," suggesting that eating meat is also Nice. Their research demonstrates that individuals who endorse the 4Ns are more likely to consume meat and other animal products regularly. Additionally, they find that the degree of endorsement of the 4Ns theory correlates with various morally relevant attitudes toward animals, including the range of animals that individuals care about and the extent to which they attribute mental capacities to animals.

Many other strategies are possible, for instance through dissociating meat from its animal origins (Benningstad and Kunst 2020). The literature on the meat paradox is flourishing; see Rothgerber (2020, page 1) for a recent conceptual framework which "explains how individuals attempt to prevent this form of dissonance from occurring (e.g., avoidance, willful ignorance, dissociation, perceived behavioral change, and do-gooder derogation) and how they reduce it once it has occurred in the form of motivated cognitions (e.g., denigrating animals, offering pro-meat justifications, or denying responsibility for eating meat)."

Note also that those strategies may not be limited to meat consumption, as their use should naturally extend to all situations where humans have a stake in the consumption, use or exploitation of animals. For instance, Ioannidou et al. (2023) show that the meat paradox extends beyond meat to other animal products. Fish consumers use more dissonance reduction strategies related to fish consumption compared to vegetarians and vegans. Similarly, dairy and egg consumers use more dissonance reduction strategies related to dairy and egg consumption compared to vegans. Vezirian et al. (2024) show that people attribute less cognitive ability to animals when they are reminded that some animals are used for laboratory testing compared to when they consider the mental lives of those animals in their natural habitat, or when people are reminded of their consumption of products that rely on animal testing.

Moreover, it is crucial to acknowledge that individuals engage in interactions with one another, and these interactions can strengthen prevailing social norms and beliefs regarding meat consumption. In essence, these interactions may bolster justifications for meat consumption, enabling individuals to maintain their dietary habits without much contemplation. Moreover, there might also exist a role for "suppliers," such as the meat industry, in facilitating these individual strategies. Suppliers may achieve this through the implementation of specific narratives, informational and marketing tactics, and even by actively sowing seeds of doubt.

Overall, the topic of the meat paradox brings to mind Paul McCartney's famous quote: "If slaughterhouses had glass walls, everyone would be vegetarian" (www.paulmccartney.com/news/

if-slaughterhouses-had-glass-walls-everyone-would-be-vegetarian). The reality is quite different: Most people are not vegetarians, slaughterhouses do not have glass walls, and, to say the least, transparency is not the rule in the meat industry. This suggests that society has probably reached an equilibrium where information about animal treatment is limited, and where prevailing beliefs may be largely misconstrued on average. Along this line, Joy (2010) emphasizes the existence of a collective belief system in our societies, coined "carnism," supported by a variety of defense mechanisms and mostly unchallenged assumptions embodied in our economic, social, and cultural environment that then leads to the supporting of the use and consumption of animals. The analysis of this system constitutes a fascinating area of investigation for researchers in human and social sciences. Chapters 14 and 16 will touch again upon these issues.

REFERENCES

Amiot CE, Bastian B (2015) Toward a psychology of human–animal relations. *Psychological Bulletin*, 141(1), 6.

Bastian B, Loughnan S, Haslam N, Radke HJ (2012) Don't mind meat? The denial of mind to animals used for human consumption. *Personality and Social Psychology Bulletin*, 38(2), 247–256.

Beck AM (2014) The biology of the human–animal bond. *Animal Frontiers*, 4(3), 32–36.

Benningstad NC, Kunst JR (2020) Dissociating meat from its animal origins: A systematic literature review. *Appetite*, 147, 104554.

Bilewicz M, Imhoff R, Drogosz M (2011) The humanity of what we eat: Conceptions of human uniqueness among vegetarians and omnivores. *European Journal of Social Psychology*, 41(2), 201–209.

Bratanova B, Loughnan S, Bastian B (2011) The effect of categorization as food on the perceived moral standing of animals. *Appetite*, 57(1), 193–196.

Butterfield ME, Hill SE, Lord CG (2012) Mangy mutt or furry friend? Anthropomorphism promotes animal welfare. *Journal of Experimental Social Psychology*, 48(4), 957–960.

Caviola L, Everett JAC, Faber NS (2019) The moral standing of animals: Towards a psychology of speciesism. *Journal of Personality and Social Psychology*, 116(6), 1011–1029.

Caviola L, Kahane G, Everett JAC et al. (2021) Utilitarianism for animals, Kantianism for people? Harming animals and humans for the greater good. *Journal of Experimental Psychology: General*, 150(5), 1008–1039.

Dacey M (2017) Anthropomorphism as cognitive bias. *Philosophy of Science*, 84(5), 1152–1164.

De Waal FB (1999) Anthropomorphism and anthropodenial: Consistency in our thinking about humans and other animals. *Philosophical Topics*, 27(1), 255–280.

Dhont K, Hodson G, Loughnan S, Amiot CE (2019) Rethinking human-animal relations: The critical role of social psychology. *Group Processes & Intergroup Relations*, 22(6), 769–784.

Gunnthorsdottir A (2001) Physical attractiveness of an animal species as a decision factor for its preservation. *Anthrozoös*, 14(4), 204–215.

Herzog HA (2007) Gender differences in human–animal interactions: A review. *Anthrozoös*, 20(1), 7–21.

Hestermann N, Le Yaouanq Y, Treich N (2017) Survey study on meat consumption and perceptions of animal welfare in France. Unpublished.

Ioannidou M, Lesk V, Stewart-Knox B, Francis KB (2023) Feeling morally troubled about meat, dairy, egg, and fish consumption: Dissonance reduction strategies among different dietary groups. *Appetite*, 190, 107024.

Jaquet F (2021) Speciesism and tribalism: Embarrassing origins. *Philosophical Studies*, 179, 933–954.

Joy M (2010) *Why We Love Dogs, Eat Pigs, and Wear Cows: An Introduction to Carnism*. Red Wheel.

Karlsson F (2012) Critical anthropomorphism and animal ethics. *Journal of Agricultural and Environmental Ethics*, 25, 707–720.

Leach S, Piazza J, Loughnan S et al. (2022) Unpalatable truths: Commitment to eating meat is associated with strategic ignorance of food-animal minds. *Appetite*, 171, 105935.

Leach S, Sutton R, Dhont K, Douglas K, Bergström Z (2023) Are we smart enough to remember how smart animals are? *Journal of Experimental Psychology. General*, 10.1037/xge0001401.

Lobue V, Bloom Pickard M, Sherman K, Axford C, DeLoache JS (2013) Young children's interest in live animals. *British Journal of Developmental Psychology*, 31(1), 57–69.

Loughnan S, Haslam N, Bastian B (2010) The role of meat consumption in the denial of moral status and mind to meat animals. *Appetite*, 55(1), 156–159.

Morewedge CK, Preston J, Wegner DM (2007) Timescale bias in the attribution of mind. *Journal of Personality and Social Psychology*, 93(1), 1.

Nozick R (1974) *Anarchy, State, and Utopia*. Basic Books.

Piazza J, Ruby MB, Loughnan S et al. (2015) Rationalizing meat consumption. The 4Ns. *Appetite*, 91, 114–128.

Plous S (1993) Psychological mechanisms in the human use of animals. *Journal of Social Issues*, 49, 11–52.

Ritvo H (2007) On the animal turn. *Daedalus*, 136(4), 118–122.

Robbins J, Franks B, Von Keyserlingk MA (2018) "More than a feeling": An empirical investigation of hedonistic accounts of animal welfare. *PloS One*, 13(3), e0193864.

Rothgerber H (2014) Efforts to overcome vegetarian-induced dissonance among meat eaters. *Appetite*, 79, 32–41.

Rothgerber H (2020) Meat-related cognitive dissonance: A conceptual framework for understanding how meat eaters reduce negative arousal from eating animals. *Appetite*, 146, 104511.

Schussler EE, Olzak LA (2008) It's not easy being green: Student recall of plant and animal images. *Journal of Biological Education*, 42(3), 112–119.

Serpell JA, Paul ES (1994) Pets and the development of positive attitudes to animals. In *Animals and Human Society*, eds. A Manning and ES Paul, 165–182. Routledge.

Sevillano V, Fiske ST (2016) Warmth and competence in animals. *Journal of Applied Social Psychology*, 46(5), 276–293.

Simion F, Regolin L, Bulf H (2008) A predisposition for biological motion in the newborn baby. *Proceedings of the National Academy of Sciences*, 105(2), 809–813.

Singer P (1990) [1975] *Animal Liberation: A New Ethics of Our Treatment of Animals*. 2nd ed. Random House.

Stanton RR (2021) *The Disneyfication of Animals*. Palgrave Macmillan.

Taylor N, Signal TD (2005) Empathy and attitudes to animals. *Anthrozoös*, 18(1), 18–27.

Trenkenschuh M, Hopwood CJ, Dillard C (2024) Personality aspects and attitudes about animal welfare legislation. *Anthrozoös*, 1–20.

Vezirian K, Bègue L, Bastian B (2024) Mindless furry test-tubes: Categorizing animals as lab-subjects leads to their mind denial. *Journal of Experimental Social Psychology*, 114, 104629.

Wilks M, Caviola L, Kahane G, Bloom P (2021) Children prioritize humans over animals less than adults do. *Psychological Science*, 32(1), 27–38.

13 Proanimal Concerns

Theoretical Aspects

13.1 ANIMAL WELFARE AS A PUBLIC GOOD

Animal welfare can be conceptually conceived as a public good, as initially argued by Cowen (2006) and Lusk and Norwood (2012). The idea is straightforward: If individuals value animal welfare, then any improvement in an animal's welfare benefits anyone who cares about animals. Importantly, this public good characteristic leads to free-riding incentives since people may not consider how their proanimal actions benefit other people, leading to an undersupply of animal welfare compared to the socially optimal level. This can potentially explain the "gap" between public opinion and market demand that I initially emphasized as one major puzzle in animal welfare economics.

From an economist's standpoint, I think the idea of animal welfare as a public good is a basic starting point for understanding the demand for animal welfare. As such, I am commencing in this chapter the formal exploration of this compelling idea. I first introduce a simple model that formalizes this idea. I build on the canonical model presented in the first part, except that I now assume that animals do not matter intrinsically but matter because altruistic consumers care about animals. I will largely follow the theoretical analysis presented in Espinosa and Treich (2023).

There are $N > 1$ identical consumers. Each consumer i chooses the quantity of animal lives consumed, that is, the number n_i of (identical) animals consumed, as well as the quality of animal lives, that is, the animal welfare level d_i. The consumer i's utility is given by

$$u(n_i) - (c + d_i)n_i + \alpha\left[\sum_{j=1}^{N} n_j v(d_j)\right], \tag{13.1}$$

where $u(.)$ is the utility derived from the consumption of meat, assumed to be increasing and concave, $v(.)$ is the farm animal's utility level, assumed to be increasing and concave, $c \geq 0$ is the baseline cost to produce an animal, and $\alpha \geq 0$ is the level of altruism.

The quality choice d_i is thus determined by the extra cost of animal welfare improvement paid by the consumer i on top of the baseline production cost c. As shown in Chapter 11, there is a lot of evidence that consumers are willing to pay some premium for more animal-friendly products.

The key property of this model is that the consumer i cares about the welfare of all animals through the term $\alpha[\sum_{j=1}^{N} n_j v(d_j)]$, while her choices n_i and d_i only affect the welfare of the animals that she actually consumes, that is, $n_i v(d_i)$. Hence, as usual in public good problems, she does not internalize the impact of her choices on the other altruistic consumers. Technically, this corresponds to a model of private provision to a public good (Bergstrom et al. 1986).

I first characterize the equilibrium in this economy. As before, I focus on interior solutions. The FOCs for the optimal symmetric choices at the equilibrium, denoted $(\hat{n}, \hat{d})$, are given by:

$$u'(\hat{n}) - \left(c + \hat{d}\right) + \alpha v\left(\hat{d}\right) = 0 \tag{13.2}$$

$$-1 + \alpha v'\left(\hat{d}\right) = 0. \tag{13.3}$$

Note that there are no strategic interactions here due to the separability of the consumer i's objective with respect to the actions of the other consumers through the additive term $\alpha[\sum_{j=1}^{N} n_j v(d_j)]$. Namely, the consumption choices of one consumer i do not affect those of another consumer j.

Let me now characterize the social optimum in this economy, denoted (n^*, d^*). It is given by maximizing over n and d the sum of the utility of all consumers given by $N[u(n) - (c + d)n + \alpha nNv(d)]$. Note that, consistent with the indirect approach, this social objective is anthropocentric: Animals matter only because they matter for the consumers. This yields the following FOCs:

$$u'(n^{\star}) - (c + d^{\star}) + \alpha N v(d^{\star}) = 0 \quad (13.4)$$

$$-1 + \alpha N v'(d^{\star}) = 0. \quad (13.5)$$

My main objective in this section is to compare $(n^{\star}, d^{\star})$ to $(\hat{n}, \hat{d})$, namely to study the impact of the public good problem on the choice variables.

First, as a preliminary inquiry, I study the much simpler case where the quality choice d is fixed, that is, $d \equiv d_0$ and $v_0 \equiv v(d_0)$. In that case, it is enough to compare (13.2) and (13.4) assuming that $\hat{d} = d^{\star} = d_0$. Since $N > 1$, it is obvious that there is more (resp. less) animal consumption at the social optimum than at the equilibrium if $v_0 > 0$ (resp. $v_0 < 0$), namely if a farm animal life is worth living (resp. not worth living) at the level of quality d_0. The intuition is similar as before: when $v_0 > 0$ the existence of a farm animal is a public good and individual consumption is too low, while when $v_0 < 0$ the existence of a farm animal is a public bad and individual consumption is too high. Again, this simple analysis shows that the concept of "life worth living" is central in the economic analysis of animal welfare.

I now study the general problem of comparing $(n^{\star}, d^{\star})$ to $(\hat{n}, \hat{d})$. It is obvious from the comparison of (13.3) and (13.5) that there is more investment in animal welfare at the social optimum: $d^{\star} \geq \hat{d}$. This is intuitive: quality d is too low at the equilibrium since each consumer does not internalize that other consumers are better-off when she consumes a more animal-friendly product. This simple result may explain part of the "gap" between public opinion and market demand emphasized in the introduction and in Chapter 11. People would like animals to be better protected, but underinvest in animal protection individually because of the public good problem.

What about animal consumption? A priori, the comparison is not obvious. On the one hand, the price of meat is higher at the social optimum, that is, $c + d^{\star} > c + \hat{d}$, providing an incentive to consume less meat. On the other hand, the animal utility level is higher at the social optimum, that is, $v(d^{\star}) > v(\hat{d})$, providing an incentive to consume more meat. Espinosa and Treich (2023) shows, after a technical manipulation (this is left as an exercise), that the socially optimal level of animal consumption is lower than the equilibrium one, that is, $n^* < \hat{n}$ if and only if the animal life is not worth living, that is, $v(.) < 0$. This is thus a similar result as in the fixed animal well-being case discussed above in this section.

One distinctive aspect of the public good model of animal welfare revolves around the two distinct choices at hand: the quantity and quality of animal lives. This suggests another comparative static analysis that could be particularly insightful in this context. Imagine a case where one of these choices is determined by the market, while the other is chosen by a regulator. This imperfect social control may stem from various economic or political constraints. For example, it might be relatively feasible to centrally regulate total meat consumption through mechanisms such as taxation or subsidies, while monitoring animal welfare across dispersed production sites could be prohibitively costly. Conversely, controlling quality might be straightforward, but it could be politically challenging to impose taxes or restrictions on meat consumption, for instance. In Espinosa and Treich (2023), we explore this question and obtain the following result: Suppose that only quantity is controlled by the regulator. Then, both quality and quality are lower than at the social optimum. Suppose alternatively that only quality is controlled by the regulator. Then, the level of quality is socially optimal, but quantity is too high if and only if the animal life is not worth living.

I finish this section with a remark. Note that an increase in the level of altruism α always increases quality both at the equilibrium and at the social optimum. Moreover, it decreases the number of animals consumed if and only if the animal life is not worth living. This implies that both $\hat{n}$ and n^* are U-shaped in α. This result was formally demonstrated in Chapter 8 in a (nonanthropocentric) model where α had another interpretation (and a different parameter was used; see the following section).

13.2 RESPONSIBLE ALTRUISM

This section considers a variant version of the model just presented. A key assumption in model (13.1) is that each consumer is concerned with the welfare of all animals, not just those they consume. This can be viewed as a strong behavioral/moral assumption regarding consumers. As an alternative, this section introduces a different assumption: that each consumer's concern is strictly limited to the animals they directly consume. This alternative model writes as follows:

$$u(n_i) - (c + d_i)n_i + \beta n_i v(d_i). \tag{13.6}$$

Model (13.6) indicates that the consumer's altruism, captured through parameter β, is tied to her actions, and, in a way, reflects her sense of responsibility. That is, the consumer is concerned only by animals she directly impacts. This is a particular case of "directed altruism" (Leider et al. 2009), where altruistic behavior is specifically targeted or directed toward certain individuals or groups, rather than being indiscriminately applied to everyone. Here, I coin this form of altruism, "responsible altruism," which emphasizes the idea that the consumer's concern is driven by personal responsibility rather than a broader, unconditional altruism toward all animals. It captures the moral perspective that care is limited to direct personal actions and responsibilities. While this is another polar case, it helps capture the modulable nature of altruism and its implications for economic outcomes.

To make things comparable with the results in the previous section, assume $\alpha = \beta$, so that the "strength" of altruism is similar in both models, only the scope of altruism differs. It is obvious then to see that this specific form of altruism leads in our simple model to exactly the same symmetric choices at the equilibrium $(\hat{n}, \hat{d})$, are given by (13.2) and (13.3). Hence, pure altruism or responsible altruism are not distinguishable from the observation of equilibrium outcomes.

What about the social optimum in that economy with responsible altruistic individuals? Social welfare is given by $N[u(n) - (c + d)n + \beta n v(d)]$. The key difference from the social optimum under standard altruism is that the social objective disregards the impact a consumer has on other consumers through his impact on animals (i.e., the public good effect). This is logical since, under responsible altruism, each consumer is indifferent to the welfare of animals consumed by others. As a result, responsible altruism eliminates the free-rider problem, aligning the equilibrium outcome with the social optimum. In other words, animal welfare is no longer a public good under responsible altruism. Therefore, no public intervention is needed, as the market outcome naturally reflects the socially optimal level of animal welfare under this model.

The absence of market failure may be seen as good news. However, it is important to realize that the welfare of animals will be larger in the regulated economy under altruism compared to under responsible altruism: $d^{*} \geq \hat{d}$. This makes sense. When consumers care about all animals and not only those under their own responsibility, more investment in animal welfare is warranted at the social optimum.

Let me now make a digression. In the rest of this section, I use this simple framework to reflect on the vote-buy gap introduced in Chapter 11. Since this gap is an important puzzle in the economics of animal welfare, it warrants a precise theoretical analysis. Here is a first attempt using the canonical model. Building on the two previous models of the altruistic consumer, we can model consumer i's utility to incorporate both standard altruism and responsible altruism as follows:

$$u(n_i) - (c + d_i)n_i + \beta n_i v(d_i) + \alpha \left[\sum_{j \neq i} n_j v(d_j) \right]. \tag{13.7}$$

Hence, when $\beta = \alpha$ we have standard altruism and when $\alpha = 0$, we have responsible altruism. To simplify, from now, I only consider the quality choicc, namely the level of animal welfare d_i (and thus assume that n_i is exogenously given). As before, the FOC characterizing the optimal d_i is simply given by:

$$-1 + \beta v'(d_i) = 0. \tag{13.8}$$

Now, I would like to explore the voting choice. To do so, I consider the simplest possible voting model I can think of. Assume that q is the consumer's perceived probability to be pivotal. Also assume that the vote concerns the legislation about animal welfare, denoted d. That is, the outcome of the vote decides the level of animal welfare. Crucially, this legislation applies to all animals. When voting, the consumer/voter i thus maximizes over d the following objective:

$$q\left[-(c+d)n_i + \beta n_i v(d) + \alpha\left(\sum\nolimits_{j\neq i} n_j v(d)\right)\right]. \tag{13.9}$$

This means that the consumer/voter accounts for the cost of the legislation in terms of increased prices relevant to his own consumption through the term $-(c+d)n_i$. He also accounts for the benefit for the animals for which the consumer is responsible through the term $\beta n_i v(d)$ as well as for the benefits to all the other animals through the term $\alpha[\sum_{j\neq i} n_j v(d)]$. After a simple manipulation, it is easy to see that the FOC for the voting decision simply equals:

$$-1 + \beta v'(d) + \frac{1}{n_i}\alpha\left[\sum\nolimits_{j\neq i} n_j v'(d)\right] = 0. \tag{13.10}$$

To study the vote-buy gap, we can now compare the buying and voting decisions, as defined by the respective FOCs (13.8) and (13.10). Assume first responsible altruism, i.e. $\alpha = 0$. Then, the FOCs are identical, and we have $d_i = d$. This suggests that the strength of animal welfare motivations is likely to be similar when the consumer makes a purchase decision as when she makes a voting decision. Therefore, the observation of a significant difference between these two types of decisions could indeed be considered paradoxical. In other words, the vote-buy gap is indeed a puzzle for this theory.

However, note that this is not true for the more standard form of altruism, that is, $\alpha > 0$. Indeed, under $\frac{1}{n_i}\alpha[\sum_{j\neq i} n_j v'(d)] > 0$, we would expect voting decisions to result in greater investment in animal welfare than purchase decisions. The intuition is simple: Voting has broader implications since it affects all animals, not just those under the direct consumer's responsibility. Thus, from a purely theoretical perspective, the vote-buy gap is not necessarily puzzling, as we can anticipate stronger animal welfare concerns to be reflected in voting decisions compared to buying decisions.

Note finally that the analysis of the vote-buy gap has important policy implications. It tells us whether the choices regarding animal welfare can be left to the market or should be resolved through the voting system. Based on the insight delivered in this section, and the discussion in Chapter 11, it seems likely that people are more friendly to animals when they vote compared to when they buy. Standard altruism and salience provide two reasons to go through voting when possible if one is willing to improve animal welfare.

13.3 DIRECT AND INDIRECT APPROACHES

In this section, I discuss the similarities and differences between the direct and indirect approaches. This builds on the analysis of the canonical model in Part II, and on the analysis presented in Section 13.1. I believe that it may be useful at this stage to build on the versions of the canonical model to reflect on the similarities and differences between the anthropocentric and nonanthropocentric approaches. To simplify, I go back to a standard form of altruism, as in Section 13.1.

First, let me discuss the quality choice. Under both approaches, we have seen that quality is underprovided at the equilibrium. However, the underlying explanation for this underprovision differs. Under the direct approach, there is no private provision of quality altogether. This stems from consumers' lack of concern for animal welfare. Under the indirect approach, there is underprovision of quality because of the public good problem. In both cases however, the use of animal welfare standards may help reach the socially optimal level of quality.

Let me now discuss the quantity choice. We have seen under both approaches that the quantity consumed at the equilibrium is too low if life is worth living and too high if it is not. Again, the outcome is similar but the explanation differs between both approaches.

Under the direct approach, this is because consumers do not account for the (positive or negative) impact of their consumption choices on animals. Under the indirect approach, this is because consumers do not take into account the impact of their choices on other altruistic consumers. In both cases, the sign of the impact is determined by the sign of the utility of the animals (life worth living).

I have also discussed the effect of an increase in animal concerns under each approach. This effect corresponds to an increase in the level of antispeciesism a under the direct approach and to an increase in the level of altruism α under the indirect approach. We have seen that the socially efficient provision of quality always increases in both a and α. Moreover, we have seen that there is a U-shaped pattern on the number of animals consumed: an increase in animal concern through either a or α first decreases then increases this number. Again, very similar results.

Going further into the reflection about the different approaches, we may also discuss the case in which both approaches are combined. As mentioned in the introduction, this presents certain challenges, specifically the issue of double counting. Under the combined approach, animal welfare is indeed accounted for twice in the SWF, once directly and again indirectly through consumers' preferences. To see this, suppose that an altruistic consumer has the following preferences:

$$u(n_i) - cn_i + \alpha \sum_{j=1}^{N} n_j v. \tag{13.11}$$

To make things simple, note that animal welfare is assumed to be fixed in equation (13.11) and equal to v as in the canonical model. I thus consider quality as exogenous and solely focus on the quantity choice. The equilibrium level of consumption in this economy is given by the following FOC:

$$u'(n) - c + \alpha v = 0. \tag{13.12}$$

Let me now explore the socially efficient level of animal consumption in this economy. It is given by maximizing over n the following social objective:

$$N\left[u(n) - cn + \alpha Nnv + anv\right]. \tag{13.13}$$

The key point here is that the animal's utility term v appears twice in this expression, reflecting the double counting of animal welfare in the social objective. Remember indeed that n is the number of animals consumed per human. Hence, animals are accounted for twice in this objective since each human cares about the Nn consumed by all humans (i.e., the anthropocentric term, αNnv), and also consumes n animals (i.e., the nonanthropocentric term, anv). This yields the following FOC:

$$u'(n) - c + \alpha Nv + av = 0. \tag{13.14}$$

By comparing (13.12) and (13.14), we can see two differences. One is due to the difference between αv and αNv, and reflects the public good problem arising when $N > 1$. That is, the consumer does not account for the impact of his consumption on the other $N-1$ altruistic consumers. Second, another difference is due to the term av, which captures the value of (non)existence of animals overlooked by individual consumers. Note that the sign of both differences depends on the sign of v. Hence, both effects go in the same direction: When life is worth living $v > 0$, then there is underconsumption of meat, and when life is not worth living $v < 0$, there is overconsumption.

Logically, this provides two justifications for policy intervention. This makes sense since there are now two sources of misalignment between the consumers' preferences and the social objective. By a similar reasoning as in Chapter 7, we can then apply an animal welfare levy. It is easy to see that it takes the following form in this economy: $t = -\alpha(N-1)v - av$. This formula for the levy indeed reflects the two justifications for policy intervention: the anthropocentric one through the term $-\alpha(N-1)v$ (indirect approach), and the nonanthropocentric one through the term $-av$ (direct approach).

Let me now make another digression. Consider an alternative model with only two individuals. Individual 1 does not care about animals and derives utility $u(n_1) - cn_1$. Individual 2 does care about animals and derives utility $u(n_2) - cn_2 + \alpha(n_1 + n_2)v$ where n_j is the number of animals consumed by individual $j = 1,2$. The anthropocentric social objective is simply to maximize the sum of both individuals' utilities. It is then easy to show that the socially optimal consumption is equal to $u(n_j) = c - \alpha v$, $j = 1,2$. This implies that, to realign individual incentives and achieve the first-best outcome, a tax $t = -\alpha v$ could be imposed on the consumption of individual 1. Note that individual 2 does not need to be taxed since she already consumes at the socially optimal level. The challenge, however, arises from the practical difficulty of implementing personalized taxes. If the same tax t must be applied uniformly to both individuals, the first-best outcome cannot typically be achieved. This limitation underscores the complexity of designing effective policies in settings with heterogeneous preferences. This is a topic that I typically set aside in this book.

13.4 ANIMAL WELFARE AS A MERIT GOOD

In economics, a merit good is a good or service that is deemed beneficial for individuals but that individuals nevertheless underconsume. The government then typically intervenes to encourage the consumption of these goods, such as healthcare or education. It is important to understand that the rationale for government intervention here is not the standard one based on market failures or distributional issues. Instead, it is motivated by the belief that individuals might make mistaken decisions. Therefore, this concept largely falls within the domain of behavioral economics.

The point explored in this section is that animal welfare may be considered a merit good. The idea is that individuals may misvalue animal welfare, as documented in previous chapters, leading to mistaken decisions involving animals. For instance, people may underestimate animal suffering in industrial farming conditions, and overconsume meat as a result. The key point is that government intervention is then justified from the perspective of benefiting individuals themselves in the sense that they would ideally want to make informed and sound decisions regarding animals but fail to do so.

Hence, this is a paternalistic form of intervention: Since individuals misestimate animal welfare, it makes sense to intervene in the economy to improve their decisions for their own benefit. Let me emphasize again, to be clear: The motive for intervention here is not because humans do not care about animal welfare, but because they do not care as they should from the point of view of the government (which is assumed to be correct for simplicity).

Following Besley (1988), I use a simple model to demonstrate that a tax or a subsidy on meat can optimally correct individual decisions when animal welfare is treated as a merit (or a demerit) good. Since the merit good argument is behavioral by nature, I am removing the public good aspect in the model of this section in order to focus solely on the individual's mistaken decisions. I assume that consumers display responsible altruism; see Section 13.2. Suppose then that individuals' preferences take the following form:

$$u(n) - cn + \alpha n(v + \theta), \tag{13.15}$$

where the parameter θ is the key parameter here: It indicates the misperception of animal welfare by the consumer compared to the "correct" perception: $\theta = 0$.

Note that the consumer does care about animal welfare. But the point is that there is a bias in how much he cares because of the misperception θ. As a benchmark, optimal consumption n^* is obtained as usual by maximizing the consumers' preferences under the correct perceptions $\theta = 0$, namely by maximizing $u(n) - cn + \alpha nv$. This leads to the following FOC: $u'(n^*) - c + \alpha v = 0$. It is immediate then that the consumption level given by the maximization of (13.15) deviates from n^* as soon as θ is different from 0. This suboptimal consumption decision is the motive for the government's intervention.

Let me now show that the first-best consumption n^* can be retrieved by using, again, a levy t. When the levy is introduced, the individual consumption choice, denoted $n(t, \theta)$, is simply given by

$$u'(n(t,\theta)) - c - t + \alpha(v + \theta) = 0. \tag{13.16}$$

The objective of the government is then to maximize over t the following objective (where the tax revenues are given back to consumers, as in the canonical model):

$$u(n(t,\theta)) - cn(t,\theta) + \alpha n(t,\theta)v. \quad (13.17)$$

Crucially, note that the government does not directly account for the misperception θ in (13.17) as the parameter θ is not added to v in the last term. This is the precise sense in which the government is paternalistic since it does not maximize the welfare of consumers based on the consumers' perception of animal welfare. Instead, the government maximizes the "true" welfare of the consumer computed under the true value of animal welfare v, corresponding to the case $\theta = 0$. However, note that the government accounts indirectly for the misperception in the behavioral response of the consumer to the tax t given the value of θ, namely through the term $n(t,\theta)$. Hence, the optimal levy depends on θ only indirectly through its effect on $n(t,\theta)$. Indeed, the FOC associated with (13.17) is equal to $u'(n(t,\theta)) - c + \alpha v = 0$, which, together with (13.16), gives

$$t = \alpha\theta. \quad (13.18)$$

The optimal levy is thus equal to the misperception gap θ multiplied by the altruism parameter. Trivially, it is a tax when consumers overestimate animal welfare ($\theta > 0$) and overconsume meat as a result, while it is a subsidy when consumers underestimate animal welfare ($\theta < 0$), and thus underconsume meat. It is immediate to see that the levy permits to reach the first-best level of consumption. Indeed, combining (13.16) and (13.18) we have $u'(n(t,\theta)) - c + \alpha v = 0$, which characterizes the first-best solution, that is, $n(t,\theta) = n^{\star}$. Similar results are formally derived in Besley (1988), with the slight difference that Besley considers a multiplicative term θ while I considered an additive term. Note that Besley's multiplicative modeling is criticized by Schroyen (2005), who employs a different approach to modeling (de)merit goods.

To conclude, let me make a few comments about those results regarding the merit goods aspect of animal welfare. First, given that it is plausible that many people overestimate animal welfare ($\theta > 0$), the analysis would tend to support the implementation of a tax on meat. Note, again, that this policy recommendation contrasts with most observed regulatory practices, which typically focus on animal welfare standards rather than imposing a levy on meat consumption. Second, it seems possible to empirically estimate the levy if one has both estimates for actual animal welfare and estimates for people's misperceptions about animal welfare. Note however that misperceptions about animal welfare are expected to be highly heterogeneous in society. Since the implementation of heterogeneous taxes is in general not feasible, the use of a uniform tax can only be justified then under a systematic perception bias in society.

Third, an alternative, and perhaps more natural, form of intervention would be to provide information to consumers to correct their perception gap. However, the merit good argument precisely rests on consumers' faulty decisions that, for various reasons, cannot be fully corrected by informational instruments alone. Again, this provides a different basis for taxation than the one based on standard market failures such as externalities or public goods. Last, the modeling of the behavioral limitation through the misperception parameter θ is very parsimonious but lacks precise behavioral foundations. From this point of view, the next chapter studies a well-founded behavioral model generating the misperception (cognitive dissonance), aligning more closely with recent advances in behavioral economics.

REFERENCES

Bergstrom T, Blume L, Varian H (1986) On the private provision of public goods. *Journal of Public Economics*, 29(1), 25–49.

Besley T (1988) A simple model for merit good arguments. *Journal of Public Economics*, 35(3), 371–383.

Cowen T (2006) Market failure for the treatment of animals. *Society*, 43(2), 39–44.

Espinosa R, Treich N (2023) Animal welfare as a public good. *Ecological Economics*, 216, 108025.

Leider S, Möbius MM, Rosenblat T, Do QA (2009) Directed altruism and enforced reciprocity in social networks. *The Quarterly Journal of Economics*, 124(4), 1815–1851.

Lusk JL, Norwood FB (2012) Speciesism, altruism and the economics of animal welfare. *European Review of Agricultural Economics*, 39, 189–212.

Schroyen F (2005) An alternative way to model merit good arguments. *Journal of Public Economics*, 89(5–6), 957–966.

14 An Economic Model of the Meat Paradox

14.1 THE MODEL

In Chapter 12, I discussed the meat paradox. Drawing from the extensive literature on cognitive dissonance, I presented psychological studies that offer compelling evidence in support of this paradox. In this chapter, I propose an economic analysis of the meat paradox. It builds on a simplified version of the model in Hestermann et al. (2020), which, in turn, adapts the architecture of the model of motivated beliefs put forth by Bénabou and Tirole (2002). This chapter is quite technical (even more than the previous one), and can perhaps be considered as the most technically advanced in this book. It indeed uses fairly recent economic theories that approach psychology with the tools of game theory. Nevertheless, I only present here a simplified version of those theories. Moreover, to make the content accessible and relatable to a wider audience, I have dedicated the last section of this chapter to discussing in simple terms the model's assumptions, interpretations, and implications.

Let me first adapt the canonical model. A consumer chooses optimal meat consumption n to maximize his utility:

$$u(n) - pn + \alpha nv, \tag{14.1}$$

in which $\alpha > 0$ could be conceived as before as the level of altruism. Crucially, I now assume that the well-being of animals v is uncertain. This uncertainty may represent the consumer's lack of knowledge regarding various aspects such as the animals' rearing conditions, the utility potential or sentience of the animals, among others. Formally, I assume that v can take two values with equal probability, either a good state $v = v_g > 0$ or a bad state $v = v_b < 0$.

Observe that the consumer always prefers the good state v_g to the bad state v_b. This is because the consumer cares about animals, and prefers them to be in a better state. Formally, let the indirect utility function for a given v:

$$V(v) \equiv u(n(v)) - pn(v) + \alpha n(v)v, \tag{14.2}$$

with optimal consumption $n(v)$ given by the FOC (as before I focus on interior solutions):

$$u'(n(v)) - p + \alpha v = 0. \tag{14.3}$$

Obviously, by the envelope theorem, the indirect utility increases with v: $V'(v) = \alpha n(v) > 0$. Hence, the consumer strictly prefers a higher animal welfare level. Note also that $n'(v) = \frac{-\alpha}{u''(n(v))} > 0$: Meat consumption increases with that level.

I now introduce the motivated belief (or cognitive dissonance) aspect of this model. This is the crucial part. Suppose that at some point the consumer observes the realized state, the good or bad one. Suppose in addition that the consumer can, at a cost k, manipulate his own beliefs about that state, namely his own beliefs about the level of animal welfare. Formally, this means the following: When observing one state, he can believe that the other state occurred. Obviously, since the consumer prefers the good state, he has no incentive to believe the bad state occurred instead of the good state. But he has an incentive to believe that the good state occurred instead of the bad state. This is because he would feel better if he thinks that animals have a good life.

In the following, I thus focus on the bad state, which is the interesting case. When observing that state, the consumer thus faces a tradeoff between realism and denial. Under realism, his welfare is equal to $V(v_b)$ corresponding to the indirect utility in the bad state, while under denial it is equal to $V(v_g) - k$, corresponding to the indirect utility in the good state minus the cost of self-deception k. There is thus a cutoff value for the cost of self-deception, $\hat{k} = V(v_g) - V(v_b)$: When the self-deception cost is low enough $k \leq \hat{k}$

then the consumer is in denial, while when this cost is high enough $k \geq \hat{k}$ then he is realistic.

Note that this simple psychological model predicts a negative association between meat consumption and realism. Indeed, under realism, meat consumption is equal to $n(v_b)$ which is lower than the consumption under denial, that is, $n(v_g)$ since $n'(v) > 0$. Hence, more realistic consumers consume less meat, other things being equal. This is intuitive: The benefit to self-deceive is greater when meat consumption is higher.

14.2 COMPARATIVE STATICS

Following the motivated beliefs literature, the primary innovation in this model lies in the endogeneity of beliefs concerning animal welfare. Consequently, an interesting question emerges: How do the model's parameters influence these beliefs? We have seen that the cutoff value $\hat{k} = V(v_g) - V(v_b)$ determines whether the consumer is realistic or not. This cutoff value thus captures the benefit from self-deception: It measures the net benefit of believing that the good state occurred instead of the bad state. I now explore how the model's parameters affect this cutoff value, and thus in turn his endogenous beliefs.

I first consider the effect of the taste for meat (or preferences for meat more generally). In the model, this taste is captured by the shape of the utility function of meat $u(.)$. Formally, a greater taste for meat implies, everything else equal, greater meat consumption $n(v)$. A simple use of this definition of a greater taste for meat is then enough to solve the comparative statics analysis. Indeed, observe that a greater meat consumption $n(v)$ leads to a greater $\hat{k}$ (since this increases $V'(v) = \alpha n(v)$). Therefore, a higher taste for meat is associated with a lower level of realism: Individuals with a higher taste for meat are more likely to resort to self-deception.

I now explore the impact of the price of meat p. It is not very difficult to see that $\frac{\partial \hat{k}}{\partial p} = n(v_b) - n(v_g) \leq 0$. Hence, an increase in the price reduces the benefit from self-deception. The reason is that a higher price decreases meat consumption, and in turn the benefit to manipulate one's own beliefs. At the limit, under vegetarianism, there is no benefit of self-deception. Hence, there is a "crowding in" effect of a change in price here, since the psychological effect reinforces the economic effect through its impact on the changes in beliefs.

I now study the impact of altruism α. It is easy to see that $\frac{\partial \hat{k}}{\partial \alpha} = v_g n(v_g) - v_b n(v_b)$, whose sign thus depends on how $vn(v)$ varies with v. Straightforward manipulations show that this depends on whether the term $\frac{-nu''(n)}{u'(n)-p}$ is greater or lower than 1. This term reflects an elasticity of consumption (net of the unit price). Hence, under inelastic demand, the consumer becomes less realistic when altruism increases, while under elastic demand the opposite result holds. The intuition is the following: Consumers with inelastic demand are unwilling to lower their consumption; as a consequence, they are more likely to resort to motivated cognition in order to alleviate the psychological disutility associated with their consumption behavior.

I conclude the comparative statics analysis by exploring the impact of information. To do so, I compare the situation with and without information about the true value of v. Without information, the consumer's expected welfare is equal to $V(\frac{1}{2}v_g + \frac{1}{2}v_b)$. With information, under realism, expected welfare is equal to $\frac{1}{2}V(v_g) + \frac{1}{2}V(v_b)$. Since V is convex $(V''(v) = \alpha n'(v) > 0)$, this implies $\frac{1}{2}V(v_g) + \frac{1}{2}V(v_b) > V(\frac{1}{2}v_g + \frac{1}{2}v_b)$. Hence a realistic consumer always prefers information. This is an illustration of the classical result that costless information is always valuable since it allows the decision-maker to make better choices. I now study the value of information under denial. In that case, expected welfare with information is equal to $V(v_g) - \frac{1}{2}k$. The point is that the comparison of this last term with the expected welfare without information $V(\frac{1}{2}v_g + \frac{1}{2}v_b)$ is generally unclear. This implies that the effect of information is ambiguous in this case. It is thus possible that under denial a consumer prefers to ignore information. The intuition is that information is costly here. Indeed, if information reveals that the bad state occurred, the consumer has to pay the cost of self-deception to change his beliefs.

14.3 INTERPRETATIONS AND IMPLICATIONS

Before discussing some implications of the results above, let me first discuss some assumptions of the model. First, the model assumes that the consumer cares about animal welfare through the parameter α. This assumption is instrumental to generate cognitive dissonance. Indeed, it highlights the tradeoff between the utility derived from meat consumption and the disutility associated with the externality of that consumption on animals. While I initially interpreted the parameter α as a measure of (responsible) altruism, this parameter can also be alternatively interpreted as warm glow, guilt, or the moral pressures exerted on an individual's behavior. These different interpretations may reflect the multifaceted nature of the underlying motivations driving consumers' attitudes toward animal welfare that we discussed before.

The model also assumes that there is a cost of self-deception k. In conventional economic models, self-deception is typically considered impossible, resulting in an implicit assumption of an infinite cost of self-deception. However, in this model, I follow the economic literature on cognitive dissonance building on Bénabou and Tirole, and I assume the cost of self-deception to be finite. What could this self-deception cost represent? Several interpretations are possible, such as the cost of repressing or forgetting a signal, the cost of actively seeking contradictory evidence, or the cost of rationalizing one's behavior. It seems clear that not all beliefs are possible, or at the cost of making serious mistakes. That is, there is also a cost of self-deception in terms of suboptimal decisions.

Although I did not mention this hypothesis explicitly in the model's presentation in this chapter, there is an implicit assumption of "naïveté." Let me try to explain why. Remember that I modeled self-deception as follows: When observing one state, the consumer can believe that the other state occurred. In fact, this can be formally captured in a more complex model by a signaling game between two consumer's incarnations (Bénabou and Tirole 2002) where the first incarnation sends a signal about the state of animal welfare to the second incarnation, who then decides on the level of consumption. To keep things simple, I assumed that the second incarnation always takes the signal at face value, disregarding any strategic motives the first incarnation may have. While Hestermann et al. (2020) explore a Bayesian signaling game building on Bénabou and Tirole (2002), they obtain similar predictions to those presented in this chapter. Hence, the findings above would also hold in a model featuring sophistication (but at the cost of a much more complex model). Whether the assumption of naïveté or sophistication is more realistic remains largely unknown, and deserves more empirical research.

I now briefly discuss the theoretical results. One basic prediction of the model is a negative correlation between realism (regarding animal welfare) and meat consumption. This finding aligns with the evidence discussed in Chapter 12: Omnivores tend to underestimate animal suffering compared to flexitarians or vegetarians. Hence, motivated beliefs lead to further increase the consumption levels of individuals with high taste for meat, inducing an exacerbation of consumption differences among individuals with varying tastes. In other words, the psychological impact associated with meat consumption intensifies the consumption gap between individuals with different levels of meat preference.

One of the most interesting results of this model is probably the one on the price. This result indicates that a "price shock" may affect beliefs about animal welfare. This effect from the price on beliefs is unusual in economics. It arises because in our behavioral model price affects meat consumption, and in turn the demand for self-deception.

An increase in the price of meat decreases meat consumption levels, and thus the incentives to self-deceive. An immediate consequence of this result is that meat consumption is more sensitive to price than in a conventional model. The reason is that there are two effects of price: the classical economic effect leading to a reduction in consumption, and the novel psychological effect, leading to more realism and a further decrease in meat consumption.

We have seen that consumers with a higher level of altruism (or warm glow, or guilt, etc.) may be more likely to resort to self-deception. This is because more altruistic consumers suffer more from the psychological cost associated with their consumption. This further suggests that altruism, perhaps paradoxically, need not induce lower meat consumption. This sounds paradoxical because more altruistic consumers are expected to consume less meat (from animals with lives not worth living). This primary intuition would hold indeed in the model with fixed beliefs about v. But the subtlety here is that beliefs are endogenous. Hence, a more altruistic individual may also be more motivated to hold optimistic beliefs about v, which in turn provides an incentive to consume more, and not less, meat. Speculating about this last observation, this also suggests that "manipulating" guilt through moral pressure may have unexpected effects on meat consumption.

Additionally, we have seen that the value of information may be negative within this model, which is a typical feature of motivated beliefs models inspired by Bénabou and Tirole (2002). The mechanism is easy to understand in our context. While acquiring more information theoretically enables consumers to make more informed consumption decisions, the revelation of the reality about animal welfare may decrease consumers' well-being. Consequently, a tradeoff arises where certain consumers may actually prefer to "look away" and avoid confronting the truth, despite the usual decision-making benefits of acquiring additional knowledge.

In the motivated beliefs literature, this result about the possible negative value of information has often been used as a test of those models. Indeed, incorrect beliefs' updating is difficult to document empirically, whereas attitudes toward information are more easily elicited. Hence, motivated reasoning is often (indirectly) evidenced by demonstrating that many subjects prefer to remain ignorant about the realities of industrial farming. Consistent with this prediction, Epperson and Gerster (2024) find that about 30 percent of their subjects avoid information on animals' living conditions in intensive farming. Moreover, Epperson and Gerster show that people respond to their beliefs. At university canteens, information avoiders reduce their meat consumption by around 30 percentage points in the first days after being obliged to watch a video about intensive farming.

Note also the following possible implication regarding the dynamics of beliefs. When individuals consistently ignore or disregard information, their beliefs may deviate significantly from what could be considered as true beliefs. Consequently, a single piece of information has the potential to exert a profound influence on their beliefs. This phenomenon may shed light on the occurrence of "epiphanies," where individuals experience sudden shifts in their beliefs after being exposed to certain stimuli, such as watching a movie or reading a book. Such experiences can act as catalysts, causing a substantial transformation in their previously held beliefs.

It is important to recognize that, in the real world, information does not simply appear out of nowhere. Instead, it is often generated by various stakeholders. This production of information can be strategically influenced to account for the consumer's psychology. In particular, producers may strategically construct narratives or sow doubt, which can be particularly effective when consumers are not genuinely inclined to seek out information. Note that even displaying an honest label about animal welfare could be counterproductive for a producer. It might make animal welfare concerns more salient, increasing consumers' self-deception costs and potentially leading to a backlash against meat products. Animal advocacy NGOs also produce pieces of information, such as undercover videos to expose the reality of animal farming, aiming to create epiphanies and to have a lasting impact on consumers. For instance, NGOs might employ "shock" campaigns to provoke strong emotional reactions.

Information may also come from observing the behavior of other consumers. In Hestermann et al. (2020), we extend the model to include multiple identical consumers. Our findings reveal that both a "collective denial equilibrium" and a "collective realism equilibrium" can exist in this economy. The intuition is as follows: If all consumers deny the evidence, their consumption decisions are not informative about the original message, thereby increasing the scope for self-deception. In other words, if consumers observe others eating large amounts of meat, it reinforces the belief that there is no problem with animal welfare, thus supporting the collective denial equilibrium. Conversely, if consumers see others eating little or no meat, it aligns with the belief that there is a problem with animal welfare. In this collective realism equilibrium, the incentives to rationalize the evidence away are limited, as observing others consuming small quantities makes it impossible for individuals to ignore the animal welfare externalities of meat consumption. Overall, the presence of other realistic agents gives individuals stronger incentives to accept the evidence.

Overall, the meat paradox raises profound questions regarding the specific circumstances that prompt consumers to modify their behavior. It highlights the tendency of individuals to evade information and, even if they acquire it, to engage in self-deception as a means to "forget" what they have learned. This begs another central question: What kind of information is truly impossible to ignore? At present, this remains largely an open question.

In conclusion, it is important to highlight that the meat paradox can offer some insights into the "gap" observed between public opinion and market demand, as emphasized in the introduction. This gap may arise from the significant variations in information presented in different contexts. During survey studies or voting processes that focus on animal welfare, information about animal welfare tends to be prominently featured and difficult to ignore. In such contexts, it becomes challenging to overlook the ethical concerns related to animal welfare. On the contrary, in markets, producers and retailers largely control the framing, and they may strategically choose to downplay or selectively avoid emphasizing animal welfare on their products. Hence, in a world where consumers display cognitive dissonance, this control over information presentation may contribute to the divide between public attitudes and market demands.

REFERENCES

Bénabou R, Tirole J (2002) Self-confidence and personal motivation. *Quarterly Journal of Economics*, 117(3), 871–915.

Epperson R, Gerster A (2024) Willful ignorance and moral behavior, mimeo.

Hestermann N, Le Yaouanq Y, Treich N (2020) An economic model of the meat paradox. *European Economic Review*, 129, 103569.

15 Some Economics of Pets

15.1 THE ECONOMICS OF PETS' OWNERSHIP

A primary question to discuss regarding the economics of pets concerns the motive for pet ownership. According to Endenburg et al. (1994), by far the main motive is companionship. Through their dependence on humans and their continuous presence, pets can satisfy various emotional needs of humans. In contrast, few people say they primarily adopt a dog for pure practical purposes such as guarding for instance. Most people see dogs as a member of the family (Schwarz et al. 2007). Weimer and Vining (2024) discuss various roles for dogs in their book "Dog Economics." They report a survey study in which respondents from the United States (N = 4,973) were asked to indicate the possible roles for their dogs (and were given the opportunity to specify more than one role). A large majority of respondents (93 percent) consider their dogs as pets, and over half of them consider them to be companions; see Table 15.1.

The decision to have pets comes with benefits, but also with significant costs. There are actually several types of costs. Many pets are bought, so there is often a significant acquisition cost. This goes along with food and veterinary expenditures. Moreover, there are what economists call the "opportunity costs." These opportunity costs include for instance the value of time spent providing care, and the loss of flexibility in terms of schedules and travel. Some people may also choose or be limited to certain housing options for living or in holidays to accommodate pets, potentially forgoing more affordable or desirable places that do not allow animals.

Pets are often viewed as an impulse purchase. However, expected benefits such as companionship and various costs seem to

Table 15.1 *Multiple dog roles reported by owners*

Role	Percent
Pet	93
Guide	4
Companion	51
Guard	25
Agriculture	1
Breeder	1

Source: Weimer and Vining (2024)

play a major role to explain the demand for pets. As an illustration of this economic approach to pet ownership, Weimer and Vining (2024) discuss the COVID-19 pandemic which spurred the demand for pets. They argue that the pandemic increased the value of pet companionship as a replacement for the loss of human companionship due to (e.g.) lockdowns and reduced work interactions. Moreover, the pandemic also reduced the opportunity cost of owning a dog, as people spent more time at home and traveled less.

Numerous studies suggest that pets can function as substitutes for children, also indicating that pet ownership is a deliberate and enduring choice. Households with very young children indeed tend to be less likely to own pets. Endenburg et al. (2014) indicate that childhood experiences and a willingness to dedicate spare time to animals increase the likelihood of pet ownership. Similarly, home ownership and income levels also increase pet ownership rates. In the United States, dog ownership peaks in the third quartile of family income. Additionally, ownership rates are highest among individuals aged 50–59 years, and households in cities are less likely to have a dog compared to those in small towns and rural areas (Weimer and Vining 2024).

The pet industry is a multi-billion-dollar global market, covering pet food, veterinary care, grooming, insurance, and accessories (see Chapter 2). The lifetime cost of a pet varies widely, but may be estimated in the range of $20,000 for a dog in the United States and about $1,000–$5,000 for smaller pets (rabbits, hamsters, birds). Weimer and Vining (2024) discuss supply side issues within the dog market, highlighting various organizational structures based on size and profit orientation. They distinguish between "backyard breeders," typically producing a small number of puppies, as opposed to pedigree breeders, who operate more professionally and yield larger litters. They also discuss the presence of illegal and unethical practices, such as black-market breeders and puppy mills. Following standard economic analysis, they discuss possible market failures, including information asymmetry favoring breeders over owners (breeders have a better knowledge about the dog than the possible future owners at the time of the purchase) and externalities stemming from the societal burden of unsold or unfit puppies. Weimer and Vining also touch upon the supply of dogs from shelters, which can be likened to a "used dog market."

15.2 A SIMPLE INVESTMENT MODEL

From now, I explore an adapted version of the canonical model to examine a few aspects related to the decision making process of pets' owners. As before, it may be useful to distinguish quantity and quality. Typically, the owner may decide how many pets to "consume" (quantity), and how much to invest in their welfare (quality). For reference, the consumption model discussed in Chapter 12 remains relevant here (see also Schwarz et al. 2007); but the current focus now shifts to the quality decision only. That is, I focus on the welfare level of the pet after it has been acquired.

As in previous analyses, I maintain the assumption of pure altruism while excluding the consideration of the public good dimension. This means that the owner cares about his own pet, but not about other pets in the society (or that this aspect concerning other pets does not matter for the decision making problem at stake and is thus ignored). This assumption is consistent with responsible altruism; see Chapter 13. Additionally, and in contrast to previous analysis in this book, this chapter places significant emphasis on the wealth of the pet owner as a crucial determinant in the decision-making process.

Formally, let $u(w)$ be the utility of the owner of the pet in which w is the owner's wealth. Assume that this utility function is increasing and concave in wealth. The owner can exert an effort e in the form of a financial investment to improve the well-being of the pet denoted $v(e)$, which is positive, increasing and concave in e. This effort may be related to financial investments in food, veterinary services or more care in general. The owner's utility can thus be written:

$$u(w-e)+\alpha v(e) \tag{15.1}$$

where α is the level of altruism of the owner toward the pet. The optimal investment in effort is simply given by the following FOC:

$$-u'(w-e)+\alpha v'(e)=0 \tag{15.2}$$

That is, the marginal cost of an extra effort is equal to its marginal benefit in terms of hedonic value for the owner associated with a marginal increase in the pet's well-being. Since an increase in α increases the marginal benefit term $\alpha v'(e)$, the optimal effort increases in α. Hence, as is intuitive, a more altruistic owner invests more in effort to improve the quality of life of the pet, other things equal. This indicates for instance that the effort may vary depending on pets, those generating more altruism from their owners getting more expenditures.

Moreover, since an increase in wealth w decreases the marginal cost term $-u'(w-e)$, the optimal effort increases in wealth. This is intuitive too since a wealthier owner can more easily afford financial expenditures, other things equal. As a result, this suggests that societies with higher wealth levels may tend to allocate more financial resources to pet care, all other factors being constant. This inference seems to corroborate the observation that pet veterinary expenditures have indeed increased over the years, as discussed in Chapter 2; see Einav et al. (2017) for the United States.

Note that this last theoretical result about the impact of wealth is related to the assumption that the effort is commensurable with wealth and thus can be interpreted as a financial effort. If, in contrast, the effort would have been incommensurable with wealth, such as one described by the following utility $u(w) - l(e) + \alpha v(e)$, then the optimal effort decision would have been independent from wealth. One could even imagine that the cost of effort reflects the opportunity cost of time, which is usually greater for wealthier people. In that case, wealthier people would invest less, and not more, for pets.

15.3 MEDICAL EXPENDITURES AND INSURANCE

In this section, I focus on a specific economic aspect: medical expenditures. Remember that medical expenditures through veterinary services represent about half of dog-related expenditures; see Chapter 2. I consider a variant version of the model presented in the previous section. Suppose that a pet has a deadly disease, and the owner can cure the pet if he spends an indivisible amount of medical expenditure, l (i.e., vet expenditures). I assume that the well-being of pets is fixed and simply equal to $v > 0$ here.

If the owner spends that amount l he gets a utility level $u(w - l) + \alpha v$, namely the utility of wealth net of the expenditure and the hedonic utility derived from the pet (the pet is saved). This particular choice is referred to as "self-insurance," wherein the owner invests in the medical treatment of the pet. Alternatively the owner may decide to forgo spending this amount; in this case, he simply gets a utility level $u(w)$, that is, initial wealth but with no utility from the pet (as the pet passes away due to the untreated deadly disease). This case could be described as "economic euthanasia" since the owner decides to let the pet die because he cannot afford the necessary medical expenditures.

What is the effect of wealth on the likelihood to choose self-insurance or economic euthanasia? Observe that, since $u'(w - l) > u'(w)$ everywhere and in particular at w such that $u(w - l) + \alpha v = u(w)$, the two utility levels can only cross once, with the self-insurance

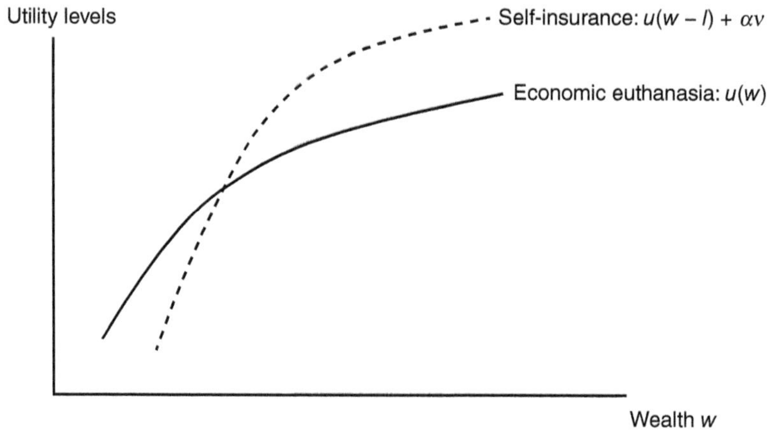

FIGURE 15.1 Utility levels as a function of wealth.

utility crossing from below. Hence, there is a critical level of wealth from which the owner invests in medical expenditures, as shown in Figure 15.1. This implies that the wealthier the pet owner, the more likely he is to rely on self-insurance.

Consider now the situation *ex ante*, before knowing if the pet will catch the disease or not. Suppose that the probability of catching the disease is p. The owner's utility levels associated with spending or not spending the necessary amount l are written respectively $(1-p)u(w)+pu(w-l)+\alpha v$ and $u(w)+(1-p)\alpha v$, reflecting exactly the same tradeoff as above. Since the decision to self-insure or to rely on economic euthanasia is made *ex post*, namely after knowing if the dog is sick, the indirect utility is the max of the two previous expressions, representing a non-concave indirect utility function of wealth *ex ante*.

Consider now another dimension to the choice: insurance. We have seen in Chapter 2 that pet insurance is a growing market, and represents significant expenditures. Suppose that it is possible to buy *ex ante* pet insurance covering the medical expenditures for the pet. In that case, the owner's *ex ante* utility is simply $u(w-\pi)+\alpha v$ where π is the insurance premium. Overall, given the insurance opportunity, the owner's utility level depends on whether he chooses "insurance" $u(w-\pi)+\alpha v$, "self-insurance" $(1-p)u(w)+pu(w-l)+\alpha v$, or "economic euthanasia" $u(w)+(1-p)\alpha v$.

Note that if the term αv is low enough, it is always optimal to resort to economic euthanasia. Indeed, when that term goes to zero, the utility level reached under economic euthanasia is greater than under insurance or self-insurance. This result holds for any positive insurance premium. Hence, this is in contrast with a traditional result in insurance economics due to Mossin (1968) that insurance should always be purchased if the insurance is actuarially fair: $\pi = pl$. Hence, Mossin's result does not hold here in our basic pet insurance model. The intuition is simple: insurance is purchased only for pets which provide high enough hedonic utility to humans. The term αv is low when the level of altruism α is low and/or the animal well-being v is low. Old animals with limited life expectancy and poor health may have a low v, and are thus less likely to be favored for medical treatment according to the model, other things equal. Using a survey study in the United States, Carlson et al. (2019) show that the owners' WTP for dog's reduction in mortality risk increases when "the dog is viewed as a companion," and with the life expectancy of the dog. Note that this effect depends ultimately on the perception of the pet's well-being by the owner, and also on the long term bond between the owner and her animal.

How does the owner's wealth w affect preferences among the three choices? Under standard risk preferences (i.e., under standard "shapes" for the utility function of wealth $u(.)$), it is well known that insurance is theoretically an inferior good (Mossin 1968): when wealth increases the agent purchases less insurance. However, it is easy to understand that for low levels of wealth the owner prefers not to invest in medical expenditures (either through self-insurance or through insurance that reimburse those expenditures). This implies that insurance is not an inferior good in this specific model. In short, poor people choose economic euthanasia while rich people choose self-insurance. Insurance is only purchased for intermediate values of wealth. Again, pet insurance is quite special as it yields different theoretical results compared to traditional insurance.

Suppose finally that if the pet dies, it can be replaced by another pet at cost c. For the sake of comparison, assume that the new pet generates the same hedonic value for the owner through the term αv. It is immediate then that the decision to buy a new pet is similar to that of investing in medical expenditures. The tradeoff is between paying for medical expenditures l and buying a new pet at a cost c. If $c > l$, then it is optimal to invest in medical expenditures. If $c < l$, then it is optimal to let the first pet die if sick and to buy a second pet. This simple case emphasizes the importance of the notion of "replaceability" in pet decision-making. Some pets may be viewed as more replaceable than others. This suggests that people may spend less on medical care and insurance for pets that are easily replaceable, like pet fish, since the human-animal bond is expected to be weaker on average compared to pets like dogs. Note finally that the notion of replaceability used here is very different from the one used in Part II, such as when I talked about the Singer's replaceability argument. Here, this is all about whether the pet is replaceable from the owner's point of view, while in Part II it was about whether the animal is replaceable from the social point of view.

15.4 OTHER ASPECTS IN THE ECONOMICS OF PETS

The preliminary analysis above explores formally the decision-making process of pet owners regarding medical expenditures, insurance and the role of (perceived) well-being and altruistic considerations in shaping those choices. It underscores the importance of considering individual pet characteristics and owners' preferences when analyzing the economic aspects of pet care and insurance. This analysis may be viewed as a natural first step. However, it is important to realize that it captures only a glimpse of the various aspects of the economics of pets. In this section, I briefly discuss a few other aspects.

I briefly discussed in the first section of this chapter the motives for owning a pet. A related, or symmetric, aspect to consider is the decision to relinquish a pet. In France, a well-known phenomenon is the surge in pet relinquishments before the summer holidays. This trend often occurs due to restrictions imposed by hotels or camping sites regarding pets' presence. This also reflects the opportunity costs of having pets that may change the desire to own them. Still, this raises the question of whether this decision is anticipated or not.

Coe et al. (2014) conducted a comprehensive scoping review, analyzing 192 papers on the subject. They identified several key factors leading to pet relinquishment, including moving to new locations, rental or housing challenges that are not pet-friendly, as well as issues related to the risk of aggressive behavior by a pet. Weimer and Vining (2024) advance the possible myopia and optimism biases of dog owners who may poorly anticipate the cost of owning a dog and their possible change in preferences towards the pet. These findings shed light on the complex reasons behind pet relinquishments and the multifaceted nature of the decisions made by pet owners. Understanding these factors, including the financial ones, can be crucial in developing strategies and policies to mitigate pet relinquishments and support responsible pet ownership, particularly during challenging times like holiday seasons when such events tend to peak.

Another concern pertains to the historical practices of dog breeders who have selectively bred for specific traits, often disregarding the impact on the overall health of dogs. Consequently, there can be a misalignment between the economic value placed on these animals by the pet owners and the actual state of well-being of the pets. This observation challenges the assumption of pure altruism of owners toward their pet, and calls for more research about the nature of proanimal concerns in the population of pet owners. It also calls for policy intervention based on a merit good argument (see Chapter 13), in the sense that policy makers may intervene to correct owners' poor decisions regarding pets. Weimer and Vining (2024) discuss at length the possible role of fashion and fads. Based on some empirical evidence, they suggest that breed popularity reflects fashion rather than function.

While pet caring is predominantly perceived as a private decision, it also encompasses a significant public good dimension. When people collectively care about pets in general (their own and those of others), they stand to benefit from owners who invest in their pets' well-being. Conversely, the relinquishment of pets can lead to adverse effects on these people. This public good aspect becomes evident through private donations made to shelters and rescue organizations aimed at assisting abandoned or homeless animals. Naturally, public authorities have a crucial role to play to address public good effects. Enacting animal protection laws and providing support to shelters can be instrumental in safeguarding the welfare of animals and addressing the broader concerns related to pet relinquishment.

A related issue is that of pet overpopulation (Coate and Knight 2010). This relates to the problem of quantity of animals that I have discussed at length in this book. However, the problem is of a different nature here compared to that studied in this book so far. Indeed, the problem does not really come from the fact that animals are created for human consumption, but rather because many pets are actually not "consumed." Namely, many pets do not find an owner. As a result, pets may live on their own or end up in shelters, with a life that may not be judged worth living, and costs for the collectivity.

This situation leading to poor pet welfare poses emotional concerns for people who genuinely care about pets, as they may empathize with the suffering and distress experienced by these animals without owners. Moreover, the burden of caring for such unowned animals usually falls on governmental bodies and NGOs, placing a strain on their resources and finances. In light of these challenges, public intervention is warranted. Effective policy measures may include controlling breeding practices, regulating the sale and illegal trafficking of pets, implementing taxation and licensing procedures, and promoting mandatory sterilization.

REFERENCES

Carlson D, Haeder S, Jenkins-Smith H, Ripberger J, Silva C, Weimer D (2019) Monetizing Bowser: A contingent valuation of the statistical value of dog life. *Journal of Benefit-Cost Analysis*, 11(1), 131–149.

Coate S, Knight B (2010) Pet overpopulation: An economic analysis. *The B.E. Journal of Economic Analysis and Policy*, 10(1), Article 106.

Coe JB, Young I, Lambert K, Dysart L, Nogueira Borden L, Rajić A (2014) A scoping review of published research on the relinquishment of companion animals. *Journal of Applied Animal Welfare Science*, 17(3), 253–273.

Einav L, Finkelstein A, Gupta A (2017) Is American pet health care (also) uniquely inefficient? *American Economic Review Papers and Proceedings.*

Endenburg N, 't Hart H, Bouw J (1994) Motives for acquiring companion animals. *Journal of Economic Psychology*, 15(1), 191–206.

Mossin J (1968) Aspects of rational insurance purchasing. *Journal of Political Economy*, 76(4, Part 1), 553–568.

Schwarz PM, Troyer JL, Walker JB (2007) Animal house: Economics of pets and the household. *B.E. Journal of Economic Analysis and Policy*, 7(1), 1–25.

Weimer DL, Vining AR (2024) *Dog Economics: Perspectives on Our Canine Relationships*. Cambridge University Press.

16 Markets and Morals

16.1 PRODUCTION COSTS

So far, my focus has centered on the demand side of animal welfare, specifically on the behavior of citizens and consumers. The reason is that I find the demand side to be the most conceptually challenging aspect to explore. I see the supply side as largely responsive to the consumer demands regarding animal welfare. From the supply side perspective, animal welfare can largely be viewed as one of the attributes of the goods that are produced, making the analysis of producers' decisions fairly standard in a sense. However, the simplicity of this view should not diminish the importance of supply-side issues. It is essential to keep in mind that improvements in animal welfare can only be implemented on the ground by producers, within their specific economic and regulatory environment. Understanding this environment is crucial, as it brings forth a range of technical, economic, and political challenges.

The animal farming sector traditionally presents a common narrative suggesting that human welfare and animal welfare are inherently aligned. This narrative is frequently tied to animal husbandry practices, which are portrayed as centered around caring for animals by providing them with food and shelter. It is clearly delusive, as we have seen repeatedly in this book. Just to give a few examples about the farming industry, the majority of animals are subject to confinement, mutilation, and ultimately slaughtered after a relatively short period, often just a few weeks or months.

Lusk and Norwood (2011) critically discuss this narrative with the help of a simple example (already briefly discussed in Chapter 2). They consider an egg producer facing the short-run problem of deciding how many hens to stock in a barn. Each hen produces more eggs when happier. If hens are too densely stocked, they will be unhappy and unproductive. Thus, providing a bit more space per hen would indeed increase both welfare and output. However, the point is that the farmer's objective is not about maximizing animal welfare or maximizing productivity per hen; rather, it is about maximizing profits. Lusk and Norwood then demonstrate that profit is expected to peak at a significantly higher stocking density than the one that maximizes productivity per hen.

In sum, the story is simple: In a market economy, producers are primarily driven by profit. As a result, animals are treated well when it is profitable to do so, but they are treated poorly when it is not profitable to treat them well. In other words, producers are not expected to view animals as sentient beings, but rather as production machines (McMullen 2015). Contrary to the notion of alignment between profitability and welfare, animal welfare in production systems tends to be minimal, as its improvement typically involves additional costs and logistical challenges. This underscores the importance of examining the production costs associated with enhancing animal welfare. This forms the central focus of the remainder of this section.

Several papers have studied the additional production cost associated with an improvement in animal welfare. For instance, Seibert and Norwood (2011), in an ex ante projection study, assess the production costs associated with four stylized hog production systems. Their findings indicate that enhancing animal welfare for all hogs in the United States would result in an increase in retail pork prices of 2 percent for a minor welfare enhancement and 5 percent for a substantial one involving free range. Hence, these costs seem modest compared to the substantial improvement of the life quality of pigs. This is because the main cost component concerns the food for pigs, which is common to the different production systems. Notably, the cost associated with banning gestation crates, as determined in this study, appears considerably lower than the consumer WTP estimates for animal welfare improvement taken from other studies.

In an ex post study, Malone and Lusk (2016) explore the cost of Proposition 2, a law which mandates a minimum floor space requirement for birds. This legislation was voted on in 2008 and enacted in 2015. It presented producers with the choice of either transitioning to cage-free barn systems, adopting larger "colony cages," or reducing stocking density in existing cages. To assess the economic impact of this law, Malone and Lusk gathered daily egg prices in California and the United States before and after the law's implementation. Their analysis indicates that Californian consumers pay between $0.48 and $1.08 more for a dozen eggs due to the reform. Furthermore, their estimates suggest an annual reduction in California consumer surplus ranging from $400 million to $850 million. In a follow-up study, Mullally and Lusk (2018) estimate that the price impact fell over time, from an initial impact of about 33 percent per dozen to about 9 percent over the last six months of their observed time horizon. Their results estimate a loss in California consumer surplus of at least $25 million in future years from higher retail egg prices.

Oh and Vukina (2022) conduct an ex ante study on the costs associated with the implementation of Proposition 12, which expands upon the regulations set forth in Proposition 2. In November 2018, California passed Proposition 12, which mandates the complete ban on selling eggs produced in any type of cages by the end of 2021. Prior to its implementation, Oh and Vukina estimate the welfare effects of Proposition 12, using a partial equilibrium model that simultaneously considers both the supply and demand sides of the market. Their findings indicate that Proposition 12 would lead to a substantial increase in the price of conventional eggs by 65 percent and thus significant welfare losses for both egg buyers and sellers in California. In an ex post preliminary study, Xie (2023) estimates that California consumers now pay an additional $0.25 to $0.73 for a dozen eggs due to the new regulation (an increase of between 11 percent to 33 percent in egg prices). With the presumed price-elasticity of demand, this results in a state-level annual loss in consumer surplus of $223 million to $664 million.

16.2 THE MORALITY OF MARKETS

The treatment of animals in our society is influenced by the choices of consumers and producers but also by the broader economic and institutional environment in which these choices are made. Therefore, it is important to expand our focus and examine the role of markets, globalization, and institutions more generally.

The economy depicted in the canonical model is basic and could be expanded in several ways. For instance, it does not account for market power, pre-existing tax distortions, or the budgetary impacts of regulation. As the model closely aligns with the textbook approach to externality regulation, existing research in public and environmental economics (e.g., Bovenberg and Goulder 2002) is directly relevant for possible extensions. One promising area of research within the industrial organization of food markets is the impact of animal welfare levies on the decision-making of meat producers in a more complex economy. For example, it would be valuable to estimate pass-through rates and market power adjustments in specific food markets.

In economics, the long-standing literature on second-best policies, introduced by Lipsey and Lancaster (1956), shows the challenge of implementing optimal policies in a complex economy. The core idea is that when a market failure in one sector remains uncorrected, attempting to address market failures in another sector to improve economic efficiency can sometimes reduce overall efficiency. Consider the canonical model in this book, which, again, assumes a competitive market. If, instead, a monopoly were in place, it becomes unclear whether an animal welfare levy would enhance total welfare (Buchanan 1969). The intuition is simple: If the levy is a tax on meat consumption, by further restricting animal production, it exacerbates inefficiencies already present in the meat market due to the monopoly situation. Market power can, in some cases, have positive implications for animals. For example, a merger between two major United States broiler producers led to higher market prices and reduced the number of chickens produced by tens of millions per year (Pi and Vukina 2025).

Other ambiguities arise at a broader scale. For instance, it is often argued that globalization may lead to an improvement in animal welfare standards through the spread of regulatory best practices. However, it may also lead to a lowering of standards due to competitive pressures given the rules of trade agreements (Stevenson and White 2015). Globalization may also lead to a phenomenon that I would coin "animal welfare leakage": If a country implements stricter regulations on animal welfare, some producers may relocate to regions with more lenient regulations, or consumers might opt for cheaper imported food that is produced under less stringent conditions (Blattner 2019, Ferguson et al. 2024). Note the parallel here with environmental issues (e.g., "carbon leakage"). Existing research in environmental economics on the impact of trade relations and market structure on environmental outcomes (Copeland and Taylor 2004, Requate 2006) thus provides a good starting point to reflect on animal welfare issues in this global context.

McMullen (2022, page 120) argues that there has been a race to the bottom in the animal industry. He emphasizes the damaging impact on animal welfare of a highly competitive environment. To illustrate, he describes the financial environment of chicken growers as follows:

> The farmers are compensated in such a way that any production choice that noticeably increases costs could threaten their ability to stay in business. Many of these growers, in fact, are operating with substantial debt and net compensation levels that are alarmingly low. One recent study found that 71% of growers whose sole source of income was from chicken production were living below the poverty line (...). In this kind of organizational structure, there is no option for a farmer to choose to raise chickens on pasture or give them more space to move around in smaller groups. Choices like these, while they would

> dramatically improve the lives of chickens, would dramatically increase the grower's costs and would violate their contract with the meat production company. The business of hog production has been moving into this contract model as well, with similar attributes (...). While it is tempting, then, to paint producers as greedy capitalists maximizing profit at the expense of animals, it is probably more accurate to frame the choice, for many farmers, as one between adopting the latest inhumane production techniques and leaving the industry entirely.

McMullen further underscores the market dynamics that perpetuate this race to the bottom. First, there is a process of natural selection among farms, where only the most efficient ones survive and expand. Second, there is a self-selection process into the industry itself. Those who establish new farms are typically those more open to adopt technological advancements – namely, those willing to adopt industrial confinement production models, and, I would venture to say, those more readily accepting of engaging in this morally contentious activity. Such a competitive environment swiftly alters the professional norms and long-standing traditions that may have once shaped the industry.

Theoretical developments in economics on this issue indicate that the market environment may, or may not, affect the incentives to behave morally depending on the form of non-standard preferences and the precise market structure. In a pioneering paper, Dufwenberg et al. (2011) derive a separability condition under which other-regarding preferences make no behavioral difference relative to selfish preferences in the sense that demand functions only depend on own consumption decisions and own budget constraints (even if preferences account for others' decisions and preferences).

To be more precise, Dufwenberg et al.'s condition states that any consumer i s' utility function u_i can be represented by the following specification $u_i(m_i(x_i), x_{-i})$ where x_i and x_{-i} represent the consumption bundle of consumer i and that of other consumers respectively. To understand the intuition for the sufficiency of their result note that, under that specification, the consumer chooses x_i to maximize $m_i(x_i)$, which is indeed independent from x_{-i}. The authors show that this specification holds in various behavioral models in the literature, and in particular in models with altruism. This restriction thus holds in several models I have considered in this book. I actually indicated several cases where optimal consumers' decisions do not depend on other consumer's choices such as in the public good model with altruism in Chapter 13. However, this does not hold in all behavioral models I have considered. Moreover, even if that restriction holds, there is still a market failure and a need for government intervention.

Several papers have discussed the implications of behavioral aspects for market outcomes and policy intervention. For instance, Dewatripont and Tirole (2024) explore economic environments in which the intensity of competition influences the morality of markets. In particular, they demonstrate an "irrelevance result": under specific but plausible conditions, the impact of moral actions on economic outcomes is independent from competitive pressure on markets. Ponthiere and Stevens (2024) revisit the Dewatripont and Tirole's irrelevance result and show that, in a slightly modified model, markets undermine moral values. This occurs either by failing to convey consumers' moral preferences or by incentivizing the replacement of ethical suppliers with less ethical ones. The relationship between market structure and morality is, in fact, a complex issue, with conflicting findings throughout the literature. For an overview, see Ziegler et al. (2024), and for broader references in the philosophy literature see Anderson (1995) and Sandel (2012).

Market structure can also directly influence individual attitudes toward animals. It can erode moral considerations for their welfare. When animals are viewed as commodities, their welfare may be secondary to other priorities. Consider the seminal study by Falk and Szech (2013) on this aspect. In their experiment, human subjects face the decision either to earn money and to accept the killing of a mouse, or to receive no money from the experimenter and to save the life of a mouse. Note that, in this study, mice that are chosen to survive because of the subjects' decisions are purchased by the experimenters and kept in an appropriate, enriched environment, and the subjects know this.

Falk and Szech analyze three different treatments: (1) an individual treatment in which subjects decide between the life of their mouse and a given monetary amount, (2) a bilateral trading market where one buyer subject and one seller subject bargain over prices in order to trade, and (3) a multilateral trading market where many buyer and seller subjects potentially trade with each other. Hence, in all treatments, subjects could exchange the life of an animal for money. Crucially, the monetary incentives are set so that they are similar across the three treatments. As a result, if an effect is observed, it is reasonable to attribute it to a behavioral explanation.

The main results are depicted in Figure 16.1. They suggest that moral standards tend to erode within market contexts. In the individual treatment, 45.9 percent of subjects indicate their willingness to kill the mouse for 10 euros. In contrast, 72.2 percent of sellers in the bilateral market and 75.9 percent in the multilateral market

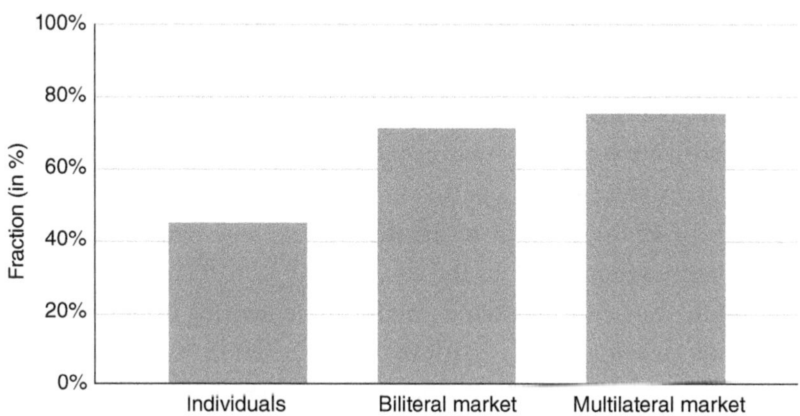

FIGURE 16.1 Fractions of subjects who are willing to kill a mouse for monetary amounts below or equal to 10 euros.
Source: Falk and Szech (2013)

are willing to trade for prices at or below 10 euros. The authors propose three potential explanations for these findings. First, in markets, trade requires the agreement of two parties, potentially diluting feelings of responsibility and guilt and thus diminishing consumers' sense of complicity. Second, markets provide information regarding the acceptability of trading, potentially making the act of killing mice more socially permissible. Third, markets impose a strong focus on materialistic aspects such as bargaining, negotiation, and competition, potentially diverting attention away from the possible adverse consequences and moral implications of trading.

The first explanation suggests that, in markets characterized by numerous buyers and sellers, the diffusion of responsibility for outcomes contributes to moral decay. This phenomenon has been corroborated by subsequent research indicating that both markets and group decision-making tend to favor moral transgressions by diffusing responsibility and notions of pivotality (Falk et al. 2020). This aspect, inherent to market interactions, is often invoked in traders' rhetoric with appeals to the replacement excuse that "if I don't do it, someone else will." This excuse may find more acceptance among those who prioritize outcomes over principles, reflecting a utilitarian perspective. In particular, the existence of a clear social norm of moral conduct can limit the impact of the availability of the replacement excuse (Bartling and Özdemir 2023).

The replacement excuse argument typically serves as a common justification for perpetuating practices that harm animals, based on the premise that if one person or company ceases such practices, others will simply step in to fill the gap, thereby perpetuating the harm. Representatives from the agricultural sector frequently assert that while they care for their animals, implementing improved rearing conditions would only result in the importation of cheaper meat, which has been produced using less humane farming methods, from competitors. Similar arguments are employed concerning animal testing. The argument extends much more broadly. Consider, for instance, the pressure exerted by various NGOs on transportation firms not to transport farmed, experimental, or hunted animals alive. Once again, these firms could rightfully argue (and some do) that if they cease their activities, other firms will simply replace them.

16.3 CORPORATE SOCIAL RESPONSIBILITY

Corporate social responsibility (CSR) refers to voluntary actions undertaken by firms with the goal of contributing to the public good. CSR involves integrating social and environmental concerns into business operations and interactions with stakeholders. This can include activities such as philanthropy, ethical labor practices, environmental sustainability initiatives, and community engagement efforts. In recent years, CSR initiatives have also gained some traction as a means of addressing animal welfare concerns (Mendez and Peacock 2022). For instance, over the past decade, numerous companies worldwide have pledged to source cage-free eggs. These commitments have emerged in response to public pressure campaigns led by advocates for farmed animals. The impact has been substantial: In the United States, the share of cage-free hens rose from 5 percent in 2015 to 40 percent within less than a decade. This shift is part of a global trend, with countries like France and Italy doubling their cage-free hen populations over the same period.

In the following discussion, I interpret CSR as voluntary efforts by firms using animals aimed at enhancing animal welfare. Historically, CSR has encountered two fundamental criticisms (Besley and Ghatak 2007). First, CSR entails additional costs, making it seemingly unfeasible in highly competitive environments. Second, there is the well-known Milton Friedman's division of task critique: Firms should focus on producing private goods while leaving the provision of public goods to the government. However, the feasibility concern dissipates if some consumers intrinsically care about the public good. As we have seen, consumers concerned about animal welfare may be willing to pay a premium for more animal-friendly products, potentially rendering CSR profitable even amid intense competition. However, since animal welfare is a public good, individual demand alone is expected to be very limited due to free-riding behavior (see Chapter 13). Consequently, the underprovision of the public good remains a prevalent issue here, leading to only marginal improvements in animal welfare through CSR initiatives (Besley and Ghatak 2007, Espinosa and Treich 2023). In other words, CSR is expected to be a niche market product, at best.

We are thus back to Friedman's critique: The government should do a better job than producers at improving animal welfare since it can a priori deal with the free-riding problem. Does this mark the end of the rationale for CSR? Not necessarily, as CSR may still be justified if the government also falls short of making socially optimal decisions. Put simply, CSR finds justification in the presence of both market failures and political failures. For instance, governmental representation may inadequately reflect the population's interests, potentially prioritizing the production sector for economic reasons or catering to specific consumer groups due to political considerations. In the face of such governmental failure, CSR initiatives have the potential to yield Pareto improvements by responding to the demands of citizens who may lack adequate representation within the government (Besley and Ghatak 2007).

However, this also raises the question of why non-profits would not assume responsibility for providing public goods instead of the producers. An additional rationale emerges then for CSR when considering the production process itself. The point is that there exists a natural "bundling effect" where the provision of a public good runs alongside the provision of a private good. For instance, farmers produce meat (a private good) as well as the welfare of animals (a public good). This bundling effect makes it logical that farmers, rather than NGOs, take the responsibility for managing animal welfare and thereby providing the public good (Besley and Ghatak 2007, Lai et al. 2017). The same point is valid for many firms using animals in their production process, such as leather or fur producers.

An additional concern relates to information asymmetry. Often, consumers have very limited access to accurate information about public goods. As previously discussed, consumers frequently misconstrue the treatment of animals within the farming industry. Information itself constitutes a public good, and there are limited incentives for individuals to get information about animal farming. Besides, potential cognitive dissonance issues may amplify the perception biases (see Chapters 12 and 14). This gives rise to a risk of "humane washing," or say "animal welfare washing," where the production sector may claim to prioritize animal welfare in its communication strategies without implementing substantive changes to improve animal rearing conditions (Hannan 2020). This mirrors the concept of "greenwashing" observed in environmental contexts.

This leads me to three final observations for this section. First, the presence of imperfect information and the risk of "animal welfare washing" suggest that collaboration between NGOs and producers could prove beneficial. NGOs could monitor producers' practices, while producers could enhance their reputation by partnering with NGOs. Note however that, due to the limited monitoring capacities of NGOs, the risk of "animal welfare washing" remains significant. Second, the informational challenges associated with CSR underscore the importance of systematically deploying benefit-cost analyses to accurately assess the true social benefits of CSR initiatives and making this information publicly available. Third, it is worth exploring how animal welfare presents unique theoretical and practical challenges compared to environmental concerns when explaining corporate decision-making. For instance, while established frameworks exist for evaluating environmental impacts, the same may not necessarily apply to animal welfare. Moreover, differing public attitudes toward animal welfare compared to environmental issues could impact the effectiveness of CSR strategies.

REFERENCES

Anderson E (1995) *Value in Ethics and Economics*. Harvard University Press.

Bartling B, Özdemir Y (2023) The limits to moral erosion in markets: Social norms and the replacement excuse. *Games and Economic Behavior*, 138, 143–160.

Besley T, Ghatak M (2007) Retailing public goods: The economics of corporate social responsibility. *Journal of Public Economics*, 91(9), 1645–1663.

Blattner C (2019) *Protecting Animals within and across Borders: Extraterritorial Jurisdiction and the Challenges of Globalization*. Oxford University Press, 2019.

Bovenberg AL, Goulder LH (2002) Environmental taxation and regulation. In *Handbook of Public Economics*, eds. AJ Auerbach and M Feldstein, Vol. 3, 1471–1545. Elsevier.

Buchanan JM (1969) External diseconomies, corrective taxes, and market structure. *The American Economic Review*, 59(1), 174–177.

Copeland BR, Taylor MS (2004) Trade, growth, and the environment. *Journal of Economic Literature*, 42(1), 7–71.

Dewatripont M, Tirole J (2024) The morality of markets. *Journal of Political Economy*, 132(8), 2655–2694.

Dufwenberg M, Heidhues P, Kirchsteiger G, Riedel F, Sobel J (2011) Other-regarding preferences in general equilibrium. *The Review of Economic Studies*, 78(2), 613–639.

Espinosa R, Treich N (2023) Animal welfare as a public good. *Ecological Economics*, 216, 108025.

Falk A, Neuber T, Szech N (2020) Diffusion of being pivotal and immoral outcomes. *The Review of Economic Studies*, 87(5), 2205–2229.

Falk A, Szech N (2013) Morals and markets. *Science*, 340(6133), 707–711.

Ferguson S, Wallenbeck A, Agenäs S, Hansson H (2024) The impact of animal welfare regulations on pork trade: Evidence from European countries. Working Paper Series/Swedish University of Agricultural Sciences, Department of Economics, (2024: 3).

Hannan J (Ed.) (2020) *Meatsplaining: The Animal Agriculture Industry and the Rhetoric of Denial*. Sydney University Press.

Lai CY., Lange A, List JA, Price MK (2017) The business of business is business: Why (some) firms should provide public goods when they sell private goods (No. w23105). National Bureau of Economic Research.

Lipsey RG, Lancaster K (1956) The general theory of second best. *The Review of Economic Studies*, 24(1), 11–32.

Lusk JL, Norwood FB (2011) Animal welfare economics. *Applied Economic Perspectives and Policy*, 33(4), 463–483.

Malone T, Lusk JL (2016) Putting the chicken before the egg price: An "ex post" analysis of California's battery cage ban. *Journal of Agricultural and Resource Economics*, 41(3), 518–532.

McMullen S (2015) Is capitalism to blame? Animal lives in the marketplace. *Journal of Animal Ethics*, 5(2), 126–134.

McMullen S (2022) Competition, regulation, and the race to the bottom in animal agriculture. In *Animals and Business Ethics*, ed. N Thomas, 113–130. Springer International Publishing.

Mendez S, Peacock J (2022) The impact of Corporate Social Responsibility on animal welfare standards: Evidence from the cage-free egg industry. Available at SSRN 4219976.

Mullally C, Lusk JL (2018) The impact of farm animal housing restrictions on egg prices, consumer welfare, and production in California. *American Journal of Agricultural Economics*, 100(3), 649–669.

Oh SE, Vukina T (2022) The price of cage-free eggs: Social cost of Proposition 12 in California. *American Journal of Agricultural Economics*, 104(4), 1293–1326.

Pi L, Vukina T (2025) Horizontal merger simulation in a Cournot oligopoly with competitive fringe: The US broiler industry case. *American Journal of Agricultural Economics*, 107(3), 869–887.

Ponthiere G, Stevens N (2024) The morality of markets: A comment. Working paper.

Requate T (2006) Environmental policy under imperfect competition. In *The International Yearbook of Environmental and Resource Economics*, eds. T Tietenberg and H Folmer, 120–207. Edward Elgar Publishing.

Sandel MJ (2012) *What Money Can't Buy: The Moral Limits of Markets*. Macmillan.

Seibert L, Norwood FB (2011) Production costs and animal welfare for four stylized hog production systems. *Journal of Applied Animal Welfare Science*, 14(1), 1–17.

Stevenson P, White S (2015) *The Impact of the World Trade Organisation Rules on Animal Welfare*. Compassion in World Farming.

Xie M (2023) Sales of cage-free eggs: The impact of proposition 12 on egg prices and consumer welfare in California. *The Journal of Purdue Undergraduate Research*, 13(1), 11.

Ziegler AG, Romagnoli G, Offerman T (2024) Morals in multi-unit markets. *Journal of the European Economic Association*, 22(5), 2225–2260.

17 Further Excursions

17.1 SOCIAL EFFECTS

Proanimal behavior may be due to a variety of factors, including self-image and social image concerns (Lai et al. 2022, Mechtenberg et al. 2024). Developing a positive self-image and overconfidence can be useful. People with a positive self-image are often seen as more attractive and may find it easier to deceive others to get what they want (Schwardmann and Van der Weele 2019, Solda et al. 2020). Regarding social image, individuals may derive social recognition by demonstrating care for animals, as this reflects values of empathy often associated with cooperative behavior. In other words, being kind to animals may yield social rewards. Just to be clear: I am not implying that people do not genuinely care about animals and only pretend to care about animals for boosting their self-confidence or their reputation. Rather, I am suggesting that our kindness toward animals may be driven by evolutionary forces promoting altruism toward others (Nowak 2006).

It is important to recognize however that social effects do not always encourage proanimal behavior. Many social norms involving animals stem from a long history of their exploitation and consumption. The widespread consumption of meat, for instance, is deeply ingrained in most societies and is largely perceived as normal practice. Consequently, deviating from this norm may result in social sanction or stigma. Typically, this may be due to a form of peer pressure. On the other hand, younger generations in developed countries often express greater concern for animal welfare, influenced by environmental and ethical considerations. This shift can lead to changing norms and expectations in families, schools, and workplaces.

People's attitudes toward animal welfare often align with their dietary choices (e.g., vegetarianism or veganism), creating group identities. These identities can not only foster solidarity within groups but also create tensions or misunderstandings between those with differing views. A phenomenon, known as vegephobia, refers to negative attitudes, biases, or discrimination against vegetarians or vegans (Markowski and Roxburgh 2019, Arpinon 2024). This phenomenon seems somewhat paradoxical, as adopting a vegetarian or vegan lifestyle can be viewed as contributing to a public good. However, there is also evidence of antisocial punishment (Herrmann et al. 2008), namely sanctioning people who behave prosocially. One explanation for such seemingly paradoxical punishment is that individuals experience moral discomfort about their own behavior when observing others' behavior or when anticipating moral reproach. Consistent with that explanation, Minson and Monin (2012) show for instance that people rate vegetarians less positively after imagining their moral judgment of meat eaters.

Moreover, people may have different interpretations about whether some behavior such as meat-eating is good or bad for the society as a whole. As we have seen, it may be argued that animal farming has positive consequences for animals if the life of farmed animals is worth living. More generally, people may care about farmers' welfare, the preservation of rural activities, or cultural aspects, and so on. Furthermore, people may be motivated to hold and share certain beliefs that are consistent with their own behavior (cf. the cognitive dissonance theory and the sections in Chapters 12 and 14 about the meat paradox). Thus, differing interpretations of the societal implications of actions with positive or negative impacts on animals can lead to varied attitudes and behaviors, highlighting the complex interplay between social norms, perceptions, and the precise individual choices impacting animals (meat-eating, hunting, carrying out experiments with animals, having pets, going to the zoo, etc.). The role of these social effects to explain our attitudes toward animals and how this should affect policymaking (Nyborg et al. 2016, Meunier and Schumacher 2020) remains a largely unexplored domain of research.

17.2 POLITICAL ASPECTS

Animal welfare is eminently a political topic. Most important decisions regarding animal welfare are taken by governments. For farmed animals, the political institutions of animal agriculture are decisive (McMullen 2022). The agricultural lobby is notoriously influential, and often obtains laws that are detrimental to animals. On the other side, there exist numerous animal advocacy NGOs that try to shape public opinion and in turn influence policy decisions in favor of animals. The issue of animal welfare thus provides an important and under-researched application of political economy (Harvey and Hubbard 2013). In this section, I will briefly outline a few ideas, recognizing that they only scratch the surface of the multitude of political aspects surrounding animal welfare issues.

To begin, I believe that research in the political economy of animal welfare must address an important puzzle: Despite widespread public concern for animals (see Chapter 1), their protection remains minimal (see Chapter 2). Animal welfare issues rarely feature prominently in major political elections. Why is this the case? I refer to this as the "political gap." Interestingly, the political economy literature has explored similar puzzles, where public support for a policy exists, but the policy essentially remains absent from political discourse or implementation. Let me highlight three key explanations from this literature:

- Interest groups: Policies that benefit the majority (the general population) but harm a concentrated minority (such as farmers) may fail to be implemented if the minority is better organized and lobbies more effectively. According to Olson (1965), politicians tend to favor small and well-organized groups that can provide campaign funding or voter mobilization.
- Institutional inertia: Political systems often resist change due to entrenched institutions, legal frameworks, or the vested interests of powerful actors. The costs of overcoming these barriers can be prohibitive, even when there is public support for change. See, for example, Fernandez and Rodrik (1991).

- Policy bundles: Even when a specific policy enjoys broad support, it may struggle to gain traction if it is bundled with other, less popular measures. For instance, green parties tend to support animal welfare more than other prominent parties, but their broader policy platforms in areas like taxation or energy may alienate the general population, undermining support for their animal welfare initiatives.

Regarding the interest groups explanation, there are several reasons for why the agricultural lobby is so powerful. First, agriculture remains a vital industry in many countries, providing food and employment. Agricultural interests, including large agribusiness corporations, often make substantial campaign contributions to political candidates and parties. Second, agricultural interests have a long history of organized advocacy and lobbying efforts. This includes powerful agricultural associations, trade unions, and lobbying groups that have built relationships with policymakers over time. Third, farmers possess "mobile capital" such as tractors that can easily be mobilized for protesting purposes to damage to public property and block transportation routes.

Regarding institutional inertia, rural constituencies often hold disproportionate political power due to the structure of representative systems, giving agricultural interests a strong political voice. Additionally, agriculture is closely tied to issues of food security and national identity. Policymakers are often hesitant to implement changes that could disrupt agricultural production or jeopardize food security, leading to a reluctance to challenge agricultural interests. Beyond this, agriculture and animal farming are deeply ingrained in the culture and identity of many countries through enduring traditions that are unlikely to change rapidly. Such transformations typically require gradual shifts over time or may occur only in response to significant external shocks.

It is also important to acknowledge that animal agriculture constitutes a substantial portion of agricultural revenues, comprising roughly half in many industrialized nations. In countries like France, around three-quarters of farms and two-thirds of agricultural jobs are linked to animal agriculture, either through direct animal production and/or the cultivation of feed for them, as evidenced by the 2020 French agricultural census. Consequently, the agricultural lobby predominantly represents the interests of animal agriculture. As a matter of fact, most agricultural subsidies (about 80 percent for the Common Agricultural Policy, Kortleve et al. 2024) go to animal farming. It is no surprise then that proposing significant changes related to animal farming, particularly those aimed at reducing meat consumption and thus animal production, faces formidable political opposition. A salient example was the 2019–2020 Dutch farmers' revolt against the government plan to reduce farms' nitrogen emissions implying a reduction in the number of livestock in the country.

With these political economy explanations in mind, the political gap may seem less surprising, as it is expected that animal welfare concerns should struggle to secure a prominent spot on the political agenda. Moreover, as discussed in Chapter 11, preferences within the population are highly heterogeneous, with only a small segment of individuals deeply concerned about animal welfare. This heterogeneity can pose a challenge to advancing animal welfare issues politically, in universal suffrage elections particularly. Note that opinion polls may also struggle to capture well the intensity of preferences (Cavaillé et al. 2024). Additionally, the political inertia may be exacerbated by the cognitive dissonance experienced by many citizens. When the issue fades from public attention, so does their concern, further hindering political momentum. See Matějka and Tabellini (2021) and Le Yaouanq (2023) for relevant economic analyses in that area.

A portion of legislation even aims to obscure transparency within the sector to keep consumers in the dark. This is epitomized by the enactment of "ag-gag" laws, which prohibit undercover filming or photography of activities on farms (Robbins et al. 2016). Advocates of ag-gag laws argue their necessity in protecting farmers from unfounded accusations, preserving trade secrets, and upholding biosecurity measures (Weiler and Zavitz 2024). However, critics perceive these laws as deliberate attempts to stifle transparency and accountability within the animal agricultural industry, thereby impeding efforts to shed light on and address issues related to animal welfare and food safety.

In this political landscape, animal advocacy NGOs encounter significant hurdles to protect animals. These organizations operate with considerably less income and political influence compared to the farming industry. However, their comparative advantage lies in their generally favorable reputation among the public, offering them a higher potential for opinion influence. NGOs invest substantial efforts into shaping public beliefs, aiming to indirectly sway companies and policymakers. Yet, they face formidable challenges due to attention scarcity and cognitive dissonance among the public, as suggested above.

An important component of NGOs' efforts is moral persuasion. Haile et al. (2021) conduct a randomized-controlled trial of pro-vegan animal-welfare pamphlets at a college campus. They observe the effect on meat consumption using an individual-level panel data set of approximately 200,000 meals. While some short-term effects are observed among certain subgroups, the findings suggest that the pamphlet had no statistically significant long-term aggregate effects. Feinberg et al. (2021) also suggest that nudges that appeal to moral values have a small impact on reducing meat consumption.

An example of a successful NGO campaign is the cage-free movement (Bollard 2023a). For decades, NGOs lobbied governments to improve animal welfare with very limited results. Then, they changed strategy and achieved significant wins. NGOs did two things: First, they targeted big food corporations and second, they focused on worst practices, namely on the ban of battery cages used to confine hens. In 2015, NGOs launched cage-free campaigns in the United States, securing initial pledges from Costco and McDonald's, followed by other top retailers and fast-food chains. These campaigns then succeeded globally. Follow-up studies show that 89 percent of the over 1,000 pledges due by 2023 have been fulfilled (https://openwingalliance.org/2024-cage-free-fulfillment-report).

In this book, I have extensively discussed the implementation of a meat tax as a natural policy instrument (Pigouvian taxation). Several commentators, public reports and scholars have recommended the implementation of a meat tax. Bonnet et al. (2020) and Funke et al. (2022) discuss the justifications for a tax for environmental, health, and animal welfare reasons. Interestingly, Perino and Schwickert (2023) find that people are more willing to support a tax for animal welfare reasons than for climate reasons. However, despite the popularity of taxation among economists, empirical evidence indicates that public backing for a meat tax remains low. Recent studies suggest that, among various climate policies, such as bans on highly polluting cars and mandatory building insulation, meat taxation ranks as the least favored option (Dechezleprêtre et al. 2024).

If the idea of taxing meat appears to face such a strong resistance, it is important to understand why. Note first that meat taxation is often perceived as regressive (Klenert et al. 2023), unless specific tax-revenue redistributional strategies are implemented. Moreover, many individuals value their freedom of choice regarding dietary preferences and identify strongly as meat eaters (Randers and Thøgersen 2023). Additionally, various factors may further dampen support for a meat tax, including attachment or addiction to meat (Zaraska 2016), political ideologies (Simmonds and Vallgård 2021), or underestimation of the externalities associated with meat consumption (Camilleri et al. 2019). Simon (2013) extensively discusses how governments obscure the true costs of meat production by failing to account for its externalities, such as environmental damage, health issues, and subsidies.

One final topic in this section concerns voting decisions. I have already mentioned referendum outcomes concerning animal welfare issues. For instance, Propositions 2 and 12 saw about two-thirds of California voters in favor of banning battery cages. However, the induced paradox (that I already mentioned many times) is that a large majority of voters were still purchasing eggs from hens confined in battery cages. The book has discussed a few explanations for the gap between voting and consumer behavior, the so-called vote-buy gap. Specifically, in Chapter 14, I proposed that this gap can be explained through a standard approach based on altruism. Additionally, in Chapter 11, I suggested that salience might play a significant role in this phenomenon.

17.3 INFORMATION AND EDUCATION

Until now, I have not much discussed information campaigns about animal welfare. In the first nonanthropocentric part, it is assumed that people do not care about animals and their welfare; hence information about animal welfare would have no effect on their behavior whatsoever. In this second part, I suggested that information is expected to have a small effect, as it would not solve the public good problem regarding animal welfare provision. Furthermore, note that there are also free-riding incentives associated with seeking information, particularly if the information scheme lacks transparency and necessitates additional search efforts, as just discussed. Additionally, under cognitive dissonance, information might even be ignored, or its impact may be largely mitigated by the desire to protect our beliefs favoring animal use and consumption. For instance, Epperson and Gerster (2024) show empirically that some people are willing to pay not to receive information about farm animal welfare. Overall, I believe that information tools are not the most effective instruments.

However, it is important to acknowledge that, in the absence of better alternatives, providing consumers with accurate information can help align food attributes more effectively with their diverse preferences. Several WTP studies indicate that consumers prioritize nutritional and animal welfare attributes over environmental considerations (van Loo et al. 2014, Bonnet et al. 2020). Despite this, the use of informational tools to promote awareness of animal welfare remains limited. For example, there is no standardized label on animal-based products indicating whether the animal was (e.g.) raised under intensive farming conditions, subjected to mutilation, or slaughtered without stunning. Currently, the most comprehensive information on animal welfare is often found in general labels, such as organic labels, which convey broad information on sustainability practices or the absence of antibiotics. An exception is the mandatory labeling of eggs in the European Union.

In recent years, we have witnessed several spontaneous animal welfare labeling initiatives by private firms. An illustrative example is the initiative by the French supermarket company Casino, which introduced a five-level label for broilers. Developed in collaboration with four French animal welfare NGOs (CIWF, LFDA, Welfarm, OABA), this label aims to go beyond European legislation standards (see Figure 17.1). While this represents a positive step forward, it also raises a common concern regarding private initiatives: the risk of "animal welfare washing," where marketing efforts prioritize enhancing brand reputation over making meaningful improvements to animal welfare (as discussed in the previous chapter).

Relatedly, there is a risk of manipulation of consumers' beliefs. Let me give an example using this labeling initiative in France. It features five levels, where Level A represents the highest standard.

	LEVEL A	LEVEL B	LEVEL C	LEVEL D	LEVEL E
Access to free-range access	✓	✓			
Daylight	✓	✓	✓ By 2022	✓ By 2024	
Implementation of mechanisms for broilers to express natural behaviors	Perch or other materials	Perch or other materials	Perch or other materials By 2022	Perch or other materials by mid-2021	
Increased space in buildings compared to legal standards	+68%	+53%	+40%	+10%	*
Minimum life duration	81 days	56 days			
Growth rate	Slow	Slow/ intermediary	Intermediary		
Maximum transport time	4 hours	6 hours	8 hours		
Document committing the transporter to respect animal welfare	✓	✓	✓	✓	
Mandatory stunning before slaughter	✓	✓	✓	✓	
Control video in certain areas in slaughterhouses where live animals are handled	✓	✓			

FIGURE 17.1 Label on broilers' welfare in France.
Source: Espinosa and Treich (2024)

However, this level still involves intensive farming practices, with confined chickens living relatively short lives (around 80 days). Consequently, Level A falls significantly short of best practices in animal rearing, posing a risk of consumer misinterpretation of the label A as "excellence," or "the top," perhaps envisioning instead idyllic backyard farming with a few chickens freely roaming. The reality of Level A is quite different. Furthermore, the long list of criteria (more than two hundred) underlying the label's construction are not easily accessible to the public, and hence the label's exact meaning probably remains largely obscure to most consumers.

There exist a number of studies about the impact of information schemes regarding animal welfare. Mathur et al. (2021) meta-analyze 100 studies assessing interventions designed to reduce meat consumption by mentioning or portraying farm animals or their living conditions, such as a factual mock newspaper article with graphic photographs and descriptions of gestation crates. They estimate that the large majority of interventions (83 percent) had significant effects in terms of meat consumption reduction. However, they stress that interventions may backfire for specific individuals.

Kunst and Haugestad (2018) investigate the effect of displaying a pork roast with the animal's head present or removed, which leads to less dissociation, and subsequently more disgust and empathy for the killed animal. Some animal welfare interventions have also leveraged the "identifiable victim effect." This psychological phenomenon highlights that individuals tend to experience heightened emotional responses when presented with a specific, named victim, compared to situations involving multiple victims (often coined statistical victims) or an abstract group. Animal welfare interventions describe farm animals with reference to specific, named individuals, such as "Leon" the pig or "Lucy" the chicken. This approach tends to be more impactful in changing behavior compared to presenting statistical descriptions of the overall number of animals affected. For instance, Rabinovitch et al. (2024) show that animal identifiability (through cartoon Peppa Pig) leads to children's higher perceived animal similarity to humans and reduces inclination to consume the animal.

NGOs can play a significant role in providing information to consumers about animal welfare. Stoeber et al. (2024) examine the impact of personality and individual differences on the effectiveness of animal advocacy. In their experiment, participants watched either an advocacy video depicting chickens suffering on a farm or a neutral control video. The results showed that participants who watched the advocacy video developed more positive attitudes toward chickens and stronger intentions to reduce egg consumption compared to those who watched the control video. The study highlights the importance of gender and speciesism as moderating factors, suggesting that certain types of animal advocacy may only be effective for certain individuals.

In Espinosa and Treich (2021), we compare the efficacy of two animal advocacy discourses: (i) a welfarist one seeking to improve the conditions in which animals are raised and reduce meat consumption and (ii) an abolitionist one, categorically rejecting animal use and calling for a vegan society. We show that the welfarist and abolitionist discourses both significantly undermine participants' pro-meat justifications. However, we also show that the welfarist discourse does not significantly affect participants' actions, while we detect a backlash effect of the abolitionist discourse. Our findings indicate that although NGOs exert a positive influence on individuals' actions through a change in beliefs, this effect is counteracted by a negative behavioral response to the discourses, a phenomenon we interpret as reactance.

One particular issue regarding information about animal welfare is its potential to evoke strong emotions. This prompts inquiry into the role of emotions as drivers for changes in beliefs and actions. In a subsequent study (Espinosa et al. 2024), we empirically evaluate the impact of undercover videos depicting animal abuse on support for animal welfare among the French population (N=3,310). Additionally, we examine whether heightened viewer engagement is driven by the negative emotional responses elicited by the videos.

Our findings indicate that the videos effectively increase actions in favor of animals, such as donations to NGOs and signing petitions. However, we do not find conclusive evidence to attribute this effect to the presence of primary emotions induced by the videos.

Willett et al. (2019) underscore the importance of implementing educational policies in the food domain. While many policies primarily target adults, focusing on the younger segment of the population may yield greater effectiveness, in particular because they can have a longer impact over people's lifetime. Eating preferences and habits often form during childhood and adolescence, persisting into adulthood. Evidence shows that this persistence is due to biological as well as behavioral reasons (Kesternich et al. 2015). Young individuals also exhibit more adaptability and may be more open to make significant behavioral choices (Belot et al. 2018). Numerous initiatives, including meat-free days in school canteens, have emerged worldwide, aiming to engage young people actively in educational efforts. Wynes and Nicholas (2017) highlight adolescents as a key demographic for promoting impactful environmental actions, such as transitioning to plant-based diets. However, they note a lack of emphasis on these actions in high-school science textbooks.

Hahn et al. (2021) argue that children might play a crucial role in normalizing plant-based diets, referring to them as "unsuspecting meat-eaters." Their study reveals that many children struggle to accurately identify the sources of various animal products. In their sample of 4- to 7-year-old children from the United States, 41 percent believed that bacon came from a plant. Foods derived from animals, especially meats, were among the most misunderstood by children. This finding highlights a significant opportunity for informational and educational policies to bridge this knowledge gap among the young.

Finally, let me add that animal literacy may be an interesting area of research when it comes to understanding proanimal concerns. As the best-selling book "Are we smart enough to know how smart animals are?" (De Waal 2016) suggests, there is evidence that humans may not fully appreciate the cognitive abilities and emotional complexity of animals. Research has shown that the way we attribute mental states to animals can be influenced by factors such as our age, our prior experiences with those animals, our cultural beliefs, and the ways in which we use and interact with animals (see Chapter 12). It seems important to help individuals to better understand and appreciate the needs and experiences of animals. This can involve educating people about the cognitive and emotional capacities of different species, as well as promoting ethical considerations when it comes to the treatment of animals.

17.4 INNOVATIONS

While altering people's behavior toward animals may present various challenges due to economic, psychological, political or cultural factors, technological innovations provide another channel to improve animal welfare. As we have seen in Chapter 2, throughout history, advancements in technology have played a pivotal role in diminishing the reliance on animals across various industries. For instance, the transition from whale oil to fossil fuels, ox plows to tractors, horse-drawn carts to automobiles, or animal-based fur to synthetic material has significantly reduced the use of animals in the corresponding sectors. Various innovative solutions, such as holographic animals replacing live animals in entertainment, show potential. Perhaps most significantly, cultured meat has emerged as a potential game changer in the meat industry (Treich 2021).

Using lab-based production methods that eliminate the need for animal slaughter, cultured meat offers the promise of reducing dependence on animal agriculture. One of its major advantages over other meat substitutes is its molecular similarity to conventional meat, potentially making it an almost perfect substitute in terms of taste and texture. However, cultured meat faces significant challenges, notably regarding production costs and consumer acceptance. Several studies have found relatively low WTP for cultured meat (van Loo et al. 2020). One key factor contributing to this is neophobia, an aversion to novel foods. Providing technical details about cultured meat production tends to decrease acceptance (Siegrist et al. 2018), as this may exacerbate the artificial or ultra-processed aspect of this food product. A related factor which may play a key role in cultured meat acceptance is the "naturalistic heuristic," the belief that natural foods are superior (MacDonald and Vivalt 2018).

Interestingly, Weinrich et al. (2020) stress that ethics is a primary motivator for the acceptance of cultured meat. Cultured meat, if proven successful, holds the potential to significantly alleviate animal suffering. Given the absence of a nervous system, cultured cells are expected to be devoid of any capacity for pain. Consequently, these cells cannot develop into sentient beings in any form throughout the process. Although cultured meat raises several moral concerns, I contend that cultured meat is a moral advancement. In Table 17.1, I present a list of moral objections to cultured meat alongside corresponding rebuttals.

To connect with the earlier discussion in this chapter, a crucial yet often overlooked factor in the adoption of innovations is the political context. Frieden and Silve (2023) highlight that incumbent producers affected by innovations frequently use their influence to either facilitate or hinder their adoption. The authors identify several key political factors that shape this dynamic, including whether the innovation is easy to replicate, whether it complements or threatens the elite's sources of income, whether it is location dependent, or whether it involves significant fixed costs. For instance, incumbent producers in the traditional meat industry may attempt to block the adoption of cultured meat due to the threats it poses to their market dominance, economic stability, and societal influence. Evidence suggests that these incumbents are already lobbying governments to impose restrictive regulations on cultured meat, such as banning its commercialization, imposing labeling rules that prevent it from being marketed as "meat," or limiting R&D funding. They have also engaged in campaigns to shape public perception, including disinformation efforts aimed at raising doubts about the safety, naturalness, or desirability of cultured meat.

Table 17.1 *Some moral objections to cultured meat and rebuttals*

Moral objection to cultured meat	Rebuttal
A risk of disappearance of farmed animals: If cultured meat is successful, farm animals could decrease significantly or vanish entirely.	This risk is small, and it is a curse only if a farmed animal life is worth living. Additionally, a decrease in farmed animal populations could result in an increase in wild animal populations.
A lack of moral respect: We lack moral respect for animals by commodifying or instrumentalizing them.	The conventional meat industry is worse because it treats the entire animal as a mere product. Cultured meat only instrumentalizes cells and tissues.
Animal integrity: Animals should not be biotechnologically altered.	The animal that provides the cells is not altered and the resulting tissue culture is not a new type of organism. The meat industry does alter animals (e.g., genetically).
Wrong moral motivation: Cultured meat is motivated by selfishness when we should be virtuous.	Our main goal is not to boost our own moral self-regard and virtue, but to improve animal welfare in this world.
Delay moral change: Hoping for a technological fix will make people more at ease with meat eating now.	Appeals against animal suffering should work when animals suffer, whether or not this suffering may be obviated in the future.
Respect for nature: We must respect and accept what nature gives. Seeking a technological fix is arrogant.	What is natural is not the same as what is good. Our desire to be humble should not trump our desire to improve animal welfare.
Cannibalism: Cultured meat opens the door for the consumption of human flesh.	Cultured meat would not involve two main moral issues with cannibalism: human killing and corpse desecration. Consumption of human cultured meat could be banned.

Source: Hopkins and Dacey (2008), Schaefer and Savulescu (2014) and Treich (2021)

Finally, let me conclude this section by discussing artificial intelligence (AI), which can be viewed as the pinnacle of innovations. AI has the potential to significantly impact animals and their welfare (Singer and Tse 2023). AI may be used to reduce costs and increase productivity. On the negative side, it may further eliminate contacts between humans and farmed animals, and make the production process even more industrialized. However, AI may have beneficial effects on animals. AI systems may help measure the animals' body temperature, body weight and growth rate (Singer and Tse 2023), and may aid in identifying, monitoring, and responding to animal emotions and suffering (Neethirajan 2021). For instance, Briefer et al. (2022) use thousands of vocal recordings from hundreds of pigs to deepen our comprehension of their grunts, offering a promising avenue for the development of an automated emotion monitoring tool. AI might also help the management of zoos for instance. Another example is self-driving cars. Hundreds of millions of mammals and birds are killed every year on the road. Self-driving cars may be designed through improved AI assistance to minimize human fatalities as well as animal fatalities.

Optimists envision that advanced AI will bring unprecedented wealth, technological advancements, and heightened moral considerations, potentially rendering factory farming obsolete (Bollard 2023b). AI might also revolutionize research on animals, for instance if it allows us to communicate efficiently with animals. Note also that extensive efforts are underway to mitigate biases in both data and algorithms to ensure fairness in AI applications. These efforts were prompted by numerous instances of biased algorithmic decision-making, such as in hiring systems, medical applications, and image recognition, which have disproportionately affected women, people of color, and minorities. However, animals have largely been overlooked in these efforts. Hagendorff et al. (2023) present evidence of speciesist biases across various common areas of AI. Therefore, further research in AI ethics should also incorporate considerations for animals.

17.5 COMPASSIONATE CONSERVATION

As we have seen in Chapter 4, conservation biology has largely developed independently from the literature on animal welfare. However, it is crucial to acknowledge that the research landscape is gradually evolving. The burgeoning field of "compassionate conservation" (Ramp and Bekoff 2015, Beausoleil et al. 2018, Sekar and Shiller 2020) puts forward the significance of individual animal welfare in wildlife conservation strategies. These initiatives recognize the sentience of wild animals – acknowledging their capacity to feel pleasure, pain, and emotions – and advocate for integrating their welfare into conservation decision-making processes. In my commentary on the Dasgupta Review on the economics of biodiversity (Treich 2022), I highlight certain synergies between animal welfare and conservation policies, such as safeguarding some animal species (e.g., the blue whale). However, I also highlight conflicts between these sentientist and ecological objectives for specific policies, such as the reintroduction of carnivores or the eradication of invasive species.

Among the most symbolic and powerful conservation laws in many countries are those that protect endangered species, such as the Endangered Species Act (ESA) in the United States. The main issue regarding animal welfare impacts is that these laws typically provide duties to preserve animal species, not to animals as individuals. In other words, these laws are species oriented, not individuals oriented. Much like many ecological paradigms, the focal point is on aggregates or systems, such as species, ecosystems, or the biosphere as a whole. From this perspective, animals are seen as interchangeable, valued primarily for their contribution to sustaining the broader ecological balance, but individually dispensable (Waltz 2020). Animal welfare is essentially absent from these considerations, or it matters only indirectly as a byproduct of environmental protection.

The moral foundation of the approach underlying various environmental laws thus appears to deviate significantly from that developed in Part II, where sentient animals are recognized as individuals possessing moral value akin to humans within the conventional normative framework of economics. However, it is important to note that this approach may not necessarily clash with the anthropocentric viewpoint outlined in Part III. Indeed, the extent to which individuals endorse these distinct moral stances toward animals and the environment remains uncertain. Are people inclined toward sentientism, biocentrism, ecocentrism, a blend thereof, or perhaps none of these approaches? More research is needed to better understand human preferences toward nature and animals.

It is also noteworthy that the presence of policies aimed at safeguarding endangered species may not solely mirror individual preferences but may also result from political compromises. Additionally, such policies may inadvertently perpetuate certain misconceptions regarding animals and their natural habitats. Are people adequately informed about the extent of suffering experienced by wildlife?

Furthermore, one might question the notion that the protection of animals should hinge on the population size of their species, a notion that would be widely considered unacceptable if applied to humans. To be provocative: Would anyone agree to protect only human tribes on the verge of extinction? Hence, do we experience a unique, perhaps irrational, emotional response when faced with the imminent disappearance of an animal species? Could this emotional reaction be influenced by psychological biases such as the identifiable victim effect (see earlier in this chapter), scope insensitivity (wherein the value of saving 10 versus 1,000 birds is perceived similarly), and proportion dominance (preference for saving lives within a smaller population; see Bartels 2006)?

Finally, I would like to briefly discuss, again, the delicate issue of the optimal intervention in the wild. Extensive suffering among wild animals raises the possibility of legitimate human intervention in nature to alleviate this suffering, whether for the benefit of humans who care about animals or for the animals themselves. Such intervention may involve providing assistance to animals in need, as well as more proactive measures like vaccination or sterilization campaigns. An even more ambitious proposal, as discussed by Cowen (2003), is to intervene in the wild with the aim of reducing predation. Johannsen (2020) suggests the use of genetic techniques such as CRISPR to diminish the fertility of certain species, reduce their capacity to suffer, or even alter the diet of predators. It is important to note that, taken to the extreme, if the lives of wild animals are not worth living, habitat destruction leading to biodiversity loss may not be viewed as an entirely negative outcome.

Undoubtedly, the debate surrounding intervention in nature is highly contentious. A prominent counterargument to intervention revolves around the concept of "human fallibility." Ecosystems are intricate and interconnected, making it extremely challenging to accurately predict the far-reaching consequences of our actions on them. Regrettably, many of our interventions have led to unintended negative repercussions. Historical evidence consistently reminds us that human intervention in nature has often resulted in more harm than good in the long term. This is thus a very complex issue that deserves much more research. Delon and Purves (2018) state that this issue is currently intractable and that "we need to develop models that predict the effects of interventions on biodiversity, ecosystem functioning, and animals' well-being." I couldn't agree more.

REFERENCES

Arpinon T (2024) The social cost of adopting a plant-based diet. *Ecological Economics*, 224, 108283.

Bartels D (2006) Proportion dominance: The generality and variability of favoring relative savings over absolute savings. *Organizational Behavior and Human Decision Processes*, 100, 76–95.

Beausoleil NJ, Mellor DJ, Baker L et al. (2018) "Feelings and fitness" not "feelings or fitness" – the raison d'être of conservation welfare, which aligns conservation and animal welfare objectives. *Frontiers in Veterinary Science*, 5, 296.

Belot M, Berlin N, James J, Skafida V (2018) The formation and malleability of dietary habits: A field experiment with low income families. *Journal of Political Economy: Microeconomics*, 2(4), 707–746.

Bollard L (2023a) A year of wins for farmed animals. Open Philanthropy farm animal welfare research newsletter.

Bollard L (2023b) What could AI mean for animals? Open Philanthropy farm animal welfare research newsletter.

Bonnet C, Bouamra-Mechemache Z, Réquillart V, Treich N (2020) Regulating meat consumption to improve health, the environment and animal welfare. *Food Policy*, 97, 101847.

Briefer EF, Sypherd CCR, Linhart P et al. (2022) Classification of pig calls produced from birth to slaughter according to their emotional valence and context of production. *Scientific Reports*, 12, 3409.

Camilleri AR, Larrick RP, Hossain S, Patino-Echeverri D (2019) Consumers underestimate the emissions associated with food but are aided by labels. *Nature Climate Change*, 9(1), 53–58.

Cavaillé C, Chen DL, Van der Straeten K (2024) Who cares? Measuring differences in preference intensity. *Political Science Research and Methods*, 13(2). 1–17.

Cowen T (2003) Policing nature. *Environmental Ethics*, 25(2), 169–182.

Dechezleprêtre A, Fabre A, Kruse T et al. (2024) Fighting climate change: International attitudes toward climate policies. *American Economic Review*, 115(4), 1258–1300.

Delon N, Purves D (2018) Wild animal suffering is intractable. *Journal of Agricultural and Environmental Ethics*, 31, 239–260.

De Waal F (2016) *Are We Smart Enough to Know How Smart Animals Are?* W.W. Norton & Company.

Epperson R, Gerster A (2024) Willful ignorance and moral behavior, mimeo.

Espinosa R, Borau S, Treich N (2024) Impact of NGOs' undercover videos on citizens' emotions and pro-social behaviors. *Scientific Reports*, 14, 20584.

Espinosa R, Treich N (2021) Moderate versus radical NGOs. *American Journal of Agricultural Economics*, 103(4), 1478–1501.

Espinosa R, Treich N (2024) Economics of animal law and welfare: Social objective and strategies. In *Oxford Handbook of Global Animal Law*, eds. Anne Peters, Kristen Stilt and Saskia Stucki. Oxford University Press, in press

Feinberg M, Kramer LA, Lacetera N (2021) A tough nudge to crack: An experimental study on behavioral cues to reduce animal-based food consumption, mimeo.

Fernandez R, Rodrik D (1991) Resistance to reform: Status quo bias in the presence of individual-specific uncertainty. *The American Economic Review*, 81(5), 1146–1155.

Frieden J, Silve A (2023) The political reception of innovations. *Economics & Politics*, *35*(2), 595–628.

Funke F, Mattauch L, Bijgaart IVD et al. (2022) Toward optimal meat pricing: Is it time to tax meat consumption? *Review of Environmental Economics and Policy*, 16(2), 219–240.

Hagendorff T, Bossert LN, Tse YF, Singer P (2023) Speciesist bias in AI: How AI applications perpetuate discrimination and unfair outcomes against animals. *AI and Ethics*, 3(3), 717–734.

Hahn ER, Gillogly M, Bradford BE (2021) Children are unsuspecting meat eaters: An opportunity to address climate change. *Journal of Environmental Psychology*, 78, 101705.

Haile M, Jalil A, Tasoff J, Vargas Bustamante A (2021) Changing hearts and plates: The effect of animal-advocacy pamphlets on meat consumption. *Frontiers in Psychology*, 12, 668674.

Harvey D, Hubbard C (2013) Reconsidering the political economy of farm animal welfare: An anatomy of market failure. *Food Policy*, 38, 105–114.

Herrmann B, Thoni C, Gachter S (2008) Antisocial punishment across societies. *Science*, 319(5868), 1362–1367.

Hopkins PD, Dacey A (2008) Vegetarian meat: Could technology save animals and satisfy meat eaters? *Journal of Agricultural and Environmental Ethics*, 21, 579–596.

Johannsen K (2020) *Wild Animal Ethics: The Moral and Political Problem of Wild Animal Suffering*. Routledge.

Kesternich I, Siflinger B, Smith JP, Winter JK (2015) Individual behaviour as a pathway between early-life shocks and adult health: Evidence from hunger episodes in post-war Germany. *The Economic Journal*, 125(588), F372–F393.

Klenert D, Funke F, Cai M (2023) Meat taxes in Europe can be designed to avoid overburdening low-income consumers. *Nature Food*, 4(10), 894–901.

Kortleve AJ, Mogollón JM, Harwatt H, Behrens P (2024) Over 80% of the European Union's Common Agricultural Policy supports emissions-intensive animal products. *Nature Food*, 5(4), 288–292.

Kunst JR, Haugestad CAP (2018) The effects of dissociation on willingness to eat meat are moderated by exposure to unprocessed meat: A cross-cultural demonstration. *Appetite*, 120, 356–366.

Lai Y, Boaitey A, Minegishi K (2022) Behind the veil: Social desirability bias and animal welfare ballot initiatives. *Food Policy*, 106, 102184.

Le Yaouanq Y (2023) A model of voting with motivated beliefs. *Journal of Economic Behavior & Organization*, 213, 394–408.

MacDonald BNJ, Vivalt E (2018) Effective strategies for overcoming the naturalistic heuristic: Experimental evidence on consumer acceptance of "clean" meat, mimeo.

Markowski KL, Roxburgh S (2019) "If I became a vegan, my family and friends would hate me:" Anticipating vegan stigma as a barrier to plant-based diets. *Appetite*, 135, 1–9.

Matějka F, Tabellini G (2021) Electoral competition with rationally inattentive voters. *Journal of the European Economic Association*, 19(3), 1899–1935.

Mathur MB, Peacock J, Reichling DB et al. (2021) Interventions to reduce meat consumption by appealing to animal welfare: Meta-analysis and evidence-based recommendations. *Appetite*, 164, 105277.

McMullen S (2022) Competition, regulation, and the race to the bottom in animal agriculture. In *Animals and Business Ethics*, ed. N Thomas 113–130. Springer International Publishing.

Mechtenberg L, Perino G, Treich N, Tyran JR, Wang S (2024) Self-signaling in voting. *Journal of Public Economics*, 231, 105070.

Meunier G, Schumacher I (2020) The importance of considering optimal government policy when social norms matter for the private provision of public goods. *Journal of Public Economic Theory*, 22(3), 630–655.

Minson JA, Monin B (2012) Do-gooder derogation: Disparaging morally motivated minorities to defuse anticipated reproach. *Social Psychological and Personality Science*, 3(2), 200–207.

Neethirajan S (2021) The use of artificial intelligence in assessing affective states in livestock. *Frontiers in Veterinary Science*, 8, 715261.

Nowak MA (2006) Five rules for the evolution of cooperation. *Science*, 314(5805), 1560–1563.

Nyborg K, Anderies JM, Dannenberg A et al. (2016) Social norms as solutions. *Science*, 354(6308), 42–43.

Olson M (1965) *The Logic of Collective Action: Public Goods and the Theory of Groups*. Harvard University Press.

Perino G, Schwickert H (2023) Animal welfare is a stronger determinant of public support for meat taxation than climate change mitigation in Germany. *Nature Food*, 4(2), 160–169.

Rabinovitch A, Myślińska-Szarek K, Cantarero K, Byrka K (2024) Eating pigs, not Peppa Pig: The effect of identifiability on children's propensity to humanize, befriend, and consume edible animals. *Appetite*, 200, 107505.

Ramp D, Bekoff M (2015) Compassion as a practical and evolved ethic for conservation. *BioScience*, 65, 323–327.

Randers L, Thøgersen J (2023) Meat, myself, and I: The role of multiple identities in meat consumption. *Appetite*, 180, 106319.

Robbins JA, Franks B, Weary DM, Von Keyserlingk MA (2016) Awareness of ag-gag laws erodes trust in farmers and increases support for animal welfare regulations. *Food Policy*, 61, 121–125.

Schaefer GO, Savulescu J (2014) The ethics of producing in vitro meat. *Journal of Applied Philosophy*, 31(2), 188–202.

Schwardmann P, Van der Weele J (2019) Deception and self-deception. *Nature Human Behaviour*, 3(10), 1055–1061.

Sekar N, Shiller D (2020) Engage with animal welfare in conservation. *Science*, 369, 629–630.

Siegrist B, Sutterlin B, Hartmann C (2018) Perceived naturalness and evoked disgust influence acceptance of cultured meat. *Meat Science*, 139, 213–219.

Simmonds P, Vallgård S (2021) "It's not as simple as something like sugar": Values and conflict in the UK meat tax debate. *International Journal of Health Governance*, 26(3), 307–322.

Simon DR (2013) *Meatonomics: How the Rigged Economics of Meat and Dairy Make You Consume Too Much–and How To Eat Better, Live Longer, and Spend Smarter*. Conari Press.

Singer P, Tse YF (2023) AI ethics: The case for including animals. *AI and Ethics*, 3(2), 539–551.

Solda A, Ke C, Page L, Von Hippel W (2020) Strategically delusional. *Experimental Economics*, 23, 604–631.

Stoeber J, Dhont K, Salmen A (2024) Individual differences in effective animal advocacy: Moderating effects of gender identity and speciesism. *Anthrozoös*, 37(3), 1–13.

Treich N (2021) Cultured meat: Promises and challenges. *Environmental and Resource Economics*, 79(1), 33–61.

Treich N (2022) The Dasgupta Review and the problem of anthropocentrism. *Environmental and Resource Economics*, 83(4), 973–997.

Van Loo EJ, Caputo V, Lusk JL (2020) Consumer preferences for farm-raised meat, lab-grown meat, and plant-based meat alternatives: Does information or brand matter? *Food Policy*, 95, 101931.

Van Loo EJ, Caputo V, Nayga Jr RM, Verbeke W (2014) Consumers' valuation of sustainability labels on meat. *Food Policy*, 49, 137–150.

Waltz D (2020) The 'embarrassing' endangered species act: Beyond collective rights for species. *Columbia Journal of Environmental Law*, 45, 1.

Weiler AM, Zavitz T (2024) Nothing to hide: How governments justify the adoption of ag-gag laws. *Canadian Review of Sociology/Revue canadienne de sociologie*, 62(1), 75–98.

Weinrich R, Strack M, Neugebauer F (2020) Consumer acceptance of cultured meat in Germany. *Meat Science*, 162, 107924.

Willett W, Rockström J, Loken B et al. (2019) Food in the Anthropocene: The EAT–Lancet Commission on healthy diets from sustainable food systems. *The Lancet*, 393(10170), 447–492.

Wynes S, Nicholas KA (2017) The climate mitigation gap: Education and government recommendations miss the most effective individual actions. *Environmental Research Letters*, 12(7), 074024.

Zaraska M (2016) *Meathooked: The History and Science of Our 2.5-million-year Obsession with Meat*. Basic Books.

18 Conclusion

The conclusion will be relatively brief. Essentially, I hope that this book has achieved at least one of its objectives: to persuade the reader that economics can be useful to reflect on animal welfare issues. I consider this book as a starting point, not a final destination. Much more research is needed. To conclude, I would like to highlight some topics that I have largely overlooked and would merit more attention in the future:

Animals in developing countries. The bulk of studies and examples discussed in this book center around developed countries, notably the United States and the European Union, with a particular emphasis on my home country and current residence, France. This focus could introduce biases into the analysis. For instance, the important topics of bushmeat and wildlife preservation in developing countries have been ignored. Moreover, residents of developing countries may have distinct relationships with farmed, wild, or companion animals, as well as differing moral perspectives. Note moreover that much of the stake regarding future meat consumption pertains to developing countries.

Variety of animal categories. In this book, the majority of applications concern farmed animals, while a smaller subset concern wild animals and pets. Arguably, these categories hold paramount significance in terms of relevance to policies, economics, and animal population sizes. While some findings in this book exhibit universality across animal categories such as the canonical model of animal use, the method for valuing animal welfare, or its nature as a public good, others do not. Consequently, there is potential to broaden the scope of analysis to encompass other animal categories, such as animals used in experiments and for entertainment purposes, or those residing in urban settings (such as rats or pigeons). Also, a greater emphasis on marine animals would be relevant. Furthermore, numerous actions and economic policies are strongly context specific, such as for hunting or horse racing for instance, and thus would deserve a specific treatment.

Heterogeneity of individual preferences. The canonical model presented in this book operates under the assumption of homogeneous agents, a huge simplification. Empirical studies reveal considerable heterogeneity in individuals' attitudes toward animals and their use, challenging this assumption. Notably, there has been limited discussion in this book regarding specific consumer categories such as vegetarians or vegans, who exhibit distinct preferences and behaviors in relation to animal welfare. Hence, it seems important for future economic studies to allocate greater focus to these categories, recognizing in particular their potential pivotal role in shaping societal attitudes toward animals.

Animal welfare assessment. The empirical assessment of animal welfare is crucial for making progress, especially in policy evaluation. While I dedicated significant space to discussing the foundational elements of animal welfare assessment such as the animal welfare score and utility potentials, I did not focus extensively on the numerical calculations. This is because I view the current estimation methods as very preliminary. There are several related but distinct methods available, such as the old COWEL or SOWEL models or the more recent AQALY and Welfare Footprint Project. If there is a follow-up to this book to make it more operational, this is clearly the key aspect to develop further.

Inequality. A related topic is inequality. Several sections of this book explore the social welfare function (SWF): a standard economic tool for capturing sensitivity to inequality. However, when considering animals, inequity takes on a distinct character compared to humans. Animals have very diverse cognitive and hedonic capacities, varying lifespans – often much shorter than those of humans – and may live primarily "in the moment," with lower capacity than humans to reflect on the past or plan for the future. How to capture the notion of "time" in a multispecies setting? More generally, how should these specific characteristics influence the properties and structure of a SWF that addresses inequalities across both humans and animals?

Uncertainty. Throughout this book, it becomes clear that significant uncertainties remain. These include uncertainties about animal sentience, the value of animal welfare, and the appropriate normative framework. Various approaches can address these uncertainties, such as fostering qualitative discussion or conducting sensitivity analyses. Additionally, economics has developed a rich toolkit for dealing with uncertainty, including concepts like risk aversion, stochastic dominance, option values, and the value of information. Integrating these tools into the analysis could help better design optimal policies, much like what was done in the early stages of the climate-economics literature.

Multiplicity of objectives. While this book centers on animal welfare, it is important to acknowledge that numerous other objectives are also significant, including environmental preservation and public health. For instance, policies aimed at reducing meat consumption may leverage one or many of these objectives. I have only briefly touched upon this topic, for instance when I emphasized some tensions between improving animal welfare and the environment. Therefore, a more comprehensive economic approach should consider the interplay between these various objectives to develop effective strategies and policies.

Broadening the regulatory landscape. In this book, the regulatory landscape is primarily limited to fiscal instruments as well as to animal welfare standards. Other regulatory instruments, such as adjustments in property rights, have largely been overlooked (there is a substantial body of literature in animal law on this topic). Additionally, given behavioral limitations, there is significant potential to use behavioral instruments such as specific nudges. Therefore, more theoretical and empirical effort is needed to study which instruments are best tailored to address specific animal welfare issues.

Salience. Continuing on the topic of behavioral instruments, I would like to highlight the potential of those that enhance the salience of animal welfare. It seems that many people genuinely care about animal welfare but simply do not think about it in various decision-making situations. This disconnect might partly explain the gap between intentions and actions, such as the vote-buy gap. My intuition is that salience is a key factor to explain the low state of animal welfare in this world. The hidden impacts on animals in many market situations seem consistent with that intuition. The production sector often attempts to make animals invisible. Animal welfare thus provides an interesting application to the fast-growing work on salience and economic behavior.

Donations. Most of the book focuses on "consumption" decisions, primarily the choice to consume meat. It also covers decisions related to the care and ownership of companion animals, as well as the indirect impact of consumption and environmental preservation choices on wild animals. However, another significant aspect of animal welfare decisions is donations to animal philanthropic activities. Although donations are relatively limited in size compared to charitable giving in general and the broader market for animal products, they represent an interesting domain of inquiry for economists. In particular, it is important to understand the drivers behind the decisions of donors to make charitable giving more effective.

Animals as economic agents. In this book, animals are assigned a passive role: They do not make decisions, they do not strategically anticipate or react to human actions, and they do not hold altruistic concerns for humans. However, there is no justification for these assumptions to be universally accepted and maintained in future economic studies on animals and animal welfare. Perhaps, the most promising research avenue is to assess animal welfare through animals' revealed preferences methods, namely through the observation of animals' choices.

Paternalism toward animals. Throughout the book, I have discussed fairly standard motives for policy interventions, such as externalities and public goods. However, there is an additional rationale that might justify policy intervention regarding animals: paternalism. This involves interventions aimed at "correcting" poor decisions made by animals for their own good, such as preventing a dog from eating a sharp bone that could injure him. The scope for such interventions is vast, given the potential for mistaken animals' decisions in rapidly evolving environments. However, the challenge for paternalistic interventions is significant due to the possible lack of understanding of animals' inherent motives and their welfare, and the limited resources and political acceptability of such interventions.

Markets and institutions. Most of the book focuses on simple economic models, particularly to examine the demand for animal welfare. In Part III, I explore the broader implications of the characteristics of this demand, suggesting that it is shaped not only by market forces but also by the institutional context more generally. However, this discussion remains largely informal and would benefit from further theoretical and empirical analysis.

Deontological approaches. In line with the tradition in economics, the book largely adopts a consequentialist, welfarist, and utilitarian approach. However, a substantial portion of the literature in animal ethics considers deontological approaches. Recently, there has been a growing body of deontological literature in economics. The topic of animal welfare thus provides an interesting application for this emerging literature in economics.

"Bridging" the direct and indirect approach. The book delineates a clear distinction between the direct (nonanthropocentric) approach and the indirect (anthropocentric) approach. I believe that this distinction provides a useful methodological and pedagogical device. Nonetheless, it may be pertinent to explore comparisons or potential combinations of the two approaches. Such exploration could give rise to significant and interesting complexities, including the possibility of double counting of animal welfare and the implications thereof.

Afterword

I encourage readers (e.g., students) to contact me at nicolas.treich@inrae.fr if they have comments or questions on the book.

Any personal financial gain resulting from this book will be dedicated to supporting animal protection associations in France and elsewhere.

As I conclude this book, my thoughts go to Heliott.

Heliott (2011–2022)

Index

Note: Page numbers followed *italics* refers to figures.